REVISION WORKBOOK

Family Law

Third Edition

MALCOLM DODDS
BA, LLM, Barrister,
Area Director of Legal Services, North Kent Magistrates' Court

GUILDHALL COLLEGE
60 NELSON STREET
LONDON E1 2DE
TEL: 020 7480 9000/1/3 Fax 020 7480 9002
Web: www.guildhall.ac
E-mail: info@guildhall.ac

OLD BAILEY PRESS

OLD BAILEY PRESS
at Holborn College, Woolwich Road,
Charlton, London, SE7 8LN

First published 1997
Third edition 2002

© The HLT Group Ltd 2002

All Old Bailey Press publications enjoy copyright protection and the copyright belongs to the HLT Group Ltd.

All rights reserved. No part of this publication may be reproduced or transmitted in any form or by any means, electronic, mechanical, photocopying, recording or otherwise, or stored in any retrieval system of any nature without either the written permission of the copyright holder, application for which should be made to the Old Bailey Press, or a licence permitting restricted copying in the United Kingdom issued by the Copyright Licensing Agency.

Any person who infringes the above in relation to this publication may be liable to criminal prosecution and civil claims for damages.

ISBN 1 85836 464 7

British Library Cataloguing-in-Publication.

A CIP Catalogue record for this book is available from the British Library.

Printed and bound in Great Britain.

Contents

Acknowledgement

Some questions used are taken or adapted from past University of London LLB (External) Degree examination papers and our thanks are extended to the University of London for their kind permission to use and publish the questions.

Caveat

The answers given are not approved or sanctioned by the University of London and are entirely our responsibility.

They are not intended as 'Model Answers', but rather as Suggested Solutions.

The answers have two fundamental purposes, namely:

a) to provide a detailed example of a suggested solution to an examination question; and

b) to assist students with their research into the subject and to further their understanding and appreciation of the subject.

Introduction

This Revision WorkBook has been designed specifically for those studying family law to undergraduate level. Its coverage is not confined to any one syllabus, but embraces all the major topics to be found in university examinations.

Each chapter contains a brief introduction explaining the scope and overall content of the topic covered in that chapter. There follows, in each case, a list of key points which will assist the student in studying and memorising essential material with which the student should be familiar in order to fully understand the topic.

Additionally in each chapter there is a key cases and statutes section which lists the most relevant cases and statutory provisions applicable to the topic in question. These are intended as an aid to revision, providing the student with a concise list of materials from which to begin revision.

Each chapter usually ends with several typical examination questions, together with general comments, skeleton solutions and suggested solutions. Wherever possible, the questions are drawn from the University of London external family law papers, with recent questions being included where possible. However, it is inevitable that, in compiling a list of questions by topic order rather than chronologically, not only do the same questions crop up over and over again in different guises, but there are gaps where questions have never been set at all.

Undoubtedly, the main feature of this Revision WorkBook is the inclusion of as many past examination questions as possible. While the use of past questions as a revision aid is certainly not new, it is hoped that the combination of actual past questions from the University of London LLB external course and specially written questions, where there are gaps in examination coverage, will be of assistance to students in achieving a thorough and systematic revision of the subject.

Careful use of the Revision WorkBook should enhance the student's understanding of family law and, hopefully, enable you to deal with as wide a range of subject matter as anyone might find in a family law examination, while at the same time allowing you to practise examination techniques while working through the book.

Introduction

Studying Family Law

The importance of statute

While family law is a heavy case law subject all the major areas are covered by legislation; eg the Matrimonial Causes Act 1973 covers the whole of the basic law on divorce, nullity and ancillary relief, three major examination areas. Accordingly students must be able to paraphrase (examiners would not expect precise repetition) the major provisions of the statutes as highlighted in this book.

The use of cases

The doctrine of precedent is not applicable to family law – per Ormrod LJ in *Sharpe* v *Sharpe* (1981) 11 Fam Law 121. While, therefore, you will come across a large number of cases these should be used to illustrate how the judiciary approach Family Law matters and how, by analogy, the problem in any particular question can be resolved both in practice and in the resolution of academic problems. When writing an answer to a problem question, it is seldom necessary to refer to large numbers of cases nor to refer to the facts of cases in any depth. The cases should be used to show principles upon which the particular problem will be resolved.

Approach to the examination

It is artificial in family law to advise a wife, for example, that she can divorce and not then go on to consider the implications of the divorce as regards maintenance, property adjustment and children. It is increasingly common for examiners to require the student to demonstrate a wide general knowledge of family law. The University of London LLB (external) examiners do this by asking questions which include up to three discrete areas whereas other examiners sometimes set a compulsory question that can include almost any of the areas studied. In short, it is dangerous to question spot in the sense of choosing to revise a limited number of topics. Whilst minor topics (eg jurisdiction and guardianship) may be superficially dealt with you must know in depth the major overlap areas, ie the law relating to divorce, ancillary relief, ouster orders and disputes concerning children.

Dealing with essay questions

Examiners have tended to favour problem questions. Consequently there tend to be more problem questions than essay questions in the examination paper.

No essay question will be asking you to write everything you know about a particular topic even though that tends to be the common approach of students to such questions.

The examiner will be seeking to see whether you are able to adapt your general knowledge of the area in question to a particular slant. The skill, therefore, is to identify the particular slant of the question and ensure that each paragraph you write is relevant to that slant. If you do this you will achieve high marks whereas if you simply write everything you know, you will achieve no more than a bare pass.

Because family law is a topical subject it is quite likely that essay questions will require comment on current proposals for reform or current issues eg the debate surrounding surrogacy.

Dealing with problem questions

Problem questions are often lengthy. Whatever the length, it is important to read the issues you are being asked to advise on at the end of the question before reading the facts. In this way you are more likely to identify the relevance of the facts. Be clear who you are asked to advise, be concise and relevant, support your answer with evidence and if you are asked to advise X be sure that you do.

Revision and Examination Technique

Revision Technique

Planning a revision timetable

In planning your revision timetable make sure you don't finish the syllabus too early. You should avoid leaving revision so late that you have to 'cram' – but constant revision of the same topic leads to stagnation.

Plan ahead, however, and try to make your plans increasingly detailed as you approach the examination date.

Allocate enough time for each topic to be studied. But note that it is better to devise a realistic timetable, to which you have a reasonable chance of keeping, rather than a wildly optimistic schedule which you will probably abandon at the first opportunity!

The syllabus and its topics

One of your first tasks when you began your course was to ensure that you thoroughly understood your syllabus. Check now to see if you can write down the topics it comprises from memory. You will see that the chapters of this WorkBook are each devoted to a syllabus topic. This will help you decide which are the key chapters relative to your revision programme. Though you should allow some time for glancing through the other chapters.

The topic and its key points

Again working from memory, analyse what you consider to be the key points of any topic that you have selected for particular revision. Seeing what you can recall, unaided, will help you to understand and firmly memorise the concepts involved.

Using the WorkBook

Relevant questions are provided for each topic in this book. Naturally, as typical examples of examination questions, they do not normally relate to one topic only. But the questions in each chapter *will* relate to the subject matter of the chapter to a degree. You can choose your method of consulting the questions and solutions, but here are some suggestions (strategies 1–3). Each of them pre-supposes that you have read through the author's notes on key points and key cases and statutes, and any other preliminary matter, at the beginning of the chapter. Once again, you now need to practise working from memory, for that is the challenge you are preparing yourself for. As a rule of procedure constantly test yourself once revision starts, both orally and in writing.

Strategy 1

Strategy 1 is planned for the purpose of quick revision. First read your chosen question carefully and then jot down in abbreviated notes what you consider to be the main points at issue. Similarly, note the cases and statutes that occur to you as being relevant for citation purposes. Allow yourself sufficient time to cover what you feel to be relevant. Then study the author's skeleton solution and skim-read the suggested solution to see how they compare with your notes. When comparing consider carefully what the author has included (and concluded) and see whether that agrees with what you have written. Consider the points of variation also. Have you recognised the key issues? How relevant have you been? It is possible, of course, that you have referred to a recent case that is relevant, but which had not been reported when the WorkBook was prepared.

Strategy 2

Strategy 2 requires a nucleus of three hours in which to practise writing a set of examination answers in a limited time-span.

Select a number of questions (as many as are normally set in your subject in the examination you are studying for), each from a different chapter in the WorkBook, without consulting the solutions. Find a place to write where you will not be disturbed and try to arrange not to be interrupted for three hours. Write your solutions in the time allowed, noting any time needed to make up if you are interrupted.

After a rest, compare your answers with the suggested solutions in the WorkBook. There will be considerable variation in style, of course, but the bare facts should not be too dissimilar. Evaluate your answer critically. Be 'searching', but develop a positive approach to deciding how you would tackle each question on another occasion.

Strategy 3

You are unlikely to be able to do more than one three hour examination, but occasionally set yourself a single question. Vary the 'time allowed' by imagining it to be one of the questions that you must answer in three hours and allow yourself a limited preparation and writing time. Try one question that you feel to be difficult and an easier question on another occasion, for example.

Mis-use of suggested solutions

Don't try to learn by rote. In particular, don't try to reproduce the *suggested solutions* by heart. Learn to express the basic concepts in your own words.

Keeping up-to-date

Keep up-to-date. While examiners do not require familiarity with changes in the law during the three months prior to the examination, it obviously creates a good impression if you can show that you are acquainted with any recent changes. Make a habit of looking through one of the leading journals – *Modern Law Review, Law Quarterly Review* or the *New Law Journal*, for example – and cumulative indices to law reports, such as the *All England Law Reports* or *Weekly Law Reports*, or indeed the daily law reports in *The Times*. The *Law Society's Gazette* and the *Legal Executive Journal* are helpful sources, plus any specialist journal(s) for the subject you are studying.

Examination Skills

Examiners are human too!

The process of answering an examination question involves a communication between you and the person who set it. If you were speaking face to face with the person, you would choose your verbal points and arguments carefully in your reply. When writing, it is all too easy to forget the human being who is awaiting the reply and simply write out what one knows in the area of the subject! Bear in mind it is a person whose question you are responding to, throughout your essay. This will help you to avoid being irrelevant or long-winded.

The essay question

Candidates are sometimes tempted to choose to answer essay questions because they 'seem' easier. But the examiner is looking for thoughtful work and will not give good marks for superficial answers.

The essay-type of question may be either purely factual, in asking you to explain the meaning of a certain doctrine or principle, or it may ask you to discuss a certain proposition, usually derived from a quotation. In either case, the approach to the answer is the same. A clear programme must be devised to give the examiner the meaning or significance of the doctrine, principle or proposition and its origin in common law, equity or statute, and cases which illustrate its application to the branch of law concerned. Essay questions offer a good way to obtain marks if you have thought carefully about a topic, since it is up to you to impose the structure (unlike the problem questions where the problem imposes its own structure). You are then free to speculate and show imagination.

The problem question

The problem-type question requires a different approach. You may well be asked to advise a client or merely discuss the problems raised in the question. In either case, the most important factor is to take great care in reading the question. By its nature, the question will be longer than the essay-type question and you will have a number of facts to digest. Time spent in analysing the question may well save time later, when you are endeavouring to impress on the examiner the considerable extent of your basic legal knowledge. The quantity of knowledge is itself a trap and you must always keep within the boundaries of the question in hand. It is very tempting to show the examiner the extent of your knowledge of your subject, but if this is outside the question, it is time lost and no marks earned. It is inevitable that some areas which you have studied and revised will not be the subject of questions, but under no circumstances attempt to adapt a question to a stronger area of knowledge at the expense of relevance.

When you are satisfied that you have grasped the full significance of the problem-type question, set out the fundamental principles involved.

You will then go on to identify the fundamental problem (or problems) posed by the question. This should be followed by a consideration of the law which is relevant to the problem. The source of the law, together with the cases which will be of assistance in solving the problem, must then be considered in detail.

Very good problem questions are quite likely to have alternative answers, and in advising a party you should be aware that alternative arguments may be available. Each stage of your answer, in this case, will be based on the argument or arguments considered in the previous stage, forming a conditional sequence.

If, however, you only identify one fundamental problem, do not waste time worrying that you cannot think of an alternative – there may very well be only that one answer.

The examiner will then wish to see how you use your legal knowledge to formulate a case and how you apply that formula to the problem which is the subject of the question. It is this positive approach which can make answering a problem question a high mark earner for the student who has fully understood the question and clearly argued his case on the established law.

Examination checklist

a) Read the instructions at the head of the examination carefully. While last-minute changes are unlikely – such as the introduction of a compulsory question or an increase in the number of questions asked – it has been known to happen.

b) Read the questions carefully. Analyse problem questions – work out what the examiner wants.

c) Plan your answer before you start to write.

d) Check that you understand the rubric before you start to write. Do not 'discuss', for example, if you are specifically asked to 'compare and contrast'.

e) Answer the correct number of questions. If you fail to answer one out of four questions set you lose 25 per cent of your marks!

Style and structure

Try to be clear and concise. Fundamentally this amounts to using paragraphs to denote the sections of your essay, and writing simple, straightforward sentences as much as possible. The sentence you have just read has 22 words – when a sentence reaches 50 words it becomes difficult for a reader to follow.

Do not be inhibited by the word 'structure' (traditionally defined as giving an essay a beginning, a middle and an end). A good structure will be the natural consequence of setting out your arguments and the supporting evidence in a logical order. Set the scene briefly in your opening paragraph. Provide a clear conclusion in your final paragraph.

Table of Cases

Table of Statutes and Other Materials

Chapter 1

Family Law and Society

As society changes so too the law must change to reflect prevailing social norms, and this is particularly the case in the study of the law that relates to the social group defined as the family. The history of family law reflects changes that have occurred in society's attitude towards divorce, to the significant changes that have occurred in the status of women, to the recognition of the separate status of children and to the acknowledgement that the state has a role to play in protecting members of a family who are 'at risk', in the sense that they are the victims of sexual abuse or violent attack.

Since the mid-1850s social reform in both public and private law which has had an impact on the regulation of family life has gained momentum. In private law, the establishment of a coherent secular divorce law, together with the development of the separate legal status of the wife within marriage, has now reached a point where a divorce petition is based on the 'irretrievable breakdown' of the marriage and husbands and wives enjoy equal rights and obligations within marriage. In public law, legislation which started by regulating child employment and introduced compulsory education has now reached a point at which the state can remove children from a family if it is established that they are 'at risk' through physical and sexual abuse.

Social change has been significant in the last 25 years. The changing role of women, the increase in reported child abuse, the increase in divorce and the increasing numbers of couples cohabiting outside marriage have posed and continue to pose problems for family law. There have been attempts to codify family law. For example, the Children Act 1989 codified the law relating to private law and public law disputes concerning children. The Family Law Act 1996 codified the law relating to matrimonial home rights and protection of spouses and partners against domestic violence. The reforms of divorce law in the Family Law Act 1996 were however abandoned in 2001, leaving the law as contained in the 30-year-old Matrimonial Causes Act 1973. As a result, questions on divorce and separation have been dealt with according to the current law and not as stated in Parts II and III of the 1996 Act.

It can be argued that family law includes the law on state benefits, taxation and housing. However, for examination purposes family law focuses on the more traditional questions of marriage and how to resolve family disputes about property or children.

Chapter 2

Nullity of Marriage

2.1   **Introduction**

2.2   **Key points**

2.3   **Key cases and statute**

2.4   **Questions and solutions**

2.1 Introduction

A marriage may be terminated in two ways: either a petition for divorce or a petition for nullity. Insofar as there are about 145,000 divorce decrees and only 1,000 nullity decrees each year the practical importance of the law relating to nullity of marriage is put into its proper perspective. A person would only seek a decree of nullity if he or she was not willing to petition for divorce (eg because of religious objection to divorce). However, despite its relative lack of practical importance it remains a regular examination topic.

2.2 Key points

The difference between a void and voidable marriage

Section 11 of the Matrimonial Causes Act 1973 lists grounds of nullity which make the marriage void; s12 those that make the marriage voidable only. The s11 grounds result in such a fundamentally flawed marriage that the law considers there to have been no marriage at all – technically a party to a void marriage can go ahead and contract another marriage without having the first marriage declared void by a court.

The s12 grounds are of less fundamental effect and the law recognises a marriage which is affected by one of the s12 grounds as valid until such time as one party petitions the court that it should be deemed void. However, a party to such a potentially void marriage cannot delay too long. Section 13 of the Matrimonial Causes Act generally bars an application to make a voidable marriage void unless the application is brought within three years of the date that the applicant knew that he/she could rely on one of the s12 grounds. It should be emphasised that s13 does not apply to s11 at all, nor does it apply to s12(a) or 12(b) – the non-consummation grounds.

The s11 grounds

a) Failure to comply with Marriages Acts 1949–70

   i) within prohibited degrees of relationship

   ii) either party under 16

This only applies to a marriage (wherever in the world it is contracted) if at least one of the parties is domiciled in England at the time of the marriage.

Compare *Pugh* v *Pugh* [1951] 2 All ER 680 with *Mohamed* v *Knott* [1968] 2 All ER 563.

   iii) failure to comply with the formalities of marriage

The purpose behind reading the banns is that publicity is given as to who is getting married, therefore the banns must be published in the name one is commonly known by even if that is not one's real name: *Dancer* v *Dancer* [1948] 2 All ER 731.

Note: The Marriage Act 1994 removed many of the restrictions on where civil marriages could take place. Local authorities can licence various places (eg hotels) to carry out wedding ceremonies. The restrictions on religious marriages remain (eg *Gereis* v *Yagoub* [1997] 1 FLR 854 in which a marriage was void because it took place in an unlicensed church and without due notice having been given).

However, there is a presumption of a valid marriage where the parties have lived as man and wife for some time and there is no evidence of guilty knowledge on their part: see *Chief Adjudication Officer* v *Bath* [2000] 1 FLR 8; *Pazpena de Vire* v *Pazpena de Vire* [2001] 1 FLR 460 and *A-M* v *A-M (Divorce: Jurisdiction: Validity of Marriage)* [2001] 2 FLR 6.

b) That at the time of marriage either party was already married – ie bigamous marriages

c) That the parties are not respectively male and female

English law only recognises marriages between parties of the opposite sex.

Difficulties arise if a person changes his or her sex. The leading case in English law is *Corbett* v *Corbett* [1970] 2 All ER 33 which held that a person's sex is fixed at birth and cannot subsequently be changed for the purposes of marriage. This decision has been reaffirmed in *Re P and G (Transsexuals)* [1996] 2 FLR 90. The English legal position has been upheld in the European Court of Human Rights in *Rees* v *United Kingdom* [1987] Fam Law 157, *Cossey* v *United Kingdom* [1991] Fam Law 362, *X, Y and Z* v *United Kingdom* [1997] 2 FLR 892, *Sheffield and Horsham* v *United Kingdom* [1998] 2 FLR 928 and *Bellinger* v *Bellinger* [2001] 2 FLR 1048. However, the student must be aware that the law in this area is under review. This was made clear by the dissenting judgment and the call for review in the majority judgments in *Bellinger*. The European Court is moving towards recognising the rights of transsexuals but is awaiting more of a consensus to emerge.

d) Actual or potentially polygamous marriages

A marriage is not polygamous if at its inception neither spouse has any additional spouse: see s11 MCA 1973 as amended by the Private International Law (Miscellaneous Provisions) Act PIL(MP)A 1995.

As a result s11(d) only applies if a marriage is actually polygamous. If a marriage is potentially polygamous, but neither spouse has an additional spouse, then s11(d) will not make the marriage void. See also s5 PIL(MP)A 1995 which confirms that a marriage entered into outside England and Wales is not void on the ground that it is entered into under a law which permits polygamy and that either party is domiciled in England and Wales (provided neither party is not already married).

The s12 grounds

a) Non-consummation through incapacity: s12(a)

Note:

The degree of consummation necessary: *W v W* [1967] 3 All ER 178.

A petitioner can rely on his own impotency: *Pettit v Pettit* [1962] 3 All ER 37.

Refusal to undergo a simple operation without danger to health which would cure the physical incapacity may amount to wilful refusal under s12(b): *D v D* [1979] 3 All ER 337.

b) Non-consummation through wilful refusal: s12(b)

Note:

The definition of wilful refusal – must be more than a temporary unwillingness due to shyness but rather a fixed and steadfast refusal come to without just excuse: *Horton v Horton* [1947] 2 All ER 871.

Therefore there will not be wilful refusal where:

i) The marriage was between elderly persons 'for companionship only': *Morgan v Morgan* [1959] 1 All ER 539; but probably not companionship marriage between those of child bearing age: see *Brodie v Brodie* [1917] P 271.

ii) The validity of the marriage was dependent as far as the parties were concerned on a religious ceremony which has not taken place: *Jodla v Jodla* [1960] 1 All ER 625; *Kaur v Singh* [1972] 1 All ER 292; *A v J (Nullity)* [1989] 1 FLR 110.

c) Lack of consent through duress, mistake, unsoundness of mind or otherwise: s12(c)

  i) Duress

   This is a very popular examination area – look for a scenario where one party is coerced into marrying another.

   A useful framework for an answer is provided by the three requirements suggested by Scarman J in *Buckland* v *Buckland* [1967] 2 All ER 300, namely:

   • a sufficient degree of fear to vitiate consent;

   • that the fear be reasonably entertained;

   • that the fear arose from some external factor which the petitioner had not brought upon himself.

   'Sufficient degree of fear'

   This was usefully defined in *Szechter* v *Szechter* [1970] 3 All ER 905 as requiring a threat to 'life limb or liberty'.

   More recently in *Hirani* v *Hirani* (1983) 4 FLR 232 Ormrod LJ adopted the phrase 'such a coercion of the will so as to vitiate consent' to indicate the degree of pressure required.

   Examples of such pressure are found in both *Szechter* v *Szechter* and *Buckland* v *Buckland* [1967] 2 All ER 300 namely consenting to marriage to escape unjust imprisonment.

   'Fear to be reasonably entertained'

   The debate here has been whether the test should be subjective or objective, ie is it sufficient that the petitioner was frightened or must it be shown that a reasonable person in her position would have been frightened as well?

   Initially the test was purely subjective: *Scott* v *Sebright* (1886) 12 PD 21. However, cases such as *Buckland* v *Buckland* and *Szechter* v *Szechter* strongly favoured an objective approach.

   The question of whether the test should be objective or subjective is of great importance in the area of arranged marriages where someone marries out of respect for his/her parents' wishes. If an objective test applies, then such marriages cannot be annulled due to duress. This was so in the case of *Singh* v *Singh* [1971] 2 All ER 828 which followed an objective approach. However, in *Hirani* v *Hirani* the Court of Appeal reverted to the subjective approach and allowed a decree in such an arranged marriage.

   After *Hirani* it is generally accepted that the test is now purely subjective: was the petitioner in fact sufficiently frightened so as to give his/her consent to marriage?

'Not brought on himself'

For example if, in *Buckland* v *Buckland*, the petitioner had in fact had sexual relations with the Maltese girl he would not have succeeded.

ii) Mistake

It must be a mistake as to the nature of the ceremony not as to its effect.

Compare *Mehta* v *Mehta* [1945] 2 All ER 690 with *Way* v *Way* [1949] 2 All ER 959 and *Vervaeke* v *Smith* [1982] 2 All ER 144.

iii) Unsoundness of mind

One does not have to be very sane to understand the nature and effect of marriage: *In the Estate of Park* [1953] 2 All ER 1411.

iv) Or otherwise

There have been no cases on this – it probably covers the situation where someone consents to marriage while under the influence of alcohol or drugs.

d) Mental disorder within meaning of Mental Health Act 1983: s12(d)

Virtually any mental illness is covered by the Act. If you do not understand the nature and effect of marriage you can annul it under s12(c); if you do understand the nature and effect but are incapable of carrying out the normal marital duties because of a mental illness then the marriage may be annulled under s12(d): *Bennett* v *Bennett* [1969] 1 All ER 539

e) Suffering from venereal disease: s12(e)

f) Pregnancy by another: s12(f)

Section 12(e) and (f) only apply if the petitioner was ignorant of the facts at the time of marriage.

The s13 requirement to petition within three years of marriage only applies to s12(c) to s12(f).

The s13 bar

Remember this section can only bar s12 petitions; it does not apply to s11 grounds.

One needs to show:

a) conduct by the petitioner (after he/she became aware that a petition for nullity was available to them) which leads the respondent to believe the marriage will not be annulled eg adopting children (*D* v *D* [1979] 3 All ER 337); and

b) that it would be unjust to grant the decree.

Note that where the marriage is an empty shell it would seldom be just not to grant the decree: *D* v *D* [1979] 3 All ER 337.

As regards the three year time limit remember this only applies to the grounds in s12(c) to s12(f) and while time generally runs from the date of the marriage this is not so when, during that period, the petitioner has suffered from a mental illness within the meaning of the Mental Health Act 1983.

2.3 Key cases and statute

- *A v J (Nullity)* [1989] Fam Law 63
  Refusal to consummate marriage

- *Bellinger v Bellinger* [2001] 2 FLR 1048
  Transsexual – validity of marriage

- *Corbett v Corbett* [1970] 2 WLR 1306
  Transsexual – validity of marriage

- *D v A* (1845) 1 Rob Eccl 279
  Consummation of marriage

- *Dancer v Dancer* [1948] 2 All ER 731
  Publication of banns

- *Park, In the estate of* [1953] 3 WLR 1012
  Consent to marriage

- *Szechter v Szechter* [1971] 2 WLR 170
  Duress in entering marriage

- Matrimonial Causes Act 1973 – the ground for nullity

2.4 Questions and suggested solutions

QUESTION ONE

a) Aziza, who is now 20, reluctantly married Bourhan, a 50-year-old wealthy businessman, in December 1992. Aziza's parents had arranged the marriage with Bourhan and told Aziza, who was then still at school, that if she did not marry Bourhan, she would disgrace her family, who would then disown and disinherit her. In 1993, Aziza was informed by a specialist that she would never be able to have any children and in 1994, she and Bourhan adopted twin boys. Aziza, who has never been happy with Bourhan, has now met Conrad, whom she wishes to marry.

   Advise Aziza whether she can successfully petition for a decree of nullity.

b) Deborah and Edward, aged 17 and 21 respectively, married at a register office in June 1994. Deborah had not told her parents that she was getting married. The marriage was not consummated because Deborah was afraid of intercourse. In November 1994, Deborah began seeing a psychiatrist so as to resolve this difficulty.

Edward, who has repeatedly urged Deborah to consummate the marriage, has discovered that she is having a sexual relationship with her psychiatrist.

Advise Edward whether he can successfully petition for a decree of nullity.

University of London LLB Examination
(for External Students) Family Law June 1995 Q1

General Comment

The two parts of the question both ask about how to petition for nullity. The first part deals with a possible lack of consent to marriage on the basis of duress, but then raises a possible defence of approbation through agreeing to an adoption. The second part deals with non-consummation of a marriage and requires discussion of both refusal to consummate and the inability to consummate.

Skeleton Solution

a) Whether Aziza did not validly consent to the marriage in consequence of duress (s12(c) MCA 1973) – defence of approbation (s13(1)(a) MCA 1973).

b) That the marriage has not been consummated due to the incapacity of Deborah (s12(a) MCA 1973) – that the marriage has not been consummated due to Deborah's wilful refusal (s12(b) MCA 1973).

Suggested Solution

a) Aziza asks for advice as to whether she can successfully petition for a decree of nullity with respect to her marriage to Bourhan. Aziza can be advised that a petition for nullity can be brought either on the basis that her marriage with Bourhan is void or that it is voidable. Her marriage with Bourhan would be void if it was fundamentally defective, namely, one or more the grounds outlined in s11 of the Matrimonial Causes Act 1973 (hereinafter referred to as the MCA 1973) applied. None of those grounds appear to apply in Aziza's case. There is no suggestion that there was any defect in the marriage formalities or that she and her husband are within the prohibited degrees of relationship or are under age or that either party was already lawfully married. There is no suggestion that they are not respectively male or female. There is also no suggestion that the marriage was entered into outside England and Wales and was a polygamous marriage and contravened s11(d) MCA 1973.

Her marriage with Bourhan would be voidable if one or more of the grounds in s12 MCA 1973 applied. There is no suggestion that the marriage has not been consummated so it appears that s12(a) and (b) MCA 1973 cannot apply. Of the remaining grounds only one could apply in Aziza's case, namely that she did not validly consent to the marriage in consequence of duress: see s12(c) MCA 1973. For these purposes 'duress' means fear which is so overbearing that it destroys any free consent to the marriage. Aziza would have to show that her will was so overborne by a genuine and reasonably held fear caused by a threat or immediate fear (for which she is not responsible) to life, limb or liberty, so that the restraint destroys the reality of consent: see *Szechter* v *Szechter* [1971] 2 WLR 170. Duress does not have to be a threat to physically harm or imprison Aziza. She can be advised that a threat from her family to disown and disinherit her may be sufficient to destroy the reality of consent and overbear her will: see *Hirani* v *Hirani* (1983) 4 FLR 232. However, a mere dislike of her husband and going through with the marriage out of respect for her parents and the traditions of the family would not constitute duress: see *Singh* v *Singh* [1971] 2 WLR 963. In Aziza's case it appears that her circumstances are more similar to those in *Hirani* than those in *Singh* because her family threatened to disown and disinherit her. She therefore appears to have a claim to petition for nullity on the basis of lack of consent.

However Aziza should be advised that should her husband oppose the petition he can raise a defence. That defence would be that Aziza, with knowledge that it was open to her to have the marriage avoided, so conducted herself in relation to her husband as to lead him to reasonably believe that she would not seek to petition for nullity and that it would be unjust to him to grant the decree of nullity: see s13(1) MCA 1973. He could argue that by Aziza agreeing to adopt the twins she has acted in such a manner. Aziza should be advised that there is conflicting authority dealing with this point. In *W* v *W* [1952] 1 All ER 858 it was held that an adoption application involved a representation to the court that the joint adopters were husband and wife so that it would be contrary to public policy to allow either to claim that the marriage was a nullity. By contrast, in *D* v *D* [1979] 3 All ER 337 it was held that public policy was irrelevant and that s13(1) related wholly to conduct between the parties. In that case a petition for nullity succeeded. Aziza can be advised that *D* v *D* is more likely to be followed so that the adoption would not be an absolute bar to a petition for nullity. If she did not know of her right to petition for nullity for lack of consent when the adoption took place then the s13(1) defence could not apply. Equally if the court was not satisfied that there would be any injustice to Bourhan by the granting of the decree then again such a defence would not succeed. Given the difference in age between them, the circumstances of the marriage and Bourhan's wealth it may be difficult for Bourhan to argue that it would be unjust for a decree to be granted.

Aziza should be advised that she must bring any petition within three years of the marriage otherwise the court could not grant her decree: see s13(2) MCA 1973. It is possible to consider a decree under s12(c) outside this period, but for reasons which do not appear to apply in Aziza's case. She must therefore not delay in bringing a petition should she wish to do so.

b) Now turning to Edward, he can be advised that the first ground which needs to be considered would be that Deborah married at the age of 17 without parental consent. The marriage would not be void on the basis of her age since the minimum age for marriage is 16: see s11(a)(ii) MCA 1973. A person aged between 16 and under 18 should obtain the consent of those with parental responsibility for her (normally both her parents if they are married): s3 Marriage Act 1949. However, the lack of consent from Deborah's parents would not make the marriage void (see s48(1)(b) MCA 1949) unless either parent has lodged a caveat with the superintendent registrar: see ss29 and 30 Marriage Act 1949. Since her parents did not seem to be aware of the marriage no caveat is likely to have been lodged. None of the other grounds under s11 MCA 1973 making a marriage void appear to apply.

The marriage may be voidable because it appears not to have been consummated. Edward is able to petition for nullity on the basis either that the marriage has not been consummated because of Deborah's incapacity to consummate it or that she is wilfully refusing to consummate the marriage: see s12(a) or (b) MCA 1973. An incapacity to consummate is normally a physical incapacity but may be a psychological one. A psychological incapacity must amount to an invincible repugnance to the act of intercourse. A mere dislike or aversion to Edward would not be sufficient: see *Singh* v *Singh*. In order for Edward to succeed on the basis of Deborah's incapacity he must be able to show that this is incurable or could only be cured by an operation which is attended by danger or which is unlikely to succeed or where Deborah refuses to undergo treatment: see *S* v *S* [1963] All ER 55. None of these features appear to apply. If Deborah is having a sexual relationship (which it is assumed involves sexual intercourse) with her psychiatrist it will be difficult to maintain that her incapacity is incurable. She has consented to treatment which appears to be working albeit in a most unfortunate manner. Therefore Edward is more likely to succeed if he petitions on the basis of her wilful refusal to consummate the marriage. In order to show wilful refusal he would have to show that Deborah has come to a settled and definite decision without just excuse: see *Horton* v *Horton* [1947] 2 All ER 871. If Deborah started out with an inability to consummate, but this has been cured by virtue of her relationship with her psychiatrist, then any refusal to consummate her marriage with Edward is likely to amount to wilful refusal. She is unlikely to be able to persuade a court that she has a just excuse for not consummating the marriage if she is having sexual intercourse with another. In these circumstances Edward is likely to succeed in a petition for nullity. None of the defences available against a petition where a marriage is voidable appear to apply.

QUESTION TWO

Alan was introduced to Bert by a mutual friend. Bert had been a member of an illegal organisation for gay rights in his own country and had come to England to escape from repression there. He offered Alan £5,000 to 'marry' him. Alan had incurred large debts and so reluctantly agreed. Although he was homosexual he did not intend to live with Bert; the 'marriage' would be in name only. Bert was anxious that his whereabouts might be traced and also wanted the 'marriage' to appear valid and so he disguised himself and gave a woman's name at the register office where they were to marry. Alan began to worry about the implication of the plan and shortly before the ceremony saw his doctor, who prescribed tranquillisers and advised him not to drink alcohol. He did, however, drink with friends on the night before the marriage and was in a confused state at the register office. A party was held after the ceremony at which he drank more alcohol. He awoke the next morning with Bert, remembering very little of the events. He then discovered that Bert was a woman. Since then they have not lived together, but Bertha, as he now knows her, has told him that she is expecting his child.

Is the marriage valid? If it is valid, how can Alan end it?

University of London LLB Examination
(for External Students) Family Law June 1997 Q2

General Comment

The question puts forward an intriguing set of facts which require the student to explore the grounds for annulling marriage. In particular the grounds on which a marriage is void must be discussed. The legal status of transsexuals is one element of that discussion. In addition, the grounds on which a marriage is voidable may be relevant. Finally, the option of divorce must be mentioned.

Skeleton Solution

Grounds for voiding the marriage: parties are not respectively male and female (s11(c) MCA 1973) and the position of transsexuals; disregard of marriage requirements (s11(a) MCA 1973) – grounds for marriage being voidable: non-consummation (s12 (a) and (b) MCA 1973); lack of consent due to duress, mistake or unsoundness of mind (s12(c) MCA 1973) – petition for divorce on basis of irretrievable breakdown – fact of behaviour (s1(2)(b) MCA 1973).

Suggested Solution

Alan asks for advice on the validity of the marriage and, if the marriage is valid, how Alan can end it.

Firstly, Alan can be advised that if one or more of the grounds in s11 Matrimonial Causes Act (MCA) 1973 can be established then the marriage can be declared to be void. This would have the effect of the law treating the marriage as if it had never existed: see *De Reneville* v *De Reneville* [1948] 1 All ER 56.

One possible ground is that the parties are not respectively male and female: s11(c) MCA 1973. Marriage is not allowed in English law between persons of the same sex. There may be some doubt as the status of Bertha, who was known as Bert. A person's sex is fixed at birth. Even if a subsequent operation or other change is such that a person claims to have changed sex this makes no difference: see *Corbett* v *Corbett* [1970] 2 WLR 1306. Though the law on transsexuals is developing at the same time as developments in the scientific understanding of sexuality the most recent cases confirm *Corbett* as representing the existing law: see *Cossey* v *United Kingdom* [1991] Fam Law 362 and *Re P and G (Transsexuals)* [1996] 2 FLR 90. Alan will need to obtain evidence of Bertha's (or Bert's) sex at birth. If it was male then the marriage will be void. If it was female then this ground cannot apply. If Bertha is indeed expecting a child then it seems likely that she must have been female at the time of her birth so the likelihood of establishing this ground appears small.

A second possible grounds is that Alan and Bertha have intermarried in disregard of certain requirements as to the formation of marriage: s11(a)(iii) MCA 1973. It is noted that Bertha gave a false name and disguised him/herself at the register office. If the marriage was by way of superintendent registrar's certificate and licence then it has been decided that the object of the giving of names is not to achieve publicity. As a result a deliberate misdescription of Bertha will not invalidate the marriage: see *Puttick* v *Attorney-General* [1979] 3 WLR 542 where a false name and particulars were given by one of the parties to the marriage but the marriage was held to be valid. The situation is likely to be different if the ceremony was a Church of England marriage, but the information supplied does not suggest this.

Alan can be advised that none of the other grounds voiding the marriage appear to apply. If neither of the above two grounds can be established then Alan can seek to establish that the marriage is voidable pursuant to one or more of the grounds set out in s12 MCA 1973. If the marriage is voidable Alan needs to obtain a decree to prove that the marriage is a nullity and it may be possible for Bertha to establish a defence under s13 MCA 1973. The first ground Alan may seek to establish is that the marriage has not been consummated, either due to the incapacity of either party or owing to the wilful refusal of Bertha: see s12(a) and (b) MCA 1973. It is difficult to see how Alan could establish non-consummation on the basis of Bertha's wilful refusal. There is no suggestion of such refusal on Bertha's part. It is likely to be difficult to establish an incapacity to consummate the marriage if Bertha is indeed a woman and is capable of 'ordinary and complete intercourse': see *D* v *A* (1845) 1 Rob Eccl 279. If Bertha is not a woman then the marriage is void. Otherwise Alan would have to rely on medical evidence to show that she has a physical incapacity to consummate the marriage. He would also have to establish that such incapacity is either incapable of remedy or can only be cured by an operation which is either dangerous or has little chance of success, or that Bertha refuses to undergo the operation: see *S* v *S* [1954] 3 All ER 736. In the absence of information suggesting an incapacity it is again difficult to see how this ground can be established.

A further ground is that Alan did not validly consent to the marriage, whether in consequence of duress, mistake, unsoundness of mind or otherwise: see s12(c) MCA 1973. It may be possible to say that Alan did not validly consent because he made a mistake as to identity of the person he was marrying – namely that Bertha was not a man but a woman. It has been held that a mistake as to the quality of the person is not sufficient: see *Moss* v *Moss* [1897] P 263 where the wife concealed that she was pregnant. A mistake as to the name would also not be sufficient to invalidate consent: see *Puttick* v *Attorney-General* (above). In addition, Alan appears to have been a party to any deception practised or, at least, aware of it. He appears to have been aware of the false name and that 'Bert' dressed up as a woman. In these circumstances he would not be advised to apply to the court on this basis.

Alan could seek to establish that he did not validly consent due to duress, namely he only agreed to the marriage because of his large debts. However, Alan should be advised that any duress must be so overbearing that the element of free consent is absent: *Szechter* v *Szechter* [1971] 2 WLR 170. The court would ask whether Alan's will was overborne by a genuine and reasonably held fear caused by the threat of immediate danger (for which Alan is not responsible) to his life, limb or liberty so that the constraint destroyed the reality of consent. The facts do not suggest such duress. There may have been some pressure due to Alan's financial state whereby Alan 'reluctantly' agreed to the marriage, but this seems to fall far short of duress. Alan should also be advised that there is uncertainty about whether any fear must be a fear for which Alan is not responsible: contrast *Buckland* v *Buckland* [1967] 2 WLR 1506 with *Griffith* v *Griffith* [1944] IR 35. If Alan has been responsible for his own debts this is likely to further weaken his case.

A further basis for lack of consent is unsoundness of mind. The combination of tranquillisers and drink may have been such that Alan was not aware of what was going on during the marriage ceremony. However, English law considers that marriage is a simple concept so no high degree of understanding is required: see *In the estate of Park* [1953] 3 WLR 1012 and *Re Roberts (Deceased)* [1978] 3 All ER 225. As a result it is likely to be difficult for Alan to establish this ground, particularly in the context of self-induced intoxication. The marriage could also be voidable if either party is suffering from a mental disorder (whether continuously or intermittently) within the meaning of the Mental Health Act 1983 so as to be unfitted for marriage: s12(d) MCA 1973. A temporary intoxication is unlikely to be classified as a mental disorder and is unlikely to be such that Alan is incapable of carrying out the ordinary duties and obligations of marriage. A temporary hysterical neurosis was insufficient in *Bennett* v *Bennett* [1969] 1 WLR 430.

If Alan does establish that the marriage is voidable Bertha can seek to satisfy the court that Alan behaved in a way that led Bertha to believe that he would not seek to have the marriage annulled: see s13(1) MCA 1973. There does not appear to be anything to suggest that Bertha could satisfy the court as to the defence of 'approbation'.

If Alan is not able to satisfy the court that the marriage is void or voidable he could seek to petition for divorce. However, he would not be able to petition until one year had elapsed from the date of the marriage: see s3(1) MCA 1973. Once the year has elapsed then he could seek to establish, first, that the marriage had irretrievably broken down and, second, that one or more of five facts is established: see s1(1) and (2) MCA 1973. One fact is that Bertha has behaved in such a way that Alan cannot reasonably be expected to live with her: see s1(2)(b) MCA 1973. Bertha's deceitful behaviour may be sufficient to establish this fact, together with the fact that they have not lived together since the marriage. A second fact is that Bertha has deserted Alan for a continuous period of at least two years immediately preceding the presentation of the petition: see s1(2)(c) MCA 1973. Alan should be advised that this ground is not easy to establish. Alternatively, Alan could establish that he and Bertha have lived apart for a continuous period of at least two years and Bertha consents to the decree: see s1(2)(d) MCA 1973. The final fact is that the parties have lived apart continuously for a period of five years: see s1(2)(e) MCA 1973. Given the delay involved in establishing the facts in s1(2)(c), (d) and (e) it is assumed that Alan would seek to rely on s1(2)(b) should he fail to challenge the validity of the marriage.

QUESTION THREE

Evaluate the view that the law of nullity, particularly in relation to voidable marriage, represents the imposition by law of moral values more pertinent to the nineteenth century than to the twenty-first.

University of London LLB Examination
(for External Students) Family Law June 2000 Q1

General Comment

This essay question invites the student to evaluate the law or nullity, particularly in relation to voidable marriage. As the student looks at the grounds he/she can critically look at them in terms of their relevance in a twenty-first century world. Recent case law on the right of transsexuals to marry is a good example of a twenty-first century situation controlled by a nineteenth- and twentieth-century moral values. Similarly, the matter of consummation concerns individual views which have changed over the years. Consent is also a matter of debate particularly in relation to arranged marriages.

Skeleton Solution

The distinction between void and voidable marriages; void marriages: prohibited degrees of relationships – either party is under sixteen – disregard to certain requirements as to formation of marriage – either party was already lawfully married – that the parties are respectively male and female – certain polygamous marriages; evaluation of these grounds in light of twenty-first century moral values particularly in relation to transsexuals and polygamous marriages; voidable marriages: non-consummation due to incapacity or wilful refusal – lack of consent – mental disorder, venereal disease and pregnancy by some other person; evaluation of these grounds in light of twenty-first century moral values particularly in relation to consummation and lack of consent.

Suggested Solution

The question invites an evaluation of the law of nullity and how it reflects the moral values of the nineteenth century compared to those of the twenty-first century. It should be stated that the number of petitions for nullity of marriage is very small, compared with many thousands of petitions presented for divorce. As a result the impact of any conflict in moral values is small in terms of the number of cases. However, it can be important in terms of the impact on the individuals concerned.

Petitions for nullity can be divided into two categories – those where it is alleged that the marriage is void and those where it is alleged that the marriage is voidable. Void marriages are those which are so defective on social and public policy grounds that the purported marriage cannot be said to have ever existed. Strictly speaking there is no need for a decree since a void marriage does not exist, but either party or a third party may apply for a degree to confirm the status of the marriage. The grounds for a void marriage include where the parties are within the prohibited degree of relationship: see s11(a)(i) Matrimonial Causes Act (MCA) 1973. The prohibited degrees are largely accepted on moral grounds as well as scientific grounds because of physical defects born of parents who share the same genes. The prohibited degrees have been relaxed in terms of in-laws – for example, by the Marriage (Prohibited Degrees of Relationship) Act 1986. A further ground is that one of the parties is under the age of 16 years: see s11(a)(ii) MCA 1973. This ground does not appear to have attracted criticism in the twenty-first century, even with changes in the behaviour of young people. A further ground is that the parties have disregarded certain essential procedural requirements: see s11(a)(iii) MCA 1973. This ground largely reflected nineteenth-century views on religious marriages – for example, the requirements to publish banns in a Church of England marriage. Now that civil marriages have more relaxed procedural requirements this ground attracts little controversy and comment. For example, marriages by Superintendent Registrar's Certificate have more relaxed requirements as to the parties' residence and as to where the marriage takes place. Even deliberate misdescriptions of the parties may not invalidate the marriage: see *Puttick* v *Attorney-General* [1979] 3 WLR 542. A further ground is that the one of the parties are already lawfully married: see s11(b) MCA 1973. Again this ground does not appear to be controversial in the twenty-first century.

There is also the ground that the parties are not respectively male and female: see s11(c) MCA 1973. This ground has attracted controversy in the late twentieth and twenty-first century mainly in relation to transsexuals. Can a person who was born a male but who then has an operation to become a woman then marry a man? The leading case remains *Corbett* v *Corbett* [1970] 2 WLR 1306 which held that sex is fixed at birth and cannot be changed by artificial means. As a result any marriage between men is void. This remains the position under English and Welsh law: see more recently *Re P and G (Transsexuals)* [1996] 2 FLR 90. This position has been challenged in the European Court of Human Rights on the basis that domestic law contravenes arts 8 (right to family life), 12 (right to marry) and 14 (prohibition on discrimination in applying Convention rights) of the European Convention on Human Rights (ECHR). These challenges have yet to be successful: see *Rees* v *United Kingdom* [1987] Fam Law 157, *Cossey* v *United Kingdom* [1991] Fam Law 362, *X, Y and Z* v *United Kingdom* [1997] 2 FLR 892 and *Sheffield and Horsham* v *United Kingdom* [1998] 2 FLR 928. However, the

European Court of Human Rights has criticised the UK government for not keeping the law under review. The UK is now in a minority of EU countries in not recognising the rights of transsexuals to have some kind of 'civil' marriage. The European Court is moving towards recognising the rights of transsexuals but awaits more of a consensus to emerge. The Home Secretary announced in November 2000 that any review would be postponed until after the next election. This ground is an example of a nineteenth-century concept of marriage being out of kilter with twenty-first century advances in medical science and in a greater acceptance of the rights of transsexuals. On a wider note the rights of same sex couples to some kind of 'civil' marriage are increasingly being recognised.

The final ground for voiding a marriage relates to polygamous marriages: see s11(d) MCA 1973. The consequences of this ground have largely been avoided in relation to potentially polygamous marriages: see Private International Law (Miscellaneous Provisions) Act 1995. As a result the ground only applies to actually polygamous marriages. The change in the law recognised that the nineteenth-century concept of marriage conflicted with a twenty-first century concept of marriage, taking into account the many British people who chose to marry abroad using a form of marriage which permitted polygamy.

A voidable marriage is defective but not in such a fundamental way. The marriage is treated as remaining valid until either party obtains a decree: see *De Reneville* v *De Reneville* [1948] 1 All ER 56. Only the parties can petition, not a third party. Since the marriage is treated as valid until a decree is obtained the consequences of marriage may remain. For example, the children of a voidable marriage will be treated as children of married parents both before and after the decree. There are special defences which can prevent the grant of a decree (see s13 MCA 1973) which are not available if the marriage is void.

The first two grounds for nullity in the case of a voidable marriage relate to the failure to consummate the marriage either because either party is incapable of consummating the marriage or because the respondent wilfully refuses to consummate the marriage: see s12(a) and (b) MCA 1973. A marriage is deemed to have been consummated as soon as the parties have sexual intercourse after the marriage ceremony. The sexual intercourse must be ordinary and complete and cannot be partial or imperfect: see *D* v *A* (1845) 1 Rob Eccl 279. The sterility of one party is irrelevant. Where a party lack the capacity to consummate the marriage the defect must be incurable or curable but only by treatment which involves danger to that party: see *S* v *S* [1962] 3 All ER 55. A party cannot petition on his or her own wilful refusal to consummate. A wilful refusal applies where the respondent has come to a settled and definite decision without just excuse: see *Horton* v *Horton* [1947] 2 All ER 871). Refusal can include situations where religious belief requires that both a civil wedding (as required by English law) and a religious wedding (as required by religious belief and custom of either or both parties) take place. If one party unreasonably refuses to take part in or arrange the religious wedding he or she can be said to be indirectly wilfully refusing to consummate the marriage:

see for example *Kaur* v *Singh* [1972] 1 All ER 292. Consummation carries with it the nineteenth-century value of marriage providing comfort to the parties and for the procreation of children. This value appears to have survived into the twenty-first century.

A marriage can also be voidable where either party did not validly consent to it, whether in consequence of duress, mistake or unsoundness of mind or otherwise: see s12(c) MCA 1973. This ground was in the past difficult to establish, particularly in relation to duress. Older cases required a threat of immediate danger to life, limb or liberty whereby the constraint destroyed the reality of consent: see *Szechter* v *Szechter* [1971] 2 WLR 170. The concept was based on a nineteenth-century concept of a Christian marriage freely entered into. In the twentieth century courts were asked to deal with non-Christian arranged marriages in which one party (usually the wife) argued that she had been pressured into the marriage by her family.

The courts have recognised that where threats, pressure or other behaviour is such as to destroy the reality of consent and overbears the will of the wife then the marriage can be voided: see *Hirani* v *Hirani* (1982) 4 FLR 232. This less restrictive approach to consent has brought the law more into line with a modern and liberal view of consent in marriage. There is, however, the potential for conflict with non-Christian concepts of arranged marriages.

The remaining grounds for avoiding a marriage relate to mental disorder (see s12(d) MCA 1973), venereal disease (see s12(e) MCA 1973) and the respondent being pregnant by some person other than the respondent at the time of the marriage: see s12(f) MCA 1973. These grounds are little used and attract little comment or case law. There are defences available to a petition relating to a voidable marriage, in particular the defence of approbation: see s13(1) MCA 1973. This defence may become more important as people live longer and may wish to marry when older without wishing to consummate the marriage.

There have been reviews of the law of nullity with a view to nullity being abolished. No change has been made to the law partly because the Christian faith places some importance on the distinction between nullity of marriage and divorce – for example, allowing remarriage in church. Non-Christian faiths can find the concept of nullity more acceptable than divorce. Divorce still carries a moral, religious and social stigma for some people which can be avoided or lessened by a petition for nullity. This view may be held more by older people than by younger persons brought up in a world more accepting of divorce. It is also possible to deal with nullity in a more confidential way, particularly in relation to medical evidence. There is also a bar to petitions for divorce in the first year of marriage (see s3(1) MCA 1973) which does not apply to nullity. In conclusion, while nullity does represent the law of moral values more pertinent to the nineteenth century it still plays an important role for a small number of petitioners each year. The area in which the law is most likely to change relates to same sex marriages the rights of transsexuals as a result of pressure from the European Court of Human Rights.

QUESTION FOUR

Anne and Bill were selected from many applicants by a national newspaper as 'the perfect strangers' to marry. The newspaper offered them a house for a year, a car and £4,000 a month for their continuing account of the marriage. They first met at the wedding ceremony arranged by the newspaper. Bill immediately knew that he did not want to marry Anne but felt he had to agree, with such wide media coverage (and with the promise of accommodation and money which he greatly needed). The marriage was consummated on their honeymoon but, when he told Anne of his reluctance to marry, they agreed to maintain the appearance of a marriage but to have no sexual relationship. In order to keep the house, the car and the monthly payments, their public image was one of marital bliss.

Ann had continued a sexual relationship with a pre-marriage boyfriend and discovered one month after the marriage that she was pregnant. Bill agreed, again for 'the sake of appearances', that he would acknowledge paternity. A son was born. Bill posed for photographs with Anne and the son and wrote in the newspapers of his happy family. However, at home he and Anne kept to the agreement. Then the newspaper promised them that if they remained a happily married couple for ten years, they would receive a lump sum of £500,000.

Bill has now decided that he wants to end the marriage and prove that the child is not his. Anne wants to keep the marriage intact and claims that Bill is the child's father.

How can Bill end the marriage? Can Anne prevent the marriage from being ended? What are Bill's responsibilities to the child?

University of London LLB Examination
(for External Students) Family Law June 1999 Q1

General Comment

The question deals with what was a topical story in the media. It uses a well publicised scenario as a a basis for discussion of various aspects of family law. The question initially asks about nullity of marriage. It looks at possible grounds based on duress and pregnancy per alium. It also deals with a possible defence to nullity of approbation. There are also possible grounds for divorce. The question then looks at the parentage of children and how to resolve disputes as to parentage. Finally, the student has to describe the responsibilities of a parent and a non-parent to the child.

Skeleton Solution

Nullity of marriage: lack of consent (s12(c) MCA 1973) – pregnancy per alium (s12(f) MCA 1973) – defence of approbation (s13(1) MCA 1973); divorce: basic ground of divorce (s1(2) MCA 1973) – fact of adultery plus intolerability (s1(2)(a) MCA 1973) – fact of behaviour (s1(2)(b) MCA 1973); dispute over paternity of child: scientific tests under ss20–23 FLRA 1969; responsibilities towards child: by father of child – by non-father who has treated the child as a child of the family – child support – application for child maintenance.

Suggested Solution

The first question is how can Bill end the marriage? The facts raise possible grounds for ending the marriage by nullity and by divorce. This answer begins with the nullity aspects since if Bill is successful in petitioning for divorce it is as if the marriage had not existed. As will be seen the grounds of nullity which could apply would make the marriage voidable rather than void. This means that a decree is necessary to prove that the marriage is a nullity and that any child of the marriage remains legitimate before and after the decree.

None of the grounds for making the marriage void under s11 Matrimonial Causes Act (MCA) 1973 appear to apply. In particular it is assumed that a proper marriage ceremony took place so s11(a)(iii) MCA 1973 does not apply. The facts suggest that the consummation grounds for voiding the marriage do not apply: see s12(a) and (b) MCA 1973. There may be an argument that Bill did not validly consent to the marriage in consequence of duress: see s12(c) MCA 1973. It is reported that Bill felt bound to go through with the marriage against his will because of the media coverage and the promise of accommodation and money. The test for duress is set out in *Szechter v Szechter* [1971] 2 WLR 170: has the will of Bill been overborne by genuinely and reasonably held fear caused by threat of immediate danger (for which Bill is not responsible) to life, limb or liberty, so that the constraint destroys the reality of consent? A later case, *Hirani v Hirani* (1982) 4 FLR 232, suggested a less stringent test, namely whether the threats, pressure or whatever is such as to destroy the reality of consent and overbears the will of the individual. Even applying the *Hirani* test it appears difficult for Bill to argue that the pressure of media coverage is such that his will was overborne. He voluntarily entered the arrangement with the media for considerable financial reward. In addition, *Szechter* suggests that any such pressure cannot be pressure for which Bill is responsible. Though there is conflicting authority on this point it is likely that the courts will not allow media pressure which Bill voluntarily invited to be a ground for voiding the marriage. The courts are likely to hold that Bill 'has made his bed and must now lie on it', namely take the consequences of his actions.

It is possible for Bill to argue that the marriage should be voided if Anne was pregnant by some other person at the time of the marriage: s12(f) MCA 1973. The question states that Anne became aware of being pregnant one month after the marriage. If she was pregnant at the time of the marriage Bill could petition on this ground.

Bill should be aware that if he petitions under s12(c) or (f) or uses both grounds Anne can defend the petition if she satisfies the court that Bill, with knowledge that it was open for him to have the marriage avoided, so conducted himself in relation to her as to lead her reasonably to believe that he would not seek to avoid the marriage and that it would be unjust to her to grant the decree: s13(1) MCA 1973. Bill has accepted the child 'for the sake of appearances'. The question does not state how long Bill has kept up this pretence, namely how long his marriage with Anne has lasted. The longer the pretence of marriage and fatherhood the more likely that Anne can mount a successful defence, provided she can show that Bill knew that he could take action to void the marriage. The courts will look at the conduct of the parties towards each other. Issues of public policy are unlikely to be applied by the court: see *D v D* [1979] 3 All ER 337. The more Anne can show that she has relied on the validity of the marriage, including the consequences for her child, the more likely she can show that it would be unjust for the marriage to be annulled. In addition, Bill must petition under s12(c) or (f) within three years of the marriage (see s13(2) MCA 1973), so if more than three years have elapsed he could not petition. There is the possibility of a court granting leave for a late petition but the circumstances do not appear to apply to Bill: see s13(4) MCA 1973. Bill could also not petition under s12(f) MCA 1973 unless he was ignorant that Anne was pregnant by another man at the time of the marriage. All in all the chances of Bill being able to successfully petition for nullity seem slim.

Bill could seek to end the marriage by petitioning for divorce. There is an absolute bar on petitioning for divorce before the expiration of one year from the date of the marriage: see s3(1) MCA 1973. Assuming one year has elapsed Bill could petition on the basis that the marriage has broken down irretrievably: see s1(1) MCA 1973. In order to show that the marriage has irretrievably broken down he must satisfy the court as to one or more of five facts: s1(2) MCA 1973. The first fact he could seek to rely upon is that Anne has committed adultery and that he finds it intolerable to live with her: s1(2)(a) MCA 1973. The facts in the question show that Anne has continued to have a sexual relationship with her pre-marriage boyfriend so it appears that adultery can be established. Bill can then argue that he finds it intolerable to live with Anne. The intolerability does not have to be as a consequence of the adultery: see *Cleary v Cleary* [1974] 1 WLR 73. The test of 'intolerability' is subjective, namely what Bill finds intolerable as opposed to a reasonable petitioner. The difficulty with a petition based on adultery is that Bill could not rely on adultery if he and Anne lived with each other for a period, or periods together, exceeding six months: s2(1) MCA 1973. There may be some argument that Bill and Anne's non-sexual sharing of the family home is not 'living together'. However, if the court held that it was 'living together' then it would be a bar to the petition. Bill and Anne would have to separate and live apart for Bill to be able to petition again on the ground of adultery. Alternatively, Bill could petition for divorce on fact that Anne has behaved in such a way that he cannot reasonably be expected to live with her: see s1(2)(b) MCA 1973. The difficulty in establishing this fact is that any unreasonableness in Anne's behaviour has been condoned by Bill who has continued to maintain the pretence of living with Anne. The court would disregard any period or periods of 'living together' of six months or less in determining whether Bill could not reasonably be expected to live with Anne: see s2(3) MCA 1973. Depending on the precise circumstances of Bill and Anne living together it appears that Bill would have difficulty in successfully petitioning using this fact. None of the other facts in s1(2) MCA 1973 appear to apply. It appears that Bill will have to separate from Anne, make it clear that his marriage to her is a sham, before he is likely to succeed in petitioning for divorce.

Bill's responsibilities to the child depend on whether he is the child's real father. A child born to a mother who is married at the time of the child's birth is presumed at common law to be the legitimate child of the mother and her husband. On this basis Bill would be presumed to be the child's father. Bill could seek to rebut this presumption on a balance of probabilities: see s26 Family Law Reform Act (FLRA) 1969. However, Bill should be advised that the courts consider the status of a child to be a serious matter and require material proof: see *W* v *K* [1988] 1 FLR 86. Bill can be advised that he can ask the courts to ascertain the child's paternity using scientific tests: see ss20–23 FLRA 1969. In particular the courts can direct DNA testing which in most cases will be conclusive in establishing whether Bill is or is not the child's real father. Even if Anne objects to the scientific tests the court can order them provided this is in the interests of the child. Bill can either make a free-standing application to establish parentage (under s55A Family Law Act 1986) or respond to an application brought against him (eg for child support) by disputing paternity and asking for the court to direct scientific tests. If Bill is found to be the child's father he will have parental responsibility for the child. This will include the responsibility to financially support the child: see s78(6) Social Security and Administration Act 1992. Anne can apply to the Child Support Agency for a child-support assessment to be made against him: see Child Support Act 1991.

If Bill is found not be the father of the child he could still be liable to provide financial support for the child. For example, in divorce or nullity proceedings Anne could seek child maintenance from Bill on the basis that he treated the child 'as a child of the family': see s52 MCA 1973. This is an objective test. It is immaterial whether Bill knew that the child was not his. Again it is not clear how long the 'pretence of marriage' has been maintained. The longer the period the more likely that Bill will be found to have treated the child as a child of the family. If he is found to have treated the child as a child of the family then Anne could ask the court to order maintenance and/or lump sum payments and/or property orders against Bill in favour of the child or in favour of Anne for the benefit of the child: see ss23–24A MCA 1973.

Chapter 3

Divorce

3.1   **Introduction**

3.2   **Key points**

3.3   **Key cases and statute**

3.4   **Questions and suggested solutions**

3.1 Introduction

The first modern law relating to divorce dates from 1937. The grounds for divorce were fault based eg adultery, cruelty and desertion and had to be proved beyond reasonable doubt – the criminal standard of proof. The term 'matrimonial offence' characterised divorce grounds as being quasi-criminal in nature. By the late sixties the need for reform had become apparent. It was argued that the divorce laws did not accord with social reality and the quasi-criminal nature of the proceedings resulting in unnecessary bitterness between the divorcing couple. Two reports published at this time, *Putting Asunder* (presented by a group appointed by the Archbishop of Canterbury) and *Reform of the Grounds of Divorce: The Field of Choice* (Law Commission Report No 6 (1966), Cmnd 3123), paved the way for reform. The objectives of the reforms were twofold, namely:

a) to buttress rather than to undermine the stability of marriage; and

b) to enable the empty shell of marriage to be destroyed with the minimum of bitterness, distress and humiliation.

The Divorce Reform Act of 1969 made irretrievable breakdown of marriage the sole ground for divorce. The breakdown had to be established by one of five 'facts' which included two years living apart with consent and five years living apart without consent. These are the no fault grounds. However adultery, desertion and behaviour were retained as evidence of irretrievable breakdown alongside the no fault grounds and it remains possible to obtain a divorce on proof of, for example, behaviour which the petitioner cannot reasonably be expected to tolerate. The law is now contained in the Matrimonial Causes Act of 1973.

In 1977 procedural changes were introduced. Undefended divorces are now dealt with by the district judge. The district judge examines the petition and a supporting affidavit and, if satisfied that the contents are proved, will issue and file a certificate to that effect.

The decree nisi is then issued in open court at a later date. The result has been that the 'ability of the court to carry out its statutory duty to enquire into the facts alleged is greatly circumscribed' (see the Booth Report – Report of the Matrimonial Causes Procedure Committee 1985) and district judges do little more than rubber stamp petitions. In some respects this is tantamount to divorce on demand. Alongside these procedural changes, parties are increasingly encouraged to resolve disputes over the residence of children and over maintenance and property themselves. This process, referred to as conciliation, has as its objective the establishment of a settlement which involves both parties and which will therefore result in less future hostility between them.

Part I of the Family Law Act 1996 has been brought into force. However, the Lord Chancellor announced in 2001 that Part II (the radical reforms to divorce law) would not be brought into force and would eventually be repealed: see Chapter 4.

3.2 Key points

One year bar

There is an absolute bar on the presentation of a divorce petition within one year of the celebration of marriage. This is strictly enforced. In *Butler* v *Butler* [1990] 1 FLR 114, 11 months after her marriage the petitioner wife presented a petition for judicial separation which was later amended to become a petition for divorce, which was granted. The divorce was set aside on the ground that the petition had been presented one month too early. There is no discretion to ignore the one year bar.

Note: The petitioner may rely on matters that occurred in the first 12 months.

The ground for divorce

A petition for divorce may be presented by either party to a marriage on the ground that the marriage has broken down irretrievably: s1(1) MCA 1973. The petitioner must satisfy the court of one of five facts set out in s1(2). It is important to emphasise that there is no causal connection between s1(1) and s1(2). In other words the petitioner has to prove two things: firstly that the marriage has irretrievably broken down and secondly that one of the facts in s1(2) is satisfied. The petitioner does not have to prove that the marriage has broken down because of one of the facts in s1(2). (See *Buffery* v *Buffery* [1988] 2 FLR 365.) Note that the ability of the court to inquire into the facts alleged is very limited in undefended cases. This is especially so as regards a petition based upon the respondent's adultery. Since October 1991 the petitioner does not have to cite the co-respondent (the person with whom it is alleged the respondent has committed adultery) even if she knows the identity of the co-respondent. It suffices for the petitioner to state that the identity of the person with whom the respondent is known to the petitioner but the petitioner prefers not to cite that person as co-respondent.

The 'five facts' – s1(2) Matrimonial Causes Act 1973

a) Section 1(2)(a): That the respondent has committed adultery and the petitioner finds it intolerable to live with the respondent.

   i) The adultery must be voluntary. This clearly excludes rape.

   ii) Sexual intercourse is the penetration by the male of the female genitalia: *Dennis* v *Dennis* [1955] 2 All ER 51.

   iii) The definition of adultery presupposes a sexual relationship with a person of the opposite sex. The respondent's homosexuality may be sufficient for a petition based on s1(2)(b).

   iv) The standard of proof is high and proof must be clear: *Bastable* v *Bastable* [1968] 3 All ER 701; *Serio* v *Serio* (1983) 4 FLR 756.

   v) The Act is not clear on whether the intolerability must arise from the act of adultery or whether it can be independent of it. The Court of Appeal took the latter view in *Cleary* v *Cleary* [1974] 1 WLR 73 and although some doubts were cast on this interpretation in *Carr* v *Carr* [1974] 1 WLR 1534 this is now the established position.

   vi) The petitioner will not be permitted to rely on this ground where the parties have lived together for a period or periods exceeding six months following disclosure to the petitioner of the adultery. The disregard of a shorter period is intended to allow the parties to attempt reconciliation: s2 MCA 1973; *Biggs* v *Biggs* [1977] 1 All ER 20.

b) Section 1(2)(b): That the respondent has behaved in such a way that the petitioner cannot reasonably be expected to live with the respondent.

   i) The test is whether a right thinking person would come to the conclusion that this husband has behaved in such a way that this wife cannot reasonably be expected to live with him taking account the whole of the circumstances and the characters and personalities of the parties.

   There exists therefore both a subjective and objective element: *Livingstone-Stallard* v *Livingstone-Stallard* [1974] 2 All ER 776; *Buffery* v *Buffery* [1988] 2 FLR 365.

   ii) A wide range of behaviour is included

   Financial responsibility: *Carter-Fea* v *Carter-Fea* [1987] Fam Law 131.

   Physical violence: *Bergin* v *Bergin* [1983] 1 All ER 905.

   Alcoholism coupled with violence: *Ash* v *Ash* [1972] 1 All ER 582.

   Acts which trivial in themselves were 'a constant atmosphere of criticism, disapproval and boorish behaviour': *Livingstone-Stallard* v *Livingstone-Stallard* (above); *O'Neill* v *O'Neill* [1975] 3 All ER 289.

iii) Some forms of behaviour will fail. It must depend on all the circumstances: *Birch* v *Birch* [1992] 1 FLR 564.

Mere lack of affection: *Pheasant* v *Pheasant* [1972] 1 All ER 587.

Extreme moodiness: *Richards* v *Richards* [1972] 3 All ER 695.

Mere drifting apart: *Buffery* v *Buffery* [1988] 2 FLR 365.

Unsatisfactory sexual performance: *Dowden* v *Dowden* (1977) 8 Fam Law 106.

iv) Involuntary behaviour. It is not necessary to prove intention and the fact that the respondent is suffering from some illness is not necessarily a bar to a decree.

Manic depressive illness: *Katz* v *Katz* [1972] 3 All ER 219.

Epilepsy: *Thurlow* v *Thurlow* [1976] Fam 32.

It is a question of fact and degree in each case: *Richards* v *Richards* [1972] 3 All ER 695.

v) Any period of less than six months cohabitation after the last incident relied upon in the petition shall be disregarded for establishing the reasonableness of continued cohabitation: s2(3) MCA 1973.

A longer period will be disregarded if the petition had no alternative but to remain with the respondent.

c) Section 1(2)(c): That the respondent has deserted the petitioner for a period of at least two years immediately preceding the presentation of the petition.

i) It is only necessary to rely on this ground where the respondent will not consent to a petition based on two years separation, there are no other grounds for divorce and the petitioner does not want to wait for the expiry of the five-year period under s1(2)(e).

ii) The fact of separation. There must be a complete withdrawal from cohabitation.

Desertion is a withdrawal from a state of affairs rather than a place: *Milligan* v *Milligan* [1941] 2 All ER 62.

Separation can be complete under the same roof: *Naylor* v *Naylor* [1961] 2 All ER 129; *Hopes* v *Hopes* [1948] 2 All ER 920.

iii) Intention to desert. Usually inferred from the fact of departure. An involuntary desertion can constitute desertion once the intention is formed and communicated: *Beeken* v *Beeken* [1948] P 302; *Nutley* v *Nutley* [1970] 1 All ER 410.

Desertion will continue through involuntary separation if the intention had been formed beforehand.

Where the respondent suffers from mental illness the question is whether he is capable of forming the necessary intention to desert.

iv) Petitioner does not consent.

Consent can be expressed – a separation agreement – or implied, but relief at departure is not consent: *Harriman v Harriman* [1909] P 123.

Consent after the de facto separation can bring desertion to an end: *Pizey v Pizey* [1961] P 101.

Consent to separation can be for a limited period in which case desertion will begin at the end of the period: *Shaw v Shaw* [1939] P 269.

The refusal of a reasonable offer of reconciliation can result in desertion beginning: *Gallagher v Gallagher* [1965] 2 All ER 967.

v) No just cause to leave.

Where the petitioner's conduct is relied upon it must be 'grave and weighty' and not merely the wear and tear of married life: *Quoraishi v Quoraishi* [1985] FLR 780.

vi) No period of six months cohabitation shall break the continuity of separation for the two year period but any period of cohabitation shall not count towards that two year period.

vii) The termination of desertion. Factors include an agreement to live apart, a decree of judicial separation, the resumption of cohabitation for a prolonged period and by the deserting spouse making a genuine offer to resume cohabitation.

viii) Constructive desertion. This is conduct by one spouse which has the effect of driving the other spouse out. Such behaviour would almost always give rise to a petition based on s1(2)(b).

d) Section 1(2)(d): That the parties to the marriage have lived apart for a continuous period of at least two years immediately preceding the presentation of the petition and the respondent consents to a decree being granted.

i) Living apart. Section 1(6) states that the parties will not be living apart if they are living in the same household. The term household is not defined.

There must be recognition by at least one of the parties that the marriage is at an end but oddly this need not be communicated to the other: *Santos v Santos* [1972] 2 All ER 246.

The parties can live apart in the same household: *Mouncer v Mouncer* [1972] 1 All ER 289; *Fuller v Fuller* [1973] 2 All ER 650.

ii) Consent. Consent must be freely given and may be withdrawn at any time up to the decree nisi. There must be capacity to give consent.

iii) No account will be taken of any period or periods not exceeding six months during which the parties resumed living together.

iv) The day of separation is excluded for the purpose of calculating the two year period.

e) Section 1(2)(e): That the parties to the marriage have lived apart for a continuous period of at least five years immediately preceding the presentation of the petition.

Interpretations of living apart are the same as considered above.

f) Financial protection to petitions based on s1(2)(d) and s1(2)(e).

   i) Under s10 the courts have powers to consider on application the respondent's financial position on divorce and to delay the decree absolute unless satisfied that the financial provision is fair and reasonable or the best that can be made in the circumstances.

   ii) Section 10(3) directs the court to consider all the circumstances including the age, health, conduct, earning capacity, financial resources and financial obligations of each of the parties and includes regard to the financial position of the respondent after the death of the petitioner: *Lombardi* v *Lombardi* [1973] 3 All ER 625.

   iii) The sole purpose is to delay the decree absolute until a financial settlement is reached. The court can refuse the application if there are circumstances which make the granting of the decree desirable and has obtained an undertaking that satisfactory provision will be made: *Grigson* v *Grigson* [1974] 1 All ER 478.

   iv) In *Garcia* v *Garcia* [1992] 1 FLR 256 the Court of Appeal held that s10 could be properly invoked to remedy the fact that the petitioner husband and father had failed to make maintenance payments for his child contrary to a previous agreement. This may be a useful authority for those mothers faced with child care costs prior to the Child Support Agency making an assessment.

g) Refusal of a decree after five years separation.

   i) Under s5 of the Act the respondent can oppose the grant of the petition on the grounds that dissolution of the marriage would result in grave financial or other hardship and that it would be wrong in all the circumstances to dissolve the marriage.

   ii) Cases on financial hardship have focused almost exclusively on the loss of pension rights, particularly where the parties are approaching retirement and the marriage has lasted many years (*Le Marchant* v *Le Marchant* [1977] 1 WLR 559), though the court will take account of the respondent's assets (*Archer* v *Archer* [1999] 1 FLR 327) and has powers to make pension provision orders to offset the hardship.

   iii) Other forms of hardship alleged have relied on the social stigma attached to divorce within certain cultures. None have been successful: *Banik* v *Banik* [1973] 3 All ER 45; *Parghi* v *Parghi* (1973) 117 SJ 582.

   iv) Grave in this context has its ordinary meaning. Accordingly young petitioners will find it hard to establish grave financial hardship: *Mathias* v *Mathias* [1972] 3 WLR 201.

v) The likely refusal of the petition can result in an improved offer of a financial settlement to offset any loss: *Le Marchant* v *Le Marchant* [1977] 1 WLR 559.

The compensation must however offset the loss: *Julian* v *Julian* (1972) 116 SJ 763.

In *Jackson* v *Jackson* [1993] 2 FLR 851 the 71-year-old husband petitioned under s1(2)(e) and his 62-year-old wife put in a s5 defence arguing that the loss of a British Rail widow's pension of £15.00 per week would cause her grave financial hardship. Her income comprised £28.00 per week state pension and £25.00 per week board and lodgings from her son. The defence failed and the Court of Appeal dismissed her appeal. Although the loss of £15.00 per week to a £60.00 per week income person might be considered a grave loss, the fact that such receipt would pro rata reduce her state provision meant that, in reality, there was no loss.

vi) The court will consider the conduct of the parties, the interests of the parties and any children or other persons concerned in deciding whether it would be wrong to dissolve the marriage.

Note that the hardship defence is retained in the Family Law Act 1996: see Chapter 4.

3.3 Key cases and statute

- *Bastable* v *Bastable* [1968] 3 All ER 701
  Ground of adultery

- *Buffery* v *Buffery* [1988] 2 FLR 365
  Ground of behaviour

- *Carr* v *Carr* [1974] 1 WLR 1534
  Adultery and intolerability

- *K* v *K* [1997] 1 FLR 35
  Defence of grave hardship

- *Santos* v *Santos* [1972] 2 WLR 889
  Meaning of living apart

- Matrimonial Causes Act 1973 – grounds for divorce

3.4 Questions and suggested solutions

QUESTION ONE

Antonia married Benjamin in 1975. Their marriage was an extremely happy one until early 1988 when Benjamin started having an affair with Clarissa, the owner of a local health club. Benjamin chose not to leave the matrimonial home, but moved out of the bedroom he shared with Antonia and into the spare room in June 1988. Antonia continued to do Benjamin's laundry for him and he ate at least four meals a week with her. In late 1991, however, Benjamin decided to move in with Clarissa.

Benjamin now wishes to divorce Antonia and marry Clarissa. Antonia does not want to be divorced as she believes that she and her husband can be reconciled. She is, further, very worried about her position with respect to the private pension plan that Benjamin has been investing in since their marriage.

Advise Antonia.

University of London LLB Examination
(for External Students) Family Law June 1993 Q2

General Comment

This question invites discussion as to whether Benjamin can satisfy one or more of the facts which establish irretrievable breakdown and so enable him to petition successfully for divorce. Particular attention has to be paid to the living apart facts, particularly the fact of five years living apart. Advice has to be given as to whether such a fact can be satisfied and, if it can, the special defences open to Antonia in ss5 and 10 Matrimonial Causes Act 1973 and how they might safeguard the position as regards her widow's pension.

Skeleton Solution

The ground of irretrievable breakdown for divorce – which of the five facts in s1(2) MCA 1973 could Benjamin seek to satisfy? – the fact of living apart for five years, in particular 'living apart' in the same household – the defence in s5 MCA 1973 of grave financial hardship and unjust to grant a divorce, with reference to Antonia and the widow's pension – the safeguard in s10 MCA 1973 with regard to the widow's pension.

Suggested Solution

Antonia should be advised that there is only one ground for divorce, namely that the marriage has 'broken down irretrievably': s1(1) Matrimonial Causes Act (MCA) 1973. Benjamin would have to satisfy the court that this was the case and also establish one or more of five facts before he could successfully petition for divorce: s1(2) MCA 1973, *Buffery v Buffery* [1988] 2 FLR 365. Before discussing whether Benjamin could establish one or more of those facts Antonia should be advised that if Benjamin does petition for divorce any solicitor acting for him has to discuss the possibility of a reconciliation with him: see s6(1) MCA 1973. It is assumed that Benjamin does not wish to be reconciled with Antonia notwithstanding her wish to be reconciled with him.

Benjamin cannot petition on the fact of his own adultery: see s1(2)(a) MCA 1973. There is no indication of adultery on Antonia's part. There is no indication that Antonia has behaved in such a way that Benjamin cannot reasonably be expected to live with her as is required to satisfy the second fact: see s1(2)(b) MCA 1973. There is no indication that Antonia has deserted Benjamin or has so behaved as to drive him out in a manner amounting to constructive desertion: see the fact in s1(2)(c) MCA 1973. Antonia has made it clear that she does not want a divorce so she would not give consent as is required to satisfy the fourth fact, that of living apart for two years and the respondent consenting to the decree: see s1(2)(d) MCA 1973.

This leaves one remaining fact upon which Benjamin might seek to rely, that of living apart for five years: see s1(2)(e) MCA 1973. The facts in this case suggest that in June 1988 Benjamin moved out of the matrimonial bedroom and moved into the spare room. However, he did not move out of the matrimonial home until late 1991. If Benjamin wishes to petition for divorce immediately using the fact of living apart for five years he must show that he and Antonia were living apart within the same household from June 1988 to the time he actually left the household. It will not be easy for Benjamin to satisfy a court in this respect. Firstly a court will look to the statutory interpretation of 'living apart' whereby a husband and wife shall be treated as living apart 'unless they are living with each other in the same household': see s2(6) MCA 1973. Benjamin may seek to argue that he and Antonia were no longer 'living with each other' from June 1988 even though he remained in the same house. He may also seek to argue that there was no 'household' from June 1988. It is important to note that Antonia continued to do Benjamin's laundry and that he continued to share at least four meals a week with her. This suggests that there was still a common household even though they did not share the same bedroom. In *Mouncer* v *Mouncer* [1972] 1 All ER 289 there were similar facts. The husband and wife slept in separate bedrooms but ate their meals together and with the children. The wife prepared the meals. They shared the cleaning though the wife in that case did not do the husband's laundry. It was held that the spouses had not been living apart. They still shared the same household. The rejection of the normal physical relationship between husband and wife and the absence of normal affection was not sufficient to constitute living apart. On the basis of that authority it would appear that Benjamin would be unsuccessful in petitioning on the basis of five years living apart.

There is another authority, *Fuller* v *Fuller* [1973] 2 All ER 650, where spouses living in the same house were held to be living apart. That case had special facts and involved a gravely ill husband going to live in the house where the wife lived with another man. The wife prepared the husband's meals which he ate with the rest of the household. She did his laundry. However both spouses clearly regarded the marriage as at an end since the wife lived with another man. The husband was no different to a lodger. That case can be distinguished from that of Antonia. Antonia did not regard the marriage as at an end during the relevant period. She and Benjamin continue to share the matrimonial household and apparently carry on as a household in terms of meals and laundry. In such circumstances it is unlikely that Benjamin could successfully petition on the basis of five years living apart at this moment in time.

Antonia should be advised that 'living apart' only requires one party to recognise that the marriage is at an end. This need not be communicated to the other party at the time the 'living apart' is said to commence though the court must be able to identify some occurrence confirming the petitioner's recognition that the marriage was at an end: see *Santos* v *Santos* [1972] 2 WLR 889. In the unlikely event that Benjamin is able to establish living apart he can show the court that this began at the moment he started his affair with Clarissa even if Antonia was not aware of that at the time.

With regard to Antonia's pension position it is assumed that if there is no divorce her position will remain unaltered. If there is a divorce she could lose her right to a share in that pension after Benjamin has retired and, after his death, her right to the widow's pension. In this respect she could defend a petition brought under s1(2)(e) if she could show that the dissolution of the marriage would result in grave financial or other hardship and that it would in all the circumstances be wrong to dissolve the marriage: see s5 MCA 1973. The court would consider all the circumstances including the conduct of the parties. Hardship includes the chance of acquiring pension rights (including a widow's pension): see s5(3) MCA 1973. A private pension plan, when compared with a state pension, is likely to be a substantial benefit to Antonia. Therefore the loss of the chance of acquiring such a pension could amount to 'grave financial hardship'. If Antonia is relatively young and able to go out to work and re-establish herself and the prospect of the pension is remote because Benjamin is also relatively young, then the loss of the pension rights may be too remote and so not grave: see *Mathias* v *Mathias* [1972] 3 WLR 201. If Antonia is older, has not worked during the marriage and so has little prospect of financial independence and the prospect of enjoying the pension rights is in the foreseeable future then the loss of those rights is more likely to be grave: see *Dorrell* v *Dorrell* [1972] 2 WLR 1087. This could be the case given that Antonia has been married to Benjamin for some 18 years. If Antonia is able to satisfy the court that she would suffer grave financial hardship she must also satisfy the court that it would be wrong to dissolve the marriage. If Antonia has been blameless and is of such an age and situation as to have little financial independence (having depended on Benjamin financially) then the court may conclude that it is unjust to allow Benjamin to divorce her. Benjamin may argue that it would be just to dissolve the marriage so that he can marry Clarissa but such an argument is likely to fail if the court considers that he has treated Antonia badly. Benjamin can also seek to compensate Antonia for any loss that she would suffer if there was a divorce: see *Parker* v *Parker* [1972] 2 WLR 21; *Le Marchant* v *Le Marchant* [1977] 1 WLR 559. Case law suggests that such compensation would have to be generous in order to safeguard Antonia's position: see *Parker* and *Julian* v *Julian* (1972) 116 SJ 763.

Antonia should also be advised that should Benjamin obtain a decree nisi of divorce under s1(2)(e) she could prevent the decree from being made absolute until Benjamin satisfies the court that he need make no financial provision for Antonia or that he has made reasonable financial provision for her or has put forward firm proposals for such provision: see s10 MCA 1973. This is likely to force Benjamin to provide for Antonia to make up for any loss in his private pension.

In conclusion Antonia can be advised that Benjamin is unlikely to be successful in petitioning for divorce at this point in time. The only fact upon which he could seek to rely is that of living apart for five years and that fact would be difficult to establish given that he remained in the same household as Antonia for most of the five years period. Even if he were successful Antonia's financial position would be safeguarded by firstly s5 and then by s10 of the Matrimonial Causes Act 1973. Benjamin will be able to bring a petition based on five years living apart in late 1996 but again Antonia's financial position is likely to be protected by ss5 and 10.

QUESTION TWO

Albert married Bridget in 1987. In December 1989, Bridget, a professional skier, was involved in a skiing accident, as a result of which she incurred permanent brain damage, leaving her with severe mental and physical disabilities.

Following the accident, Bridget spent six months in hospital. On her release in June 1990, she returned to the matrimonial home where she has been cared for ever since by Albert and his mother.

Albert's initial reaction to Bridget's misfortune was that, given his view of marriage as a life-long commitment, he would stay with his wife, although he might have affairs from time to time. As the years have passed, however, and there has been no improvement in Bridget's condition, he has changed his mind. Albert would now like his marriage to be dissolved.

Advise Albert.

University of London LLB Examination
(for External Students) Family Law June 1994 Q1

General Comment

The question requires discussion of the grounds of divorce in the difficult circumstances of a spouse suffering brain damage after an accident. The question as to whether such a spouse has 'behaved' in such a way that the petitioning spouse can no longer reasonably be expected to live with her requires particular discussion. The living apart grounds should also be mentioned.

Skeleton Solution

Single ground for divorce: irretrievable breakdown (s1(1) Matrimonial Causes Act 1973) – need to satisfy one or more of the five facts (s1(2) MCA 1973) – fact of behaviour (s1(2)(b) MCA 1973) and whether a brain damaged spouse could be said to have 'behaved' in such a way that Albert could not reasonably be expected to live with her – whether Bridget has the capacity to consent in order to satisfy the living apart for two years with consent ground (s1(2)(d) MCA 1973) – living apart for five years (s1(2)(e) MCA 1973) – financial provision for Bridget (ss5 and 10 MCA 1973).

Suggested Solution

Albert should be advised that there is only one ground for divorce, namely that his marriage with Bridget has irretrievably broken down: see s1(1) of the Matrimonial Causes Act 1973 – hereinafter referred to as the MCA 1973. In addition, the court cannot hold the marriage to have broken down irretrievably unless he satisfies the court of one or more of five facts: see s1(2) MCA 1973. These are two separate requirements which must individually be satisfied: see *Buffery* v *Buffery* [1988] 2 FLR 365. Even if Albert is able to satisfy the court that the marriage has irretrievably broken down, a divorce cannot be granted to him unless one or more of the five facts is satisfied. Establishing one or more of the five facts is likely to be the main difficulty facing Albert when he tries to obtain a divorce from Bridget.

The first fact is based on adultery. There is no suggestion of any adultery on Bridget's part so this fact is not available to Albert. He could not rely on his own adultery. The second fact is that Bridget has behaved in such a way that Albert cannot reasonably be expected to live with her (s1(2)(b) MCA 1973). In order to satisfy this fact Albert must demonstrate that Bridget behaved in a particular way and that this behaviour had a particular impact on him. The court will then apply an objective test as to whether Albert can reasonably be expected to live with Bridget but taking into account the individual personalities, characteristics, disposition and behaviour of the parties: see *Ash* v *Ash* [1972] 2 WLR 347. Put in another way, the court would ask itself whether a right thinking person would come to the conclusion that Bridget has behaved in such a way that Albert cannot be reasonably expected to live with her taking into account the whole of the circumstances and the characteristics and personalities of the parties: see *Livingstone-Stallard* v *Livingstone-Stallard* [1974] 3 WLR 302.

The difficulty for Albert is that it may be difficult for him to satisfy a court that Bridget has 'behaved' in such a way that he cannot reasonably be expected to live with her. She has suffered an accident which incurred permanent brain damage leaving her with severe mental and physical disabilities. In *Katz* v *Katz* [1972] 1 WLR 955 the husband was mentally ill and behaved badly towards his wife. It was held that 'behaviour' was more than a mere state of affairs or a state of mind. It was action or conduct by one spouse which affected the other and which had some reference to the marriage. The court applied the test for s1(2)(b), after making allowances for the husband's disabilities, and granted a decree of divorce. It is important to note that in that case the mentally ill spouse was abusive towards his wife, so 'behaved' in an identifiable way. His wife was badly affected by his behaviour and attempted suicide. By contrast in *Richards* v *Richards* [1972] 1 WLR 1073 the mentally ill husband was moody and taciturn and did not sleep properly, which disturbed his wife. There was a minor incident of violence. The wife's petition was dismissed since the court made a value judgement about the husband's behaviour and the effect of that behaviour on the wife. Though the marriage had irretrievably broken down the wife had failed to satisfy s1(2)(b). In a third case, *Thurlow* v *Thurlow* [1975] 2 All ER 979 a wife's behaviour gradually deteriorated due to a brain disorder. She became incontinent, was bad-tempered and threw objects about. She wandered the streets. Her behaviour caused her husband considerable distress. He tried to hold down a job, care for his wife and run the household. The strain made him ill. It was held that where 'behaviour' stemmed from misfortune which stemmed from accidental injury the court would take full account of all the obligations of being married. This included the normal duty to accept and to share the burden imposed on the marriage as a result of the physical or mental ill-health of one spouse. This had to be balanced against the capacity of the petitioner to withstand the stress imposed by the behaviour, the steps taken to cope with it, the length of time during which the petitioner had been called upon to bear it, and the actual or potential effect upon his health. Since the wife in that case required indefinite institutional care, and the strain on the husband was so great, a decree was granted. Whether Albert will succeed in satisfying s1(2)(b) will depend on how Bridget's condition manifests itself and the effect her condition has had on him. If her behaviour is similar to that of the wife and the effect on the husband as in *Thurlow* then a petition is likely to succeed. If the circumstances are more akin to that in *Richards* then a petition is likely to fail.

The next fact is based on desertion (see s1(2)(c) MCA 1973), but since there is no evidence of this it will not be discussed further. The next fact is based on Albert and Bridget having lived apart for a continuous period of two years and Bridget consenting to the petition: see s1(2)(d) MCA 1973. Albert does not appear to be living apart from Bridget at the moment. Indeed, he and his mother are caring for her in the matrimonial home. Should arrangements be made whereby he and Bridget live part then this ground may come to apply. However, Bridget may not have the mental capacity to give the required consent even if she wanted to. She must have the capacity to be able to understand what she is consenting to. This capacity is similar to that needed in order to consent to marriage: see *Mason v Mason* [1972] 3 All ER 315. If Bridget refuses to consent or does not have the capacity to consent then Albert may have to wait for five years and rely on the ground of five years of continuously living apart (when Bridget's consent would not be required): see s1(2)(e) MCA 1973. Should Albert rely on either s1(2)(d) or (e) there are provisions which oblige him to make financial provision for Bridget: see ss5 and 10 MCA 1973. If he failed to make financial provision for her then she could defend or delay any petition he brought.

In conclusion, should Albert want an immediate divorce, the only fact he might be able to satisfy would be based on behaviour: see s1(2)(b) MCA 1973. This may be difficult to satisfy unless Bridget's condition is such that it causes her to act in a way that puts a considerable strain on Albert's health. If her condition is passive then a petition is likely to fail. Given the likely difficulties involved in obtaining any consent to a petition Albert would be left with the fact of living apart for a continuous period of five years.

QUESTION THREE

Mary married Nicolas in 1980 and they have two children, now aged ten and eight respectively. When they married, Mary and Nicolas agreed that should Olive, Mary's schizophrenic sister, ever be in need of care or accommodation, she could come and live with them. The couple both knew that it would be very difficult if Olive ever did come to live with them, but nevertheless, in 1990, after she contracted pneumonia, Olive moved in with Mary and Nicolas. Olive's presence in the house resulted in domestic discord. Nicolas told Mary that the situation was impossible and that he would leave her if Olive remained. Mary told Nicolas that she would not abandon her sister.

In January 1992, Nicolas left the matrimonial home, telling Mary that although he still loved her and the children, he could not live in the same house as Olive. Nicolas returned in December 1992 for Christmas, but, as Olive was still there and the situation had not improved, he left again in early July 1993. Nicolas remained in touch with Mary both by telephone and letter and recently wrote to her asking to ensure that Olive would leave so that he and Mary could resume their marriage. Mary replied that she could never do this because she was afraid that Olive would commit suicide.

Nicolas has decided that his marriage is now over and wishes to divorce Mary.

Advise Nicolas.

University of London LLB Examination
(for External Students) Family Law June 1995 Q5

General Comment

The question invites discussion of various facts which must be shown in order to obtain a divorce. The fact of behaviour, whereby one party finds it unreasonable to live with the other, requires particular examination, especially in light of the unusual circumstances involving the mentally ill sister. There is also the fact of desertion. In this case it may be possible to show constructive desertion. Finally, there are the living apart facts. The fact of the parties living apart is complicated by the husband returning to the household. How this affects the period of living apart needs to be explained. Indeed, the reconciliation provisions in s2 of the Matrimonial Causes Act 1973 are a particular feature of the question in relation to all the available facts for divorce.

Skeleton Solution

Need to establish irretrievable breakdown (see s1(1) Matrimonial Causes Act 1973) – in addition need to establish one or more of five facts (s1(2) MCA 1973) – fact of wife behaving in such a way that not reasonable to expect husband to live with her (s1(2)(b) MCA 1973) – effect of wife's insistence that mentally ill sister live in family home – relevance of husband returning (s2(3) MCA 1973) – fact of desertion for a period of two years (s1(2)(c) MCA 1973) – can constructive desertion be shown and, if so, for what period? – relevance of husband returning (s2(4) MCA 1973) – fact of living apart for two years with consent (s1(2)(d) MCA 1973) – has two-year period been satisfied? – relevance of reconciliation provisions in s2(5) MCA 1973) – fact of living apart for five years (s1(2)(e) MCA 1973).

Suggested Solution

Nicolas should be advised that if he wishes to petition successfully for divorce he must satisfy the court that his marriage with Mary has irretrievably broken down (see s1(1) Matrimonial Causes Act 1973 – hereinafter referred to as the MCA 1973). Given the troubled state of the marriage and the differences between the parties Nicolas should be able to satisfy this requirement.

He should be further advised that in addition he must satisfy the court of one or more of five facts in order to obtain a divorce (see s1(2) MCA 1973). Both requirements are separate and each must be satisfied. If he establishes irretrievable breakdown, but not one or more of the facts, he will be unsuccessful in his petition: see *Buffery* v *Buffery* [1988] 2 FLR 365.

The first possible fact is that the respondent has committed adultery and that the petitioner finds it intolerable to live with her (see s1(2)(a) MCA 1973). Since there is no evidence of adultery on Mary's part Nicolas cannot make use of this fact. The second is that she has behaved in such a way that it is not reasonable to expect him to live with her: see s1(2)(b) MCA 1973. The court will ask whether any right-thinking person would come to the conclusion that Mary has behaved in such a way that Nicolas cannot reasonably be expected to live with her, taking into account the whole of the circumstances and the characteristics and personalities of the parties: see *Livingstone-Stallard* v *Livingstone-Stallard* [1974] 3 WLR 302. In other words can Nicolas, with his character and personality, with his faults and other attributes, good or bad and having regard to his behaviour during the marriage, be reasonably expected to live with Mary taking into account her character and personality and good and bad attributes?: see *Ash* v *Ash* [1972] 2 WLR 347. When they married in 1980 Nicolas and Mary agreed to allow Olive to come and live with them if the need arose. In 1990 they honoured that agreement. It is not clear what particular aspects of her behaviour then led Nicolas to change his mind, and to the domestic discord with his wife. If Olive's behaviour was obviously extreme and disturbed, and remains so, then Mary's insistence that Olive remain in the household is more likely to be considered unreasonable despite what was agreed in 1980 and then in 1990. If Nicolas and/or the children's physical or mental health has been adversely affected by Olive's behaviour then this would considerably strengthen Nicolas's case: see *Katz* v *Katz* [1972] 1 WLR 955 and *Thurlow* v *Thurlow* [1975] 3 WLR 161. The court is unlikely to rule that the obligations of marriage include an obligation to keep and care for a seriously disturbed relative. If Olive's behaviour is no more than a nuisance and has not adversely affected Nicolas or the children then his claim would be weaker, since the court may take the view that he should honour what he agreed with his wife. Nicolas should be advised that the only decided cases in this area deal with mentally ill spouses and how far the obligations of the petitioning spouse go in terms of remaining married to the ill spouse. The circumstances in this case are different in that the cause of the dissension is an invited guest. Mary's obligations to her sister are likely to be considered less than her obligations to her husband and children. As a result Nicolas is more likely to succeed in establishing that Mary has behaved in such a way that s1(2)(b) is satisfied. Nicolas left in January 1992, then returned in December 1992 and stayed for what appears to a period of between six and seven months in 1993. This may weaken his claim that he cannot reasonably be expected to live with Mary since he in fact returned to live with Mary despite the incidents which persuaded him to leave in the first instance. If he had returned for a period of six months or less then the court would have disregarded this in deciding whether s1(2)(b) had been satisfied: see s2(3) MCA 1973. The fact that he appears to have returned to live with her for more than six months would be not be a bar to his case but may weaken it. If he returned because he was forced to (eg he had accommodation problems) this might persuade the court to ignore the time he stayed with Mary. If fresh incidents occurred during the December 1992 to July 1993 period he could use these in his petition, rather than rely on incidents prior to his return in December 1992.

The next fact is that Mary has deserted Nicolas for a continuous period of at least two years: see s1(2)(c) MCA 1973. Since Nicolas is the person who has left he could not rely on this fact unless he could establish constructive desertion, namely that Mary drove him out of the home by her behaviour in relation to Olive and that by virtue of expelling Nicolas she has constructively deserted him: see *Lang* v *Lang* [1954] 3 All ER 571. Whether Nicolas can establish this will depend on the nature of Olive's behaviour and its effect on Nicolas and the children. Since constructive desertion requires 'grave and weighty' behaviour on Mary's part this may be more difficult to establish than satisfying s1(2)(b). For this reason it may be better for him to rely on s1(2)(b) than s1(2)(c). The fact that Nicolas returned to live with Mary for over six months will have interrupted any continuous period of desertion: see s2(5) MCA 1973. This means that the two years would only have started again from July 1993 and the court would have ignored the early period of separation in calculating the two years. If Mary makes a reasonable offer of reconciliation to Nicolas this would end the desertion: see *Gallagher* v *Gallagher* [1965] 1 WLR 1110. The court is unlikely to consider any offer from Mary reasonable if it involves Olive remaining in the household, assuming the court has found Mary's insistence that her sister live there had unreasonably driven Nicolas out in the first place.

Nicolas may also petition on the fact that he has lived apart from Mary for a continuous period of two years, and that Mary consents to a divorce: see s1(2)(d) MCA 1973. Mary would have to positively give her consent to the petition. If she is not willing to give her consent then no use can be made of this fact. Second, Nicolas would have to show that he has lived apart from Mary for a continuous period of at least two years. 'Living apart' means not living in the same household, and at least one of the parties being of the view that the marriage is over: see s2(6) MCA 1973 and *Santos* v *Santos* [1972] 2 All ER 246. Since they have lived apart since July 1993 this appears to have been satisfied. The earlier period of living apart could not be counted since it was interrupted by Nicolas returning to live with Mary for a period of over six months: see s2(5) MCA 1973. The final fact Nicolas should consider is that of the parties having lived apart continuously for a period of five years: see s1(2)(e) MCA 1973. No consent from Mary is required. However, since Nicolas interrupted the period of living apart, which commenced in 1992, by returning to live with Mary for over six months, this means that the five-year period only commenced from July 1993: see s2(5) MCA 1973. As a result, this fact is of no assistance to Nicolas should he want an immediate divorce.

In conclusion, Nicolas may be advised that he is most likely to succeed on the basis of irretrievable breakdown, coupled with the fact of two years living apart and Mary's consent or, failing that, the fact of behaviour under s1(2)(b). The fact of desertion under s1(2)(c) by way of constructive desertion is also available to him, but it is hard to see what advantages there are in using this fact when s1(2)(b) is available.

QUESTION FOUR

Mary and John, aged respectively 34 and 30, married in 1990. They have two children, Tom and Jerry, now aged six and four. John is an IT specialist who works for an international company. Following the birth of Tom, Mary, at John's insistence, gave up her employment as a trainee solicitor. In 1997 John had a brief affair with Sandra, which he terminated in December 1997. Mary suspected that John had been unfaithful, and in September 1998 discovered a hotel bill which confirmed it. Realising that her marriage was breaking down, Mary became depressed and started to drink excessively. Unfortunately, drink made Mary aggressive and on two occasions she hit John. John decided that he was leaving Mary, and arranged to travel on a two-year overseas work contract. He did not consult Mary. He left home in March 1999.

Mary wishes to have her marriage dissolved. Advise Mary as to whether she can divorce John under the Matrimonial Causes Act 1973.

University of London LLB Examination
(for External Students) Family Law June 1999 Q3

General Comment

This is a fairly straightforward question on divorce. It involves particular discussion of the fact of adultery with the complication of the parties living together after the adultery. It also involves the living apart for two years with consent fact, with the complication of an uncommunicated decision by one party to live apart. The facts of the question also raise the possibility of behaviour, desertion and living apart for five years. All in all the question invites a fairly full discussion of the grounds for obtaining a divorce.

Skeleton Solution

Demonstrating irretrievable breakdown of the marriage; discussion of five facts: fact of adultery and intolerability and effect of reconciliation provisions – fact of behaviour – fact of desertion – fact of living apart for two years with consent and application of *Santos* v *Santos* on unilateral decision to live apart – fact of five years living apart;

mention of delaying decree absolute in two years and five years living apart case and special defence to five years living apart case.

Suggested Solution

Mary can be advised that there is one ground for divorce, namely that the marriage has broken down irretrievably: s1(1) Matrimonial Causes Act (MCA) 1973. However, she must satisfy the court as to one or more of five facts in order to demonstrate that the marriage has broken down irretrievably: see s1(2) MCA 1973. The two requirements are separate and both need to be satisfied. On the facts it appears that the marriage has broken down irretrievably so advice will concentrate on whether or not one or more of the five facts can be established.

The first fact she may be able to satisfy the court of is that John has committed adultery and Mary finds it intolerable to live with him: see s1(2)(a) MCA 1973. Mary should be advised that proof of adultery is a serious matter and the court will require clear proof of John's adultery: see *Bastable* v *Bastable* [1968] 3 All ER 701. She may able to establish adultery if John provides a confession statement. It is not clear whether he would provide such a statement. If he wishes to end his marriage he may be willing to do so. Otherwise Mary would have to prove the adultery. The hotel bill may be sufficient evidence. If she can show that John and Sandra spent the night in the same room that will raise a rebuttable presumption of adultery: see *Woolf* v *Woolf* [1931] P 134. Assuming that Mary can establish adultery then she must also establish that she finds it intolerable to live with John. The intolerability need not be in consequence of the adultery: see *Cleary* v *Cleary* [1974] 1 WLR 73. The test of intolerability is subjective, namely what Mary finds intolerable, not what a reasonable petitioner would find intolerable. The circumstances since Mary discovered the adultery seem to show that she does find it intolerable to live with John. Her depression, drinking and physical arguments with him seem to bear this out. The potential difficulty with establishing this fact is that Mary cannot rely on adultery if, after the adultery became known to her, she and John lived together for a period or periods together exceeding six months: see s2(1) MCA 1973. Mary discovered the adultery in September 1998. John left in March 1999. The question is then whether Mary and John were living together for all this period. If they were then s2(1) provides a bar to Mary's petition: see *Biggs* v *Biggs* [1977] 1 All ER 20. If they were living apart for most of that period or for sufficient period(s) to make any living together less than six months then Mary could petition on this ground. It is possible for parties to share the same household and not be treated as living together. This is further discussed in relation to the two years living apart fact. Any period(s) amounting to less than six months can be ignored in terms of Mary establishing that she finds it intolerable to live with John: see s2(2) MCA 1973.

The next fact Mary may be able to rely on is that John has behaved in such a way that Mary cannot reasonably be expected to live with him: see s1(2)(b) MCA 1973. The court will apply the test whether Mary, bearing in mind her character, personality, disposition and behaviour, can reasonably live with John, having regard to his character, personality, disposition and behaviour: see *Buffery* v *Buffery* [1988] 2 FLR 365. The court will have to make findings of fact of what John did and then as to the impact of that conduct on Mary. On the facts disclosed John's affair with Sandra could amount to such behaviour (as an alternative to establishing the fact of adultery). Other examples of John's behaviour are not clear from the question. His insistence on Mary giving up her work is too long ago. His arrangement to work abroad for so long may amount to s1(2)(b) behaviour given his responsibilities to his family, particularly his young children. John could argue that his working abroad is a reasonable consequence of his work. Since John also appears to want a divorce he may not oppose a petition brought on this ground. Indeed, he may petition on the basis of Mary's behaviour, namely her drinking and assaults on him. However, the court will not 'rubber stamp' a divorce petition. It will not grant a petition if there is insufficient behaviour to justify s1(2)(b). If the court finds that John and Mary have simply drifted apart this may be insufficient: see *Buffery* v *Buffery*. The fact that the circumstances have caused Mary to drink excessively and have violent arguments with John would tend to show that this is more than a case of drifting apart. Again Mary needs to be aware of the reconciliation provisions. If she and John have lived together for a period or periods amounting to less than six months since the date of the final incident relied upon, then the court will disregard this: see s2(3) MCA 1973. If they have lived together for a period or periods of six months or more this would not be a bar to the petition but would be taken into account in deciding whether it was reasonable for Mary to live with John. In this context Mary could rely on John's adultery as behaviour and avoid the bar in s2(1) MCA 1973. In addition, if Mary and John continued to live in the same household but lived largely separate lives then this may allow the court to find that she cannot reasonably be expected to live with him: see *Court* v *Court* [1982] 3 WLR 199.

The next fact that Mary may seek to establish is that John has deserted her for a continuous period of at least two years preceding the date of the petition: see s1(2)(c) MCA 1973. Mary can be advised that desertion involves: the fact of separation; an intention to desert by John; a lack of consent by Mary; and that the separation was without just cause. The difficulty for Mary is that she does not appear to have been aware that John intended to desert Mary when he left home in March 1999. If Mary agreed to John leaving because of the work contract then desertion could not be established until Mary became aware that John did not intend to return to her: see *Nutley* v *Nutley* [1970] 1 WLR 217. In addition, Mary could not be shown to be in agreement with the desertion. Since both parties appear to want the marriage to be at an end it could be argued that Mary supports John's desertion. In all the circumstances Mary is advised that desertion would be difficult to establish.

Mary could seek to establish that she and John have lived apart for a continuous period of at least two years immediately preceding the petition and that John consents to a decree of divorce being granted: see s1(2)(d) MCA 1973. The living apart appears to have started in March 1999. Mary can be advised that any living apart could have started earlier if she and John, though living in the same house, lived separate lives in the same household: see *Fuller* v *Fuller* [1973] 2 All ER 650. However, if they continued to share important aspects of family life (eg ate meals together, shared household chores) then they could not be treated as living apart: see *Mouncer* v *Mouncer* [1972] 1 All ER 298. The fact that John has not consulted with Mary that he was leaving Mary would not prevent the 'living apart' from commencing in March 1999 provided John could offer some evidence of his decision or recognition that the marriage was at an end: see *Santos* v *Santos* [1972] 2 WLR 889. The court is able to ignore a period or periods amounting to less than six months in calculating the two years period: s2(5) MCA 1973. It appears that John will consent to a decree once the two years have elapsed. In these circumstances Mary would be able to petition for divorce on this fact in March or April 2001 (depending on when the two years period elapses).

Finally, Mary could rely on the fact of five years living apart: see s1(2)(e) MCA 1973. It is assumed that Mary is unlikely to wish to rely on this fact since she would have to wait a significant time for a divorce. The same provisions on the meaning of living apart apply as for s1(2)(d).

If John seeks to divorce Mary under s1(2)(d) or (e) MCA 1973 then there are special provisions to protect Mary's financial position: see ss5 and 10 MCA 1973. These will not be discussed since it is more likely that Mary will petition for divorce (or will not defend any petition brought by John).

In conclusion, the most likely fact Mary could establish is the two years living apart with consent (provided she does not object to waiting until the two-year period has elapsed) and the behaviour ground (provided there is sufficient behaviour to satisfy the court). There may be difficulties with the fact of adultery if the parties have lived together for six months or more since Mary learned of the adultery. The circumstances suggest that Mary would not be able to establish desertion.

Chapter 4

Divorce Law Reform

4.1 **Introduction**

4.2 **Key points**

4.3 **Key statute**

4.4 **Questions and suggested solutions**

4.1 Introduction

Students are expected to be aware of the abandoned reforms to divorce law in Parts II and III Family Law Act 1996. Examiners may ask for discussion on the proposed reforms and the Lord Chancellor's decision in 2001 not to proceed with them.

In 1988 the Law Commission published a discussion paper concerning the possible reform of divorce law. This was followed in 1990 with its report *The Ground for Divorce* (Law Com No 192). In 1993 the Lord Chancellor published a Green Paper called *Facing the Future: Mediation and the Ground for Divorce.* This was followed by a White Paper in 1995 called *Looking to the Future: Mediation and the Ground for Divorce.* The White Paper drew much from the Law Commission's proposals, and was also based on responses to the Green Paper in addition to research commissioned by the Lord Chancellor's Department.

This action was taken against a background of public concern about divorce and the numbers of divorcing couples. Great Britain has the highest rate of divorce in Europe. Criticisms were made of the existing law. As has been seen most petitioners make use of the fault-based facts in order to obtain a divorce (since this enables them to obtain a speedier divorce). It was said that the present law encourages petitioners to make allegations (sometimes exaggerated) against their spouses in order to obtain a quick divorce. This could result in needless conflict, unfairness and a sense of injustice which does nothing to save marriages.

The government therefore introduced proposals with the following objectives:

a) to support the institution of marriage;

b) to include practical steps to prevent the irretrievable breakdown of marriage;

c) to ensure that spouses understand the practical consequences of divorce before taking any irreversible decision;

d) where divorce is unavoidable to minimise the bitterness and hostility between the parties and reduce the trauma for the children;

e) to keep to the minimum the cost to the parties and the taxpayer.

The proposals were that the single ground for divorce should remain that of the marriage having broken down irretrievably. After one or both parties have applied for a divorce this ground will be demonstrated by the passing of a period for reflection and consideration. During this period couples will be required to settle arrangements for their children, property and finances (unless the court dispenses with this requirement, for example, in the interests of the children). The spouse applying for the divorce will be obliged to attend an information-giving session which will inform him/her of the various options open to him/her (eg marriage guidance, counselling, family mediation and the legal consequences of divorce). The other spouse will be encouraged to attend. The Government proposed to limit legal aid to specific legal advice during this process so that it should no longer be necessary for parties to be legally represented to the extent they currently are now. The Government wished to make mediation available through the block funding of contracts for mediation services. Though mediation was not be made compulsory it is hoped that divorcing couples should keep control of their own affairs through mediation rather than be steered by lawyers.

The end result of this process of reform is the Family Law Act 1996 which was passed on 4 July 1996. Part I came into force on 21 March 1997. This lays down the general principles underlying Parts II and III (which deal with divorce and separation orders). The principles largely reflect the objectives already mentioned. The Lord Chancellor announced in 2001 that Parts II and III would not be brought into force and would in due course be repealed. Pilot projects were run to test the various aspects of the new legislation (eg providing information to divorcing couples). The Lord Chancellor considered the results of the pilot projects disappointing (though others disagreed with this view).

4.2 Key points

The existing law – Matrimonial Causes Act 1973

a) The sole ground – irretrievable breakdown: s1(1).

b) The only ways to prove it – the five facts: s1(2)(a)–(e).

It is possible for a marriage to have irretrievably broken down but for no divorce to be possible because no fact can be established – is that fair or sensible?

c) Three 'facts' are based on fault – in order to obtain an immediate divorce have to rely on fault-based fact. 77 per cent of wife petitioners and 62 per cent of husband petitioners rely on fault-based facts.

Therefore, there is still much bitterness associated with divorce which does nothing to assist continuing relationships between divorced parents and their children.

d) There are about 145,000 divorce petitions a year – 40 per cent of marriages end in divorce – high cost to legal aid – high cost to spouses and children involved.

e) The existing 'special procedure' for divorce allows divorces to be dealt with by paperwork and does not oblige the parties to reflect on the process or on the consequences for any children.

The Family Law Act 1996

The general principles of divorce (s1(a)–(c) FLA 1996):

'The court and any person in exercising functions under or in consequence of Parts II and III [of the FLA 1996], shall have regard to the following general principles –
(a) that the institution of marriage is to be supported;
(b) that the parties to a marriage which may have broken down are to be encouraged to take all practicable steps, whether by marriage counselling or otherwise, to save the marriage;
(c) that a marriage which has irretrievably broken down and is being brought to an end should be brought to an end –
(i) with minimum distress to the parties and to the children affected;
(ii) with questions dealt with in a manner designed to promote as good a continuing relationship between the parties and any children affected as is possible in the circumstances; and
(iii) without costs being unreasonably incurred in connection with the procedures to be followed in bringing the marriage to an end ...'

Divorce order (s2(1)(a) FLA 1996)

Application is made for a divorce order (which is what an order dissolving the marriage will be called).

A diagram on p45 provides a simplified illustration of the new provisions for divorce.

Applying for the divorce order

Application cannot be made for the divorce order until:

a) the period for reflection and consideration fixed by s7 FLA 1996 has ended; and

b) the application for a divorce order is accompanied by a declaration by the party making the application under s5(1) FLA 1996 that:

   i) having reflected on the breakdown of the marriage; and

   ii) having considered the requirements of Part II FLA 1996 as to the parties' arrangements for the future

   the applicant believes that the marriage cannot be saved.

The statement of marital breakdown and the application for a divorce order do not have to be made by the same party: s5(2) FLA 1996.

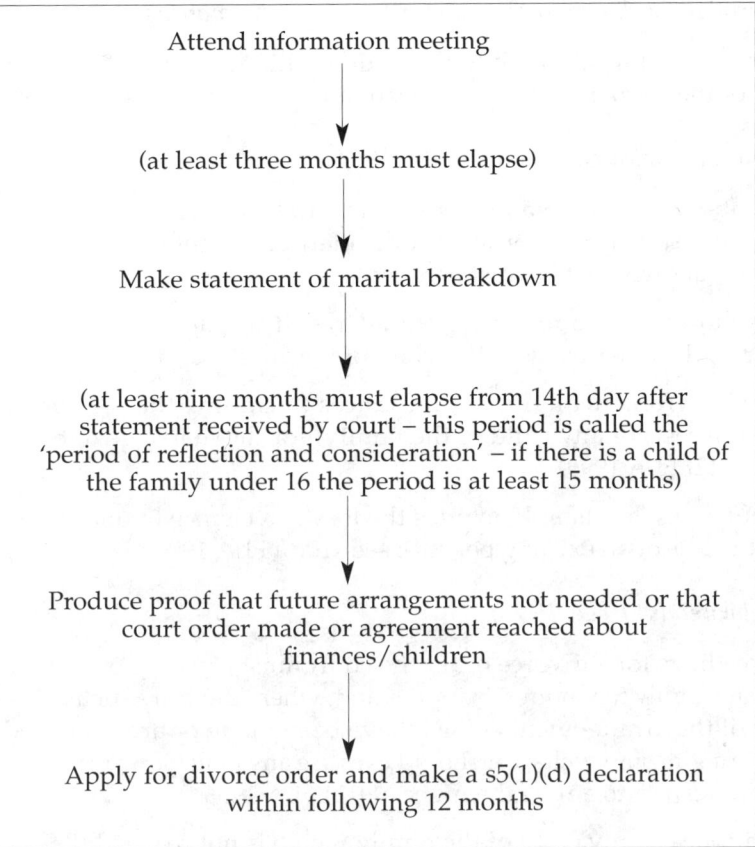

Attend information meeting

(at least three months must elapse)

Make statement of marital breakdown

(at least nine months must elapse from 14th day after statement received by court – this period is called the 'period of reflection and consideration' – if there is a child of the family under 16 the period is at least 15 months)

Produce proof that future arrangements not needed or that court order made or agreement reached about finances/children

Apply for divorce order and make a s5(1)(d) declaration within following 12 months

Arrangements for the future

Under s9(2) FLA 1996 a divorce order cannot be made unless one of the following is produced to the court:

a) a court order (made by consent or otherwise) dealing with the financial arrangements; or

b) a negotiated agreement as to their financial arrangements; or

c) a declaration by both parties that they have made their financial arrangements; or

d) a declaration by one of the parties (to which no objection has been notified to the court by that other party) that he/she has no significant assets and does not intend to make any application for financial provision; and he/she believes that the other party has no significant assets and does not intend to make an application for financial provision; and there are therefore no financial arrangements to be made.

Bar on application for divorce order within one year of the marriage

A statement as to marital breakdown made within the first year of the marriage is ineffective for the purposes of any application for a divorce order: see s7(6) FLA 1996.

Special defence to a divorce order (s10 FLA 1996)

If an application has been made by one party to the marriage the court may on the application of the other party order that the marriage is not to be dissolved. The court may only so order where it is satisfied that:

a) the dissolution of the marriage would result in substantial financial or other hardship to the other party or to a child of the family; and

b) it would be wrong in all the circumstances (including the conduct of the parties and the interests of any child of the family) for the marriage to be dissolved (see s10(1) and (2) FLA 1996).

For these purposes 'hardship' includes the loss of a chance to obtain a future benefit (as well as the loss of an existing benefit): see s10(6) FLA 1996.

Welfare of children (s11 FLA 1996)

In any proceedings for a divorce order the court must consider whether there are any children of the family to whom s11 applies and, where there are such children, whether in the light of the arrangements which have been made or are proposed to be made for their upbringing and welfare it should exercise any of its powers under the Children Act 1989 with respect to any of them: see s11(1) FLA 1996.

Section 11 applies to any child of the family who has not reached the age of 16 at the date when the court considers the case in accordance with s11, and any child who has reached that age at that date and in relation to whom the court directs that s11 shall apply: see s11(5) FLA 1996.

Where it appears to the court that the circumstances require it or are likely to require it to exercise any of its powers under the Children Act 1989 with respect to any child and it is not in a position to exercise the power(s) without giving further consideration to the case and there are exceptional circumstances which make it desirable in the interests of the child that the court should give a direction, then the court may direct that the divorce order is not to be made until the court orders otherwise: see s11(2) FLA 1996.

The court must treat the welfare of the child as paramount in considering whether the circumstances of the case require the court or are likely to require it to exercise any of its powers under the Children Act 1989 with respect to that child: see s11(3) FLA 1996.

Under s11(4) FLA 1996, in making that decision the court must have particular regard on the evidence before it to:

a) the wishes and feelings of the child considered in the light of his/her age and understanding and the circumstances in which those wishes were expressed;

b) the conduct of the parties in relation to the upbringing of the child;

c) the general principle that in the absence of evidence to the contrary the welfare of the child will be best served by his having regular contact with those who have parental responsibility for him and with other members of his/her family and the maintenance of as good a continuing relationship with his parents as is possible; and

d) any risk to the child attributable to:

   i) where the person with whom the child will reside is living or proposes or reside;

   ii) any person with whom that person is living or with whom he/she proposes to live; or

   iii) any other arrangements for his care and upbringing.

Observations on the Family Law Act 1996

Would the Family Law Act 1996 have achieved the objectives it set out for itself?

Would a year's period of cohabitation and reflection have done anything to buttress a marriage capable of being saved?

Do petitioning spouses need to 'blame' the other spouse by using a fault-based fact for therapeutic purposes? Would a no fault-based divorce have been acceptable?

Were the proposals really designed to save legal aid money by involving mediators more than lawyers?

4.3 Key statute

• Family Law Act 1996, Part I (which is in force) and Parts II and III which are not being brought into force.

4.4 Questions and suggested solutions

QUESTION ONE

'The current law of divorce is confusing and misleading, discriminatory and unjust, provokes unnecessary hostility and bitterness and does nothing to save the marriage.' Discuss. What reforms, if any, to the law of divorce do you consider appropriate?

University of London LLB Examination
(for External Students) Family Law June 1991 Q2

General Comment

This question requires a consideration of the Family Law Act (FLA) 1996 which derives from the Law Commission's report *The Ground for Divorce* (1990). Candidates should review the existing law and consider whether its aims have been met, and thereafter consider to what extent the FLA 1996 will fulfil these aims.

Skeleton Solution

Discuss differing views relating to object of divorce law expressed by Archbishop of Canterbury's group in *Putting Asunder* and Law Commission – outline current divorce law – consider criticism of current law made by Law Commission in its report *The Ground for Divorce* (1990) and recommendation for reform accepted in the Government's White Paper *Looking to the Future* and enacted in the FLA 1996 – does reliance on fault facts add to the distress, bitterness and humiliation? – can divorce law save marriages? – is the current law confusing and misleading? – is it unjust and discriminatory? – consider the Law Commission's proposals and FLA 1996 reforms – one ground, but divorce to be granted only after a transitional period to allow for reflection and the making of arrangements for children and property.

Suggested Solution

The Divorce Reform Act 1969 which forms the basis of the current law on divorce was a compromise between two basic principles expounded by the Archbishop of Canterbury's Committee in its report *Putting Asunder* published in 1966, and the Law Commission.

The Archbishop of Canterbury's group favoured the substitution of 'breakdown' for the matrimonial offence as the basis of divorce law, taking the view that a divorce decree should be seen as a judicial recognition of a state of affairs with a consequent redefinition of status. The Committee favoured the view that the divorce court should carry out a detailed inquest into the alleged facts and causes of the breakdown of the marriage relationship in each case to avoid possible abuse of the law.

However, the Law Commission, which was appointed to investigate the reform of divorce law following the publication of *Putting Asunder*, did not agree that there should be such a detailed inquest, arguing that such a course would be impracticable. The Commission recommended that the grounds that existed already for divorce should be retained but that an additional ground as evidenced by a period of separation, which would be shorter if the respondent consented than if he or she did not, should be introduced. The Commission's aims were to preserve the stability of marriage but it recognised also the social function of divorce, that is to allow parties to enter new legal relationships if they so wished while giving any necessary protection to the children of the family and dealing with financial and property adjustment as required. Further, it believed that a machinery to allow for reconciliation should be provided if there was any possibility that a marriage could be preserved.

Under the Divorce Reform Act 1969 irretrievable breakdown of the marriage became the sole ground for divorce. However, it could only be inferred by proof of one or more of the specified facts which are akin to the old matrimonial offences, although they included two new facts based on separation.

This legislation has been described as an uneasy compromise between two inconsistent views on divorce policy. One view is that divorce should be available to either party to the marriage where it has irretrievably broken down and that the old matrimonial offences are mere symptoms of that breakdown. Another view, however, is that it would be fundamentally unjust to allow a party to petition for divorce on the basis of irretrievable breakdown alone as that could allow a party to rely on his or her own wrongdoing and to obtain a divorce even against the will of the innocent spouse.

Under the current law a divorce is obtainable only where there is evidence of irretrievable breakdown as evidenced by one of the 'facts' set out in s1(2) Matrimonial Causes Act 1973 and a divorce cannot be granted in the absence of one of these facts even where it is clear that the marriage has broken down irretrievably: *Richards* v *Richards* [1972] 1 WLR 1073. This requirement of proof of one of the facts is to ensure that the innocent spouse cannot be divorced against his or her will, at least until five year separation is established and even then the respondent can prevent the divorce if grave financial or other hardship can be established along with injustice in granting the decree.

It is recognised that this reformed law has made it possible for virtually all broken marriages to be dissolved, even though in some cases it may only be after a period of delay. However, it is also recognised that the most commonly used 'facts' on which irretrievable breakdown is evidenced are the fault based ones and in particular adultery and behaviour. One of the objectives of the reformed law was to bury decently a dead marriage and enable the 'empty legal shell' of marriage to be destroyed with the maximum fairness and the minimum bitterness, distress and humiliation. It could be argued that reliance on the fault based facts would only add to the contention between the parties and this view was expressed by the Law Commission in its report *The Ground for Divorce* (1990) Law Com No 192. This would be particularly the case where serious allegations of behaviour were made. However, many practitioners also recognise that the fault facts are frequently used by their clients merely as a device on which to hang the decree nisi, and that any bitterness and hostility arise not really because of the divorce petition, but as a result of the consequences which flow from divorce, namely loneliness, a reduced standard of living and in some cases loss of close contact with one's children. It is argued that even if the basis for divorce was changed to allow a more civilised process, these consequences would still arise and the resultant bitterness would still be present: see Mears [1991] Fam Law 231.

The present law is also criticised by the Law Commission for failing to do anything to save marriage. However, it could be argued that because a petitioner is unable to obtain a divorce (except where the spouses have been separated for five years) without showing one of the fault facts is established or without the consent of the respondent, the law does go some way to saving marriages. In any event it is difficult to see how divorce law can save marriages except by making a divorce more difficult to obtain, and that may have the effect of adding to the tension and acrimony felt by the parties. It is recognised that it is pointless to try to keep any obviously dead marriage alive and by the time spouses seek legal advice on how to dissolve their marriage they have decided their marriage is dead. Therefore any counselling or mediation aimed at saving the marriage is futile at that stage. Divorce does not make a marriage break down. It is merely the mechanism by which the marriage is legally dissolved. The process should be as constructive as possible and the Law Commission stated in its report *The Ground for Divorce* that the aim of the law must be to promote the amicable resolution of practical problems in relation to finance and property and children, to minimise the harm suffered by children and to promote shared parental responsibility.

The Law Commission argued that the current law is confusing and misleading in that, for example, the facts relied upon to obtain a divorce may not really be the true reason for the marriage breakdown. This may be a valid point, for many spouses will seek to rely on a fact which will provide a speedy divorce and this may mean that the facts are used as a convenience rather than as a true reflection of the problems in the marriage. Some writers would question whether anyone is really confused or misled by the law, however, and argue that if the law worked well in practice, this would not be an important criticism.

The Law Commission also argued that the present law is unjust and discriminatory in that inter alia it is unfair that divorce is not readily available at the behest of one party and that the other party may use the requirement of his or her consent (where a petition under s1(2)(d) MCA 1973 only is relevant) as a basis for bargaining on other ancillary matters. However, given that the divorce may cause other adverse consequences such as a reduced standard of living or loss of home, it is questionable whether it is unfair to a petitioner that the respondent should seek to exact a price for his or her consent. Under the present law the 'innocent' spouse cannot be divorced without his or her consent (except where the parties have been separated for five years, subject to the s5 MCA 1973 defence). The Law Commission considered this to be unfair and favours the principle of divorce on demand (albeit after a period of reflection). But the divorce procedures cannot be looked at without also considering their consequences in relation to money, property and children, and given that these are the most important concerns of the parties it should be asked why an innocent spouse should have those consequences unilaterally imposed upon him or her.

The Law Commission's main proposals for reform of the divorce law was followed by the Government's White Paper *Looking to the Future: Mediation and the Ground for Divorce* (April 1995) which led to the Family Law Act (FLA) 1996. The Act is based on the principle that divorce should be available after a period of transition in which the parties are given the time to reflect on this step and to make necessary arrangements with regard to money, property and children.

The FLA 1996 provides for one ground for divorce, namely the irretrievable breakdown of the marriage. This would be established by a sworn statement by either or both parties. Statements giving details of any minor children of the family and the arrangements made for them, and where financial relief and property adjustment is sought, giving information relating to the financial positions of the parties, would also be filed in court.

The parties would be given information regarding the effects of divorce and counselling and conciliation services. These services could provide the forum in which the parties can air their grievances and resolve disputes with each other, a process which is recognised as essential to reduce future conflict and encourage co-operation between the parties.

On the expiration of a period for reflection and consideration either party will be entitled to apply for a divorce order. In their discussion paper *Facing the Future* (1988) Law Com No 170, the Law Commission suggested that a decree could be postponed where the issues in relation to the children had not been resolved or where proper financial or property arrangements had not yet been made. In *Principles of Family Law* (5th ed) S M Cretney and J M Masson argue that if such postponements were allowed this would encourage hostile litigation to resolve these disputes. The objects of the period for reflection and consideration must include the opportunity to allow the parties to address the feelings of bitterness and hostility attendant on the marital breakup in an unpressured environment. These potential postponements could operate to exert further pressure on the parties.

It is argued that the FLA 1996 has much to recommend it if it means that the aims of the divorce process will be to provide support for families, particularly children, and to avoid conflict if possible. Any divorce process will involve pain and upheaval for the parties concerned and perhaps the most that can be expected of a divorce law is that it does not add to these problems. It must be remembered however that the real areas of conflict, namely financial and property matters and children, remain.

QUESTION TWO

'The retention of some notion of fault in the law of divorce is essential so as to maintain the sanctity of marriage.'

Discuss this statement in the light of the proposals for divorce law reform contained in the current Family Law Bill [now the Family Law Act 1996].

University of London LLB Examination
(for External Students) Family Law June 1996 Q5

General Comment

The Family Law Act 1996 has had a troubled and controversial passage through Parliament. It has provoked much criticism, some of it misguided and misleading. This is not surprising given the strength of feeling about the rate of divorce in Great

Britain and its consequences. The difficulty the critics of the Act face is that the sanctity of marriage and the high divorce rate appear to be more a matter of social and historical forces rather than shaped by statute and the courts. The question invites a discussion behind the reasons for the Family Law Act, particularly in relation to its proposals to eliminate the need to find fault as the basis for divorce.

Skeleton Solution

Existing law of divorce – the ground of irretrievable breakdown and the need to satisfy the court of one or more of five facts (s1(1) and (2) MCA 1973) – the extensive use of the fault facts of adultery and behaviour and consequences of this – Law Commission proposals for reform of divorce law – government's approach to divorce law reform through the Family Law Act, in particular the imposition of a period for reflection and to prepare for the consequences of the divorce – the use of mediation – whether divorce law reform can maintain the sanctity of marriage – the wider social and historical forces which shape divorce.

Suggested Solution

The current divorce law reform contained in the Family Law Act 1996 has provoked considerable controversy in its passage through Parliament. It seeks to remove the notion of fault in the law of divorce. The question asks whether this aim is a laudable one or whether the retention of some notion of fault in the law of divorce is essential to maintain the sanctity of marriage.

It should be remembered that divorce law went through a similar period of reform in the 1950s and 1960s. A Royal Commission (the Morton Commission) published a report on divorce law reform in 1956. This was followed by a report from the Church of England entitled *Putting Asunder* and a Law Commission report. The Law Commission report recommended that the aims of a good divorce law are to 'buttress, rather than undermine, the stability of marriage, and when, regrettably, a marriage has irretrievably broken down, to enable the empty legal shell to be destroyed with the maximum fairness and the minimum bitterness, distress and humiliation'. The consequence was the passing of the Divorce Reform Act 1969. The existing law is contained in the Matrimonial Causes Act 1973 (which replaced the Divorce Reform Act 1969). This law replaced the notion of the matrimonial offence as being the basis for divorce with the notion of irretrievable breakdown of the marriage: see s1(1) Matrimonial Causes Act 1973 – hereinafter referred to as MCA 1973. A petitioner has to establish that the marriage has broken down irretrievably. In addition, he or she must satisfy the court of one or more of five facts: see s1(2) MCA 1973. Three of these facts retain an element of fault. The first is that the respondent has committed adultery and that the petitioner finds it intolerable to live with the respondent: see s1(2)(a) MCA 1973. The second is that the respondent has behaved in such a way that the petitioner cannot be reasonably be expected to live with the respondent: see s1(2)(b) MCA 1973. The third is that the respondent has deserted the petitioner for a continuous period of at least two years immediately preceding the presentation of the divorce petition: see s1(2)(c) MCA 1973. The other two facts are not fault based. One is that the parties have lived apart for a continuous period of at least two years immediately preceding the presentation of the petition and the respondent consents to the decree being granted: see s1(2)(d) MCA 1973. The second is that the parties have lived apart for a continuous period of at least five years immediately preceding the presentation of the petition: see s1(2)(e) MCA 1973. There is protection for respondent spouses who would suffer grave financial or other hardship – they can defend divorces based on five years living apart on the basis of such hardship: see s5 MCA 1973. These is a limited form of protection to safeguard other respondent spouses in divorces relying on s1(2)(d) and (e): see s10 MCA 1973. Petitions are barred within the first year of marriage: see s3 MCA 1973.

When the existing law was first proposed it was thought that the non-fault-based facts would be relied upon in the majority of cases. In fact the fault-based facts of adultery and behaviour are the most commonly used in divorce petitions. For example, the fact of adultery is used by female petitioners in 22 per cent of cases and by male petitioners in 37 per cent of cases. The fact of behaviour was used by female petitioners in 53 per cent of cases. The reason for the use of the fault-based facts appears to be that this is the quickest way to obtain a divorce in many cases. As a result it was argued that petitioners were encouraged to make allegations (sometimes exaggerated) against their spouses in order to obtain a speedy divorce. This can lead to spouses taking up opposing situations from the beginning of the divorce process.

In May 1988 the Law Commission published a discussion paper *Facing the Future* dealing with the possible reform of divorce law. In 1990 it published its report *The Ground for Divorce* which argued that the objectives of the law should be to support marriages which could be saved and to dissolve as painlessly as possible those marriages which could not be saved. These aims were the same as the previous report which led to the 1969 reforms. It also argued that divorce law should encourage parties to resolve issues relating to the children, the home and finance as amicably as possible having regard to their responsibilities to their children and to each other. In particular the law should aim to reduce the harm suffered by children at the time of divorce and afterwards, and to encourage the continued sharing of parental responsibilities towards the children. The existing law was criticised as being confusing, misleading, discriminating and unjust. The use of the fault-based facts were said to encourage unnecessary hostility and bitterness. It argued that the law did little to save marriage, little to help the children and did not help the parties to consider the future in a calm and reasonable manner. The Commission argued that while irretrievable breakdown should remain the sole ground for divorce it should be proved by a single fact, namely the expiry of a minimum period of one year for the consideration of the practical consequences of the divorce and for reflection upon the possibility of reconciliation. In practice this period would commence by either or both parties making a formal statement that the marriage had broken down and lodging that statement with the court. The court would then supply both parties with an information pack explaining the objectives of the ensuing one year period, the court's powers and about opportunities for reconciliation, counselling, mediation and conciliation. Within that year the court could make orders regarding the children, finance and property. Contested matters could be referred to conciliation before being determined by the court. After 11 months of the one-year period had elapsed either party could apply for a divorce order (or a separation order as judicial separation would be termed) and after one month had elapsed from the making of that application a divorce (or separation) order could be issued. These suggestions for reform came against a background of public concern about divorce and the number of divorcing couples. Great Britain has the highest divorce rate in Europe.

The Lord Chancellor published a Green Paper in December 1993 called *Facing the Future: Mediation and the Ground for Divorce* which followed the recommendations of the Law Commission. He proposed a no-fault divorce after only one year of separation and focusing on mediation rather than the courts. Following consultation, a White Paper was published in 1995 detailing the decisions taken on divorce reform – it largely reflected the views of the Law Commission and the Green Paper. The single ground for divorce would be irretrievable breakdown which would be demonstrated by the passing of a one-year period for reflection and consideration and for the parties to settle the arrangements for the children and financial provision. There would be a compulsory attendance at an information-giving session for the petitioner with the respondent encouraged to attend. At this session couples would be informed of the legal consequences of divorce and of options such as counselling and mediation. Local mediation services would be state funded. While supporting the objectives proposed by the Law Commission, the government was also concerned to minimise the cost to the taxpayer and to the parties of the existing divorce process. The government therefore proposed that legal aid would be limited in the new divorce process so that parties keep control of their own affairs preferably through mediation rather than through lawyers. These provisions were then introduced to the 1995/96 Parliament through the Family Law Bill. They attracted considerable controversy and the passage through Parliament has led to a number of amendments and concessions being made.

The difficulty in the reforms and for those who criticise them is that amendments to the law of divorce do not necessarily maintain the sanctity of marriage. If spouses wish to separate they are likely to go ahead regardless of the law or the ease or difficulty with which they can obtain a divorce. The volume of divorce appears to be largely a product of wider historical and social forces rather than changes in the law. For example, there was a significant increase in marriage breakdowns as a result of the enforced separations and upheavals of the Second World War. This increase has continued ever since. The attitude to divorce has changed considerably and religious attitudes have become far less rigid. There is an argument that reforms to divorce law follow social trends rather than shape them. Even with the extensive use of the existing fault-based facts, most divorces are undefended and amount to divorce by consent. One Member of Parliament put it this way: 'I am nervous about whether we in the House can pick up where 2,000 years of Judeao-Christian traditions appear to have failed to singly and, by the stroke of a legislative pen, safeguard marriage for the foreseeable future. That is wishful thinking.'

In conclusion, the Family Law Act 1996 was designed to meet the principal criticisms of the existing law. The statute was designed to eliminate the unjust and arbitrary use of the fault facts which can engender bitterness. It sought to eliminate fault altogether, and to concentrate on the consequences of divorce and to encourage spouses to prepare for them. It is laudable in these aims. It is unfortunate that some seek to criticise the Act as not maintaining the sanctity of marriage when its aims and objectives are principally to make the end of marriage less painful. A fault-based divorce law is unlikely to change people's behaviour and lead to fewer marriages ending in divorce. As has already been said, this is likely to be 'wishful thinking'.

QUESTION THREE

The Law Commission has stated that the law of divorce is 'confusing, misleading, discriminatory and unjust'. What do you understand to be the reasons for the Law Commission's view? Are there any strengths in the present law of divorce? To what extent do you think that the Family Law Act 1996 will improve the law of divorce?

University of London LLB Examination
(for External Students) Family Law June 1997 Q3

General Comment

This essay-style question invites the student to outline the background to the enactment of Parts I to III of the Family Law Act 1996. An understanding of the criticisms of the existing law needs to be demonstrated, together with a description of how the new law seeks to meet those criticisms. In conclusion, the student is required to give his/her view as to whether the Family Law Act 1996 is likely to succeed in improving on the existing law of divorce.

Skeleton Solution

Existing law of divorce – the ground of irretrievable breakdown and the need to satisfy the court of one or more of five facts (s1(1) and (2) MCA 1973) – the extensive use of the fault facts of adultery and behaviour and consequences of this – whether this amounts to the law being 'confusing, misleading, discriminatory and unjust' – Law Commission proposals for reform of divorce law – government's approach to divorce law reform through Parts I to III Family Law Act 1996, in particular the imposition of a period for reflection and to prepare for the consequences of the divorce – the use of mediation – whether the Family Law Act 1996 meets the criticisms of the existing law and avoids confusion, discrimination and injustice.

Suggested Solution

The reform of divorce law enacted in the Family Law Act 1996 (but not substantially in force) has proved to be controversial. The new Act seeks to overcome the criticisms of the existing law but the new proposed framework has itself been subject to criticism.

It should be remembered that divorce law went through a similar period of reform in the 1950s and 1960s. A Royal Commission (the Morton Commission) published a report on divorce law reform in 1956. This was followed by a report from the Church of England called *Putting Asunder* and a Law Commission report. The Law Commission report recommended that the aims of a good divorce law are to 'buttress, rather than undermine the stability of marriage, and when, regrettably, a marriage has irretrievably broken down, to enable the empty legal shell to be destroyed with the maximum fairness and the minimum bitterness, distress and humiliation.' The consequence was the passing of the Divorce Law Reform Act 1969. The existing law is contained in the Matrimonial Causes Act 1973 (which replaced the Divorce Reform Act 1969). This law replaced the notion of the matrimonial offence as being the basis for divorce with the notion of irretrievable breakdown of the marriage: see s1(1) Matrimonial Causes Act 1973 – hereinafter referred to as the MCA 1973. A petitioner has to establish that the marriage has broken down irretrievably. In addition, he or she must satisfy the court of one or more of five facts: see s1(2) MCA 1973. Three of these facts retain an element of fault. The first is that the respondent has committed adultery and that the petitioner finds it intolerable to live with the respondent: see s1(2)(a) MCA 1973. The second is that the respondent has behaved in such a way that the petitioner cannot be reasonably be expected to live with the respondent: see s1(2)(b) MCA 1973. The third is that the respondent has deserted the petitioner for a continuous period of at least two years immediately preceding the presentation of the divorce petition: see s1(2)(c) MCA 1973. The other two facts are not fault based. One is that the parties have lived apart for a continuous period of at least two years immediately preceding the presentation of the petition and the respondent consents to the decree being granted: see s1(2)(d) MCA 1973. The second is that the parties have lived apart for a continuous period of at least five years immediately preceding the presentation of the petition: see s1(2)(e) MCA 1973. There is protection for respondent spouses who would suffer grave financial or other hardship who can defend divorces based on five years living apart on the basis of such hardship: see s5 MCA 1973. There is a limited form of protection to safeguard other respondent spouses in divorces relying on s1(2)(d) and (e): see s10 MCA 1973. Petitions are barred within the first year of marriage: see s3 MCA 1973.

When the existing law was first proposed it was thought that the non-fault based facts would be relied upon in the majority of cases. In fact the fault based facts of adultery and behaviour are the most commonly used in divorce petitions. For example, the fact of adultery is used by female petitioners in 22 per cent of cases and by male petitioners in 37 per cent of cases. The fact of behaviour was used by female petitioners in 53 per cent of cases. The reason for the use of the fault based facts appears to be that this is the quickest way to obtain a divorce in many cases. As a result it was argued that petitioners were encouraged to make allegations (sometimes exaggerated) against their spouses in order to obtain a speedy divorce. This can lead to spouses taking up opposing situations from the beginning of the divorce process.

In May 1988 the Law Commission published a discussion paper 'Facing the Future' dealing with the possible reform of divorce law. In 1990 it published its report *The*

Ground for Divorce which argued that the objectives of the law should be to support marriages which could be saved and to dissolve as painlessly as possible those marriages which could not be saved. These aims were the same as the previous report which led to the 1969 reforms. It also argued that divorce law should encourage parties to resolve issues relating to the children, the home and finance as amicably as possible, having regard to their responsibilities to their children and to each other. In particular, the law should aim to reduce the harm suffered by children at the time of divorce and afterwards, and to encourage the continued sharing of parental responsibilities towards the children. The existing law was criticised in the terms quoted in the question. The use of the fault based facts were said to encourage unnecessary hostility and bitterness. It argued that the law did little to save marriage, little to help the children and did not help the parties to consider the future in a calm and reasonable manner. The Commission argued that while irretrievable breakdown should remain the sole ground for divorce it should be proved by a single fact, namely the expiry of a minimum period of one year for the consideration of the practical consequences of the divorce and for reflection upon the possibility of reconciliation. In practice, this period would commence by either or both parties making a formal statement that the marriage had broken down and lodging that statement with the court. The court would then supply both parties with an information pack explaining the objectives of the ensuing one year period, the court's powers and about opportunities for reconciliation, counselling, mediation and conciliation. Within that year the court could make orders regarding the children, finance and property. Contested matters could be referred to conciliation before being determined by the court. After 11 months of the one-year period had elapsed either party could apply for a divorce order (or a separation order as judicial separation would be termed), and after one month had elapsed from the making of that application a divorce (or separation) order could be issued. These suggestions for reform came against a background of public concern about divorce and the number of divorcing couples. Great Britain has the highest divorce rate in Europe.

The Lord Chancellor published a Green Paper in December, 1993 called *Facing the Future: Mediation and the Ground for Divorce* which followed the recommendations of the Law Commission. He proposed a no fault divorce after only one year of separation and focusing on mediation rather than the courts. Following consultation, a White Paper was published in 1995 detailing the decisions taken on divorce reform: this largely reflected the views of the Law Commission and the Green Paper. The single ground for divorce would be irretrievable breakdown which would be demonstrated by the passing of a one-year period for reflection and consideration, and for the parties to settle the arrangements for the children and financial provision. The petitioner would be obliged to attend an information-giving session, and the respondent would be encouraged to attend. At this session couples would be informed of the legal consequences of divorce and of options such as counselling and mediation. Local mediation services would be state funded. While supporting the objectives proposed by the Law Commission, the government was also concerned to minimise the cost to the taxpayer and to the parties of the existing divorce process. The government therefore proposed that legal aid would be limited in the new divorce process so that parties kept control of their own affairs, preferably through mediation rather than through lawyers. These provisions were then introduced to the 1995/96 Parliament in the Family Law Bill. They attracted considerable controversy and the passage through Parliament led to a number of amendments and concessions being made.

The Family Law Act 1996 has now been enacted. Part I, which deals with the general principles underlying the divorce reform, has been brought into force. However, it was then announced by the Lord Chancellor that Parts II and III would not be brought into force and would, in due course, be repealed.

The volume of divorce appears to be largely a product of wider historical and social forces (in particular the Second World War) rather than changes in the law. The attitude to divorce has changed considerably and religious attitudes have become far less rigid. There is an argument that reforms to divorce law follow social trends rather than shape them. Even with the extensive use of the existing fault based facts most divorces are undefended and amount to divorce by consent. One Member of Parliament put it this way: 'I am nervous about whether we in the House can pick up where 2,000 years of Judeao-Christian traditions appears to have failed to singly and, by the stroke of a legislative pen, safeguard marriage for the foreseeable future. That is wishful thinking.' The Family Law Act 1996 is designed to meet the principal criticisms of the existing law. The Act is designed to eliminate the unjust and arbitrary use of the fault facts which can engender bitterness. The Act seeks to eliminate fault altogether, concentrating on the consequences of divorce and encouraging spouses to prepare for them. The Act is laudable in these aims and objectives of making the end of marriage less painful. However, there is still an element of divorcing parties wishing to allocate blame for the failure of their marriage. The existing law allows parties to allocate that blame whereas the new law does not. There is the danger that the new provisions do not allow for a 'safety valve' in this respect and this may prove a weakness. Human nature may conspire to defeat the aims and objectives of the new law.

QUESTION FOUR

'The government's decision not to implement the reformed divorce law under the Family Law Act 1996 characterises official uncertainty as to the extent to which law can and should control the dissolution of family units.'

Discuss. What is your preferred solution to the reform of divorce law?

University of London LLB Examination
(for External Students) Family Law June 2000 Q2

General Comment

This question was very topical following closely on the announcement by the Lord Chancellor that Part II of the Family Law Act 1996 would not be brought into force. It allows the student to examine the shortcomings of the existing law, the aims of the proposed new law and the reasons why it was abandoned. Finally, the student is asked for his/her view on a preferred solution to the reform of divorce law, preferably avoiding the pitfalls in the existing law and retaining some of the better features of the abandoned reforms.

Skeleton Solution

Existing law of divorce: the ground of irretrievable breakdown and the need to satisfy the court of one or more of five facts (s1(1) and (2) MCA 1973); the extensive use of fault facts of adultery and behaviour and consequences of this; Law Commission's proposals for reform and the resulting Family Law Act 1996: Part I (the objectives of divorce) – Part II (the period of reflection and to prepare for the consequences of divorce, information meetings and the role of mediation); the extent to which the law can and should control the dissolution of family units; a preferred solution to the reform of divorce law.

Suggested Solution

Divorce law has long been a controversial area. Great Britain has the highest divorce rate in Europe. There is considerable concern about the consequences of divorce for divorcing couples and particularly for the children. The recently abandoned reform of divorce law followed a similar period of reform in the 1950s and 1960s. A Royal Commission (the Morton Commission) published a report on divorce law reform in 1956. This was followed by a report from the Church of England entitled *Putting Assunder* and a Law Commission Report. The Law Commission Report recommended that the aims of a good divorce law are to 'buttress, rather than undermine, the stability of marriage, and when, regrettably, a marriage has irretrievably broken down, to enable the empty legal shell to be destroyed with the maximum fairness and the minimum bitterness, distress and humiliation'. The consequence was the passing of the Divorce Law Reform Act 1969 which formed the basis for the current law in the Matrimonial Causes Act (MCA) 1973. This law replaced the notion of the matrimonial offence as being the basis for divorce with the notion of irretrievable breakdown of the marriage: see s1(1) MCA 1973. In addition, the petitioner has to satisfy the court of one or more of five facts: see s1(2) MCA 1973. Three of these facts retain an element of fault.

The first is that the respondent has committed adultery and the petitioner finds it intolerable to live with the respondent: see s1(2)(a) MCA 1973. The second is that the respondent has behaved in such a way that the petitioner cannot be reasonably expected to live with him/her: see s1(2)(b) MCA 1973. The third is that the respondent has deserted the petitioner for a continuous period of at least two years immediately preceding the presentation of the petition: see s1(2)(c) MCA 1973. The other two facts are not fault based. One is that the parties have lived apart for a period of at least two years immediately preceding the presentation of the petition and the respondent consents to the petition (see s1(2)(d) MCA 1973), and the second is that the parties have lived apart for at least five years immediately preceding the presentation of the petition: see s1(2)(e) MCA 1973. For these latter two facts there is protection for the respondent's financial position where appropriate: see ss5 and 10 MCA 1973.

It was thought that non-fault facts would be relied upon in the majority of cases. In reality the fault-based facts of adultery and behaviour are the most commonly used in divorce petitions. For example, the behaviour fact is used in over half of all petitions brought by female petitioners and the fact of adultery used in over a third of petitions brought by male petitioners. The reason for the use of fault-based facts appears to be that they offer the opportunity to obtain divorces quickly and without waiting for specified periods of elapse. The main criticism of the present divorce law is that it encourages petitioners to make allegations (sometimes exaggerated) against their spouses in order to obtain a speedy divorce. It is argued that this can lead to spouses taking up confrontational positions from the beginning of the divorce process. The courts have emphasised that they will not rubber stamp divorce petitions. They have a duty to enquire into the facts alleged by the petitioner (and any alleged by the respondent): see s1(3) MCA 1973. While the courts will not engage in pointless enquiries into conduct and fault (see *Grenfell* v *Grenfell* [1977] 3 WLR 738) it is required to make complete findings when allegations are either disputed or require more detailed investigation: see for example *Butterworth* v *Butterworth* [1998] 1 FCR 159. This may encourage petitioners to make stronger and more numerous allegations against the respondent in order to satisfy s1(1) and the relevant fact in s1(2).

In 1988 the Law Commission published a discussion paper on the possible reform of divorce law. In 1990 it published its Report *The Ground for Divorce*. The Report supported the objectives of divorce law as stated in the 1960s, namely to support marriages which could be saved and to dissolve as painlessly as possible those marriages which could not be saved. It went further in stating that divorce law should encourage parties to resolve issues relating to the children, the home and finance as amicably as possible having regard to their responsibilities to their children and to each other. It criticised the existing divorce law as being confusing, misleading, discriminating and unjust. It argued that the law did little to save marriage or to help children or help the parties to consider the future in a calm and reasonable manner. The Commission agreed that irretrievable breakdown should remain as the sole ground for divorce but that it should be proved by a single fact, namely the expiry of a minimum period of one year for the consideration of the practical consequences of the divorce and for reflection on the possibility of reconciliation. In practice the parties would commence the period by one or both making a formal statement that the marriage had broken down and lodging it with the court. It was then intended that the court would supply information to the parties about opportunities for reconciliation, counselling, mediation and conciliation. Within the one-year period the court would make orders regarding the children, finance and property. Contested matters would be subject to conciliation before being dealt with by a court. After 11 months of the one-year period either party could apply for a divorce order and then a month later be granted the divorce order.

The Law Commission Report was followed by a Green Paper in 1993 which agreed with the recommendations of the Law Commission. A White Paper followed in 1995 which included compulsory attendance at information meetings for the petitioner with the respondent encouraged to attend. At these sessions parties would be informed of the consequences of divorce and of options such as counselling and mediation. The government was also concerned about minimising the cost to the taxpayer and to the parties of the existing divorce process. The provisions were then introduced in the Family Law Bill in 1995 and 1996. There was considerable controversy and debate leading to a number of amendments and concessions. The final result was the Family Law Act (FLA) 1996 which received Royal Assent in July, 1996. Part I of the Act was brought into force in March 1997. This lays down the general principles of divorce, namely:

a) the institution of marriage should be supported;

b) the parties to a marriage which may have broken down are to be encouraged to take all practicable steps, whether by marriage counselling or otherwise, to save the marriage;

c) that a marriage which has irretrievably broken down and is being brought to an end should be brought to an end:

   i)   with minimum distress to the parties and to the children affected;

   ii) with questions dealt with in a manner designed to promote as good a continuing relationship between the parties and any children affected as is possible in the circumstances;

   iii) without costs being unreasonably incurred in connection with the procedures to be followed in bringing the marriage to an end;

d) that any risk to one of the parties to a marriage and to any children, of violence from the other party should, so far as reasonably practicable, be removed or diminished: see s1 FLA 1996.

A divorce order dissolving a marriage could only be made once the following conditions were satisfied:

a) there has been a required attendance at an information meeting followed by a statement of marital breakdown (see ss5 and 6 FLA 1996);

b) the period for reflection and consideration has passed indicating that the marriage has broken down irretrievably (see s7 FLA 1996);

c) adequate financial arrangements for the future have been made;

d) the welfare of any child has been properly provided for (see s11 FLA 1996);

e) the application has not been withdrawn.

There were some exceptions to the above conditions but this is the general framework laid down by Part II of the 1996 Act.

Before implementing Part II the government decided to pilot the information meetings' process. In 1999 the Lord Chancellor announced that the government would delay the implementation of Part II indefinitely. He was of the view that the interim results from the pilots had been disappointing, with only 7 per cent of those attending information meetings being diverted to mediation. In 2000 he announced that Part II would not be implemented and would eventually be repealed. These announcements attracted considerable surprise and criticism. For example, the Advisory Board on Family Law expressed surprise and disappointment in its Third Annual Report in June 2000. It took a more optimistic view of the research findings from the pilots. The research did show that parties found the information meetings valuable, increased knowledge and empowered people to make more informed decisions. At the present time the government has given no indication of what reforms, if any, will replace the existing divorce law.

The reaction of the government did display official uncertainty as to the extent to which the law can and should control the dissolution of married family units. The research from the pilots highlighted the variety of expectations people have in difficult circumstances. Some had made definite decisions but did not know how to implement them. Others had little or no idea how to react to the marriage breakdown and associated issues. The standardised nature of information meetings made it difficult to meet this variety of needs. The government seemed to have too high expectations about the results of information meetings. It expected them to lead to a high take up of mediation as an alternative to lawyer and court-based solutions. It expected large savings in legal costs. When these did not happen the Lord Chancellor could see no advantage in implementing Part II. It is submitted that he took a mistaken and short-term view. There has been no direct criticism of the concept of divorce following a period of reflection and consideration (as opposed to the fault-based facts under the MCA 1973). Insufficient time was allowed and insufficient consideration given to the pilots and the resulting research. The fact that the interim research results did not provide the kind of 'significant' results the government was looking for does not mean that the whole of Part II could not have improved the divorce process in the long term.

What options are there for further reform ? There is a minority view that the fault-based system should apply in order to do justice to the 'wronged' spouse. It is submitted that this would provide little benefit and continue, if not exacerbate, the problems in the existing system. There could be the elimination of fault-based facts leaving 'living apart' facts based on consent and lack of consent (as in s1(2)(d) and (e) MCA 1973). At present the five-year period when there is lack of consent would be unacceptable to many parties because of the length of time leaving them unable to settle the remainder of their lives. Different and lesser periods could be set (eg one year living apart with consent and two years living apart without consent). It is submitted that there are few advantages in having different periods depending on consent. A single period without consent would be more appropriate since the courts can provide protection of a party and/or any children. Given the relatively small use of the present fact of two years living apart with consent it appears that most parties would prefer a shorter period even if they agree on divorce. As a result there appears to be some logic to the one-year period fixed in Part II. Any shorter period might encourage the 'impetuous' divorce. However, there is a serious shortcoming to any 'living apart' fact. Some parties cannot 'live apart'. A spouse in a weak financial position may have no accommodation to go to. As a result any period should be a time for reflection rather than a requirement for living part. Many spouses would indeed be living apart following a marriage breakdown, but others for good reason may not but would have an equally valid claim for a divorce. It is submitted that the preferred solution to the reform of divorce law is that of in Part II of the Family Law Act 1996. The reforms follow a long period of consultation from the Law Commission and from Parliament. The removal of the fault-based facts and replacement with a minimum set period of one year of reflection is a sensible reform. It would deal with much which is wrong with the present divorce law and provide potential for parties to deal with the consequences of divorce in a more considered manner. There is criticism of the detail in how Part II could operate. The information meetings need to be more flexible in dealing with the variety of expectations, knowledge and fears parties have. Assistance should be provided when parties need it, not when the dictates of a legal process permit it. Expectations of big savings in legal costs are probably unrealistic. This however does not take away the benefits of parties being able to make decisions on a more informed basis, whether by themselves or with lawyers and courts to assist them.

Chapter 5

Rights and Obligations during Marriage

5.1   Introduction

5.2   Key points

5.3   Key cases and statutes

5.4   Questions and suggested solutions

5.1 Introduction

This chapter looks at the right to maintenance during marriage as part of the mutual rights and obligations of marriage. It must be emphasised that the chapter is *not* concerned with powers to award maintenance as part of divorce proceedings (which is dealt with in Chapter 6).

5.2 Key points

Application for maintenance under s27 MCA 1973

A spouse can apply for maintenance to the High Court or county court under s27(1) MCA 1973 under one or both of the following grounds:

a) that the respondent has failed to provide reasonable maintenance for the applicant; or

b) that the respondent has failed to provide or make a proper contribution towards reasonable maintenance for any child of the family.

If one of the grounds is satisfied then the court can make lump sum orders or maintenance orders. The court has regard to the considerations in s25 MCA 1973.

The court is unlikely to have jurisdiction to make child maintenance orders since this is dealt with by child support.

Application for maintenance under DPMCA 1978

A spouse can apply for maintenance to the magistrates' court under the Domestic Proceedings and Magistrates' Courts Act 1978. Application may be made for an order under s2 DPMCA 1978 if one or more of the following grounds under s1 DMPCA 1978 is satisied:

a) the respondent has failed to provide reasonable maintenance for the applicant; or

b) that the respondent has failed to provide or make a proper contribution towards reasonable maintenance for any child of the family;

c) the respondent has behaved in such a way that the applicant cannot reasonably be expected to live with the respondent;

d) the respondent has deserted the applicant.

There is no need to show any *wilful* failure to maintain. The ground of behaviour is dealt with in the same way as the divorce fact under s1(2)(b) MCA 1973: see *Bergin v Bergin* [1983] 1 WLR 279.

If one or more of the grounds is satisfied then under s2 DMPCA 1978 the magistrates' court can make:

a) a maintenance order for the applicant;

b) a maintenance order for a child of the family;

c) a lump sum for the applicant (subject to a maximum of £1,000);

d) a lump sum for a child of the family (subject to the same maximum).

In deciding whether to make any order and, if so, in what manner, the court must take into account particular considerations: see s3 DPMCA 1978. These considerations are virtually the same as those in s25(1) and (2) MCA 1973. The clean break provisions do not apply. The authorities on s25 MCA 1973 apply to s3 DPMCA 1978: see *Macey v Macey* (1982) 3 FLR 7 and *Vasey v Vasey* [1985] FLR 589. The one-third principle may apply but this may be inappropriate for low income families: see *Cann v Cann* [1977] 3 All ER 957.

The court also has power to make consent orders for maintenance which have been agreed between the parties. There is no need for the applicant to prove any grounds. The court will make the agreed order where there is nothing to suggest that so to do would be contrary to the interests of justice and the court is satisfied that proper provision is being made for any child. There is no upper limit on lump sum provisions so long as the other party agrees: see s6 DPMCA 1978.

The magistrates' court is unlikely to have the jurisdiction to make child maintenance orders whether under s2 or s6 DPMCA 1978 since this is largely dealt with by the Child Support Agency.

Applications to the magistrates' court have the advantage of being cheaper and speedier than applications to the county court. Where an applicant is legally aided he/she may be obliged to apply to the magistrates' court to reduce costs.

Reforms under Family Law Act 1996

The Law Commission in its report *The Ground for Divorce* (1990 (Law Com No 192) recommended the abolition of the grounds of behaviour and desertion in s1 DPMCA 1978 in order to avoid bitterness and conflict which could hinder prospects of saving the marriage. These recommendations have been included in the Family Law Act 1996. The grounds for making a maintenance order under s2 DPMCA 1978 are amended to delete the grounds of behaviour and desertion: see s18(1) FLA 1996 deleting s1(c) and (d) DPMCA 1978. This part of the Family Law Act 1996 has not been brought into force. Given the abandonment of Part III of the 1996 Act the provisions may never be brought into force.

Child support under the Child Support Act 1991

A parent with children can apply to the Child Support Agency for a child support assessment against the absent parent. Indeed, in most cases the courts have no jurisdiction to deal with child maintenance (though they retain the right to make capital and/or property orders under the MCA 1973, the DPMCA 1978 or the Children Act 1989). The courts retain the power to make child maintenance orders where:

a) the child is not the natural child of the absent parent (eg a step-child who has been treated as a child of the family);

b) in the case of a wealthy absent parent where the amount of child maintenance he/she could pay is in excess of the maximum amount of child support which could be assessed;

c) the child is over 19 (or is between 16 and 19 and not in education);

d) where one of the child's parents is not habitually resident in the UK;

e) where the child maintenance is intended solely for educational purposes;

f) where the child is disabled and the child maintenance is to meet expenses attributable to the child's disability.

Child support is calculated according to a fixed formula which can be summarised as follows:

a) calculating the maintenance requirement (based on income support allowances for the child and parent);

b) calculating the assessable income of both parents (ie net income less 'exempt income' which is made up of fixed outgoings);

c) calculating the deduction rate;

d) comparing the deduction rate with the absent parent's protected income.

From April 2002 the formula should have been greatly simplified as follows:

a) a normal rate which obliges the non-resident parent (NRP) to pay 15 per cent of his net income for one qualifying child, 20 per cent for two qualifying children and 25 per cent for three or more qualifying children (with discounts if he had qualifying children living with him);

b) a reduced rate where the NRP has a low income;

c) a flat rate of £5 a week for NRPs on benefit or on a very low income;

d) a nil rate for NRPs with a net income of less than £5 a week.

As with the existing system there would have been reductions where the care of a child is shared. There would have been a maximum rate of child support. Account would also have been taken of capital or property transfers to reflect pre-April 1993 clean break settlements.

However, in March 2002 the government announced that computer problems have indefinitely delayed these reforms. The student should be aware of the continued controversy surrounding child support and how the proposed reforms might have met those criticims.

5.3 Key cases and statutes

- *Crozier* v *Crozier* [1994] 2 WLR 444
  Child support and the clean break

- *Delaney* v *Delaney* [1990] 2 FLR 457
  Maintenance in low income cases

- *Mawson* v *Mawson* [1994] 2 FLR 985
  Child support and ancillary relief

- Child Support Act 1991 – child support for children

- Domestic Proceedings and Magistrates' Courts Act 1978 – financial position through the magistrates' court

- Matrimonial Causes Act 1973 – financial provision through the county court

5.4 Questions and suggested solutions

QUESTION ONE

Arthur and Betty married in 1978 and have two children. Early in 1982 Arthur developed a mental illness, as a result of which he erroneously believed that his wife was having an affair with their bank manager. After many heated arguments, which caused distress to the children as well as to Betty, Betty announced that she was leaving home, taking the children with her, and that she was not going to return. Arthur replied that he was glad she was leaving, as he had never wanted to live with an adulteress, but that he was sorry to see the children go and that he would pay Betty £40 a week for their upkeep. Betty left home a few days later and went to stay with her mother.

Arthur was admitted to a mental hospital a few months later but continued to pay Betty £40 a week out of capital he possessed. Betty visited him occasionally both out of a genuine concern for his health and because she was anxious that he should keep up the payments.

In April 1987 Arthur met Celia, a new nurse at the mental hospital, whom he wishes to marry. Betty does not want a divorce because she thinks Arthur will stop paying her the money if he marries Celia.

Assuming that Arthur does not obtain a divorce, how, if at all, can Betty ensure that Arthur makes financial provision for herself and the children?

Adapted from University of London LLB Examination
(for External Students) Family Law June 1987 Q2

General Comment

Financial provision during marriage is regularly examined; in its original form this question also dealt with whether Arthur could divorce Betty – see chapter 3: *Divorce* for this. In answering the question candidates must remember to discuss, in relation to the magistrates' court proceedings, orders under s7 as well as s2 DPMCA 1978. Advice must also be given on an application by Betty to the Child Support Agency for child support for the two children.

Skeleton Solution

Discuss the two major jurisdictions available to a spouse to obtain financial relief during a marriage, namely s27 MCA 1973 and s1 DPMCA 1978 – explain the grounds to be relied upon, and the orders available under s27 MCA 1973 and ss2 and 7 DPMCA 1978 and the factors to be considered by the court applying the guidelines in s25 MCA 1973 and s3 DPMCA 1978 – explain how to make an application for child support and how this is likely to be assessed.

Suggested Solution

On the assumption that Arthur does not obtain a divorce at this time there are two procedures available to Betty to ensure that he makes financial provision for herself.

Betty could apply to the High Court or county court under s27 MCA 1973 for financial provision for herself on the ground that Arthur has failed to provide reasonable maintenance for herself and/or the children, and even though Arthur has been paying maintenance regularly, the sum of £40 for the family's support may not be deemed reasonable. However this will depend on Betty's resources as well as Arthur's and it may be that the provision he has been making is reasonable in all the circumstances.

Alternatively she could apply to the magistrates' court for an order under s2 Domestic Proceedings and Magistrates' Courts Act 1978 (hereinafter DPMCA 1978) on one of the grounds set out in s1, namely that Arthur has failed to provide reasonable maintenance for Betty and/or the children (which ground is similar to that set out in s27 MCA 1973 and therefore the reservations mentioned above must be applied to it); or on the ground of Arthur's unreasonable behaviour (which has the same meaning as under s1(2)(b) MCA 1973); or on the ground that Arthur has deserted her (and desertion in the magistrates' court has the same meaning as under s1(2)(c) MCA 1973 although there is no minimum period of desertion so long as it is continuing at the date of the hearing, and will include constructive desertion).

Betty could rely on Arthur's behaviour, ie his false accusations of adultery, which gave rise to arguments between the parties, and even though such behaviour is attributable to his mental illness the court will take it into account having made allowances for the illness and the performance of marital obligations: *Katz* v *Katz* [1972] 1 WLR 955. Alternatively she could rely on s7 DPMCA 1978 which provides that where the spouses have been separated for a continuous period exceeding three months, neither party being in desertion (which may be the case here particularly in view of Arthur's mental illness which may have prevented him from forming the intention to desert), and one spouse has been making periodical payments for the benefit of the other party and for a child of the family, that other party may apply to the magistrates for an order, specifying in the application the aggregate amount received during the three months preceding the application. On hearing such an application the court may order the respondent to make such periodical payments to the applicant, but the amount ordered must not exceed the aggregate amount stated in the application. However, if as a result of this limitation the magistrates feel that reasonable maintenance cannot be awarded, they may refuse to make an order on this ground and treat the application as one for financial provision under s1 and make a suitable order under s2.

So Betty has a choice of applications before her. If the maintenance paid by Arthur is not reasonable she can rely on s27 MCA 1973 or s1(a) DPMCA 1978. Alternatively, she could rely on s1(b) DPMCA 1978, namely on Arthur's behaviour. If she is satisfied with the maintenance paid by Arthur voluntarily, then a s7 DPMCA 1978 application would seem appropriate.

The orders that can be made under s27 MCA 1973 and s2 DPMCA 1978 are similar and include a periodical payments order in favour of the applicant, but which in the county court can be secured although this cannot be done in the magistrates' court. Further, in both jurisdictions the court may make a lump sum order. However, whereas in the county court there is no limit on the amount of the lump sum, in the magistrates' court it is subject to a limit of £1,000, although on application for variation further lump sum awards can be made. It is unlikely that Betty will require a lump sum in excess of £1,000 in any event. It should be noted that under s7 DPMCA 1978 the magistrates have no power to make lump sum provision so if Betty requires a lump sum, say to pay off existing debts, then a s7 application would be inappropriate.

Under s27 MCA 1973 the court will take into account all the circumstances of the case first consideration being given to the welfare of any minor child of the family, including the matters set out in s25(2) MCA 1973 as substituted by s3 Matrimonial and Family

Proceedings Act 1984 (hereinafter MFPA 1984), insofar as they apply to an application which does not affect the status of the marriage. Similarly in the magistrates' court, s3 DPMCA 1978 as substituted by s9 MFPA 1984 which sets out the guidelines to be considered when deciding what if any order to make, follows the provisions of s25 MCA. Therefore in this case the relevant factors will include the income, earning capacity, including any increase in that capacity which the court considers it reasonable to expect a party to take steps to acquire, property and other financial resources of the parties (as well as the income and resources of the children, if any); the financial needs, obligations and responsibilities of the parties (and the children) both immediately and in the foreseeable future; the standard of living enjoyed by the family before the breakdown; the age of the parties and the duration of the marriage; the contribution made by each party to the marriage, including a contribution made by looking after the home; any mental or physical defect of the parties (here Arthur's mental illness must be considered particularly as it may affect his earning capacity and general resources); and the conduct of the parties if the court considers that it would be inequitable to disregard it. Conduct is unlikely to be deemed relevant here as although Arthur seems solely to blame for the breakdown of the marriage there is no evidence to show that it would affect the financial claims. In *Robinson* v *Robinson* (1983) the conduct of a wife reduced her periodical payments award but conduct such as Arthur's is unlikely to increase Betty's award.

Finally the court will consider in respect of the children, the manner in which they were being, or were expected to be trained or educated.

No clear information as to the parties' financial status has been given in this question save that Arthur has been paying maintenance out of capital since he was admitted to hospital. If Betty is working, or can be expected to work at this time (and this will depend largely on the age of their children), then any financial provision for herself will be relatively small and may be of a temporary nature to allow her to adjust to a new job and independence. If she already has a job and sufficient income to provide for her own needs then Arthur will not be ordered to make any periodical payments in her favour. In view of his illness it is difficult to say whether he will be able to work and if not, and he has to pay maintenance out of his capital then this may mean that his capacity to pay maintenance is more restricted. However, more information as to his general resources would be required before full advice on this point can be given. Further it is unclear whether Betty will require lump sum provision and if she does, her needs must be balanced against Arthur's ability to pay.

If Betty obtains orders in either the county court or the magistrates' court under the MCA 1973 or the DPMCA 1978, they can be enforced through the court process if Arthur should default in the payment of the same.

Should Betty wish to pursue financial support for the two children she would have to apply to the Child Support Agency for child support. The courts are unlikely to have any jurisdiction to make maintenance orders for them (see s8 Child Support Act 1991). The courts could make lump sum or property adjustment orders but not maintenance.

If Betty did apply for child support she should be advised that the CSA calculate the amount due according to a fixed formula. One of the elements of the formula is Arthur's income. If he has no or a limited income of his own then either a nil or a limited child support assessment will be made. No assessment can be made from any capital or property Arthur has: see *J v C (Child: Financial Provision)* [1999] 1 FLR 152. Further advice is difficult in the absence of more information on Arthur's finances.

QUESTION TWO

'The Child Support Act 1991 has largely failed because of the absence of any discretion in the new child maintenance system. When fully implemented, the addition of "departures" from the formula will make the system workable.'

Discuss.

University of London LLB Examination
(for External Students) Family Law June 1996 Q2

General Comment

The Child Support Agency and the formula for calculating child support have been highly controversial since they started to operate. As a result child support has been the subject of a discussion question over the past few years. This has required an outline of how the child support system is meant to operate, together with an analysis of its weaknesses and shortcomings. It also involves a discussion of why it was introduced in the first place and whether it has met the promises made when it first came into force. There has been a steady stream of amendments to the Child Support Act 1991 and its accompanying regulations. One of the most recent has been the introduction of a limited right of appeal (called 'departures') which allow some discretion in an otherwise rigid system. Whether the addition of 'departures' from the formula will make the system workable remains to be seen, but the student is required to set out the arguments for and against.

Skeleton Solution

Why the Child Support Act 1991 replaced the court-based system for child maintenance with the child support formula – the components of the child support formula – the difficulties created by the formula-based system – the recent reforms to improve the child support formula, including the addition of 'departures' – whether the reforms will make the system workable.

Suggested Solution

The Child Support Act 1991 (hereinafter referred to as the CSA 1991) came into force in April 1993. It has caused considerable controversy ever since. As a result of this controversy the Act has been amended on a number of occasions. In particular, the

Child Support Act 1995 has made important reforms to the original formula laid out in the CSA 1991.

From April 1993 the jurisdiction of courts to make maintenance for 'qualifying children' came to an end. The definition of 'qualifying children' includes virtually all children who were the subject of court child maintenance orders so courts largely ceased to make such orders and the Child Support Agency assumed responsibility for most child support. As a result the discretion- based court system with a hearing which both parents were able to attend was replaced by a non-discretionary formula calculated by a government agency behind closed doors. The parents' role is confined to supplying information about their financial circumstances to the Child Support Agency which is then fed into the formula and an assessment of child support is automatically produced.

The government introduced the child support system because it considered that court-based maintenance was not working. It argued that because the calculation of levels of child maintenance was a matter of discretion (with broad guidelines given as to the matters to be considered) there was no consistency between courts in the levels of maintenance fixed. It also argued that the levels of maintenance were too low and did not reflect the true costs of bringing up a child. It further pointed out that few child maintenance orders were actually paid regularly. Most were said to be in arrears and enforcement was perceived to be patchy and ineffective. The government was of the view that this was not fair to separated or divorced parents bringing up children. It also meant that the state was paying large amounts of income support and family credit to families where one parent had left and was either paying too little or no maintenance towards the costs of bringing up the children. As a result it decided to abandon the court-based system and replace it with one operated by a government agency. In order to avoid inconsistency and to increase the levels of financial payments for children it introduced a fixed formula to be used to calculate child support. This formula involves a number of stages and these need to be outlined to show the difficulties caused by this approach.

The first stage is to calculate the maintenance requirement which is the starting point for child support. This is the income support allowance for each qualifying child, plus the income support allowance for the caring parent (ie the rate for a claimant over 25 – though this reduces as the child gets older), plus the income support family premium, plus the income support lone parent premium (where the parent caring for the children – called the 'caring parent' – has no partner) but less the child benefit received. This stage continues to cause controversy because it includes an element for the caring parent, unlike the court-based system. This can cause a perceived unfairness where separating parents have negotiated a clean break order in terms of property and capital, whereby the parent who has left (called the 'absent parent') has surrendered his/her interest in property or capital in return for reduced or no maintenance payments for the former spouse (the parent with care). This difficulty was highlighted in the case of *Crozier* v *Crozier* [1994] 2 WLR 444 where an absent parent attempted to recover his interest in the former matrimonial home because of this element in the child support assessment made against him. He failed to persuade the court to change its original order.

This stage also caused controversy because it produced much higher amounts of child support than the old child maintenance system. The following stages of calculating child support are meant to ensure that the final amount of child support to be paid could be afforded by the absent parent, but the level of protest from absent parents indicated that this was often hotly disputed. The next stage in the calculation of child support is to work out the 'assessable incomes' of the parent with care and the absent parent. This is done by calculating the net income of each parent and deducting from that what is called 'exempt income'. 'Exempt income' is the income support allowance for a claimant over 25, plus housing costs up to a certain amount, plus other allowances if a parent is a lone parent or is disabled and/or has dependent children. This part of the of the calculation has perhaps caused the greatest controversy since it makes little or no allowance for many kinds of expenditure. Payments for debts taken on when the parents were together and in the absent parent's name are not considered. Travelling costs for work or the costs of travelling to see children for contact visits were not considered. The full costs of an absent parent's second family were not allowed. This latter point represented a radical departure from the court-based system. The courts took the view that an absent parent was allowed to start life afresh and allowed him or her to treat the reasonable costs of maintaining a second family as priority items of his or her expenditure. The first family would be maintained out of any balance (if any) even if this left the first family dependent on state benefit because the absent parent could not reasonably maintain two families: see *Barnes* v *Barnes* [1972] 1 WLR 1381 and *Delaney* v *Delaney* [1990] 2 FLR 457. The child support formula makes a full allowance for the financial support of the first family with only a limited allowance for the costs of keeping the second family – a complete reversal of the court approach.

The next stage of the child support formula is the deduction rate. This involves sharing the assessable income of the absent parent equally between the children and the absent parent until the maintenance requirement is met. If the parent with care has an assessable income he or she will also contribute towards the maintenance requirement. If the absent parent is particularly well off and his or her income allows more than the maintenance requirement to be paid there are provisions to allow for an extra amount of child support to be paid (called the 'additional element'). The deduction rate for the absent parent is then compared with his or her 'protected income' which is designed to provide a safety net whereby his or income is not reduced to poverty levels by the amount of child support to be paid. 'Protected income' is the income support allowance for a single claimant over 25 (or the allowance for a couple if he or she has a partner), plus other allowances, plus £30 a week, plus council tax payments, plus 15 per cent of any spare income after the allowances have been taken off. This part of the formula was also subject to considerable criticism since many absent parents argued that they were left with insufficient to live on.

The above general outline of the formula for calculating child support gives an indication of how complicated the formula actually is. The formula is meant to be rigid in order to produce consistency. However, it is also designed to take into account the different situations families find themselves in after separation. As a result further complications are introduced. This has led to the Child Support Agency being accused of incompetency in that it takes too long to collect the required information to make the necessary calculations, and then takes too long to do the calculations. It is also accused of getting many of the calculations wrong because of the complexity of the formula. As a result the CSA has been criticised not only by the absent parents (who complain that they are required to pay too much) but also by parents with care (who face delays and mistakes in the calculation of child support). As a result of the perceived injustices of the system there has been a concerted campaign by a number of absent parents to avoid having to pay child support. In other cases the CSA has failed to trace or enforce payments against absent parents who prefer to avoid payment. This has led to critics saying that the child support system has failed to provide the advantages over the court-based system which the government promised.

The criticisms of absent parents have been supplemented by criticisms from some parents with care. While some parents with care have benefited from the child support system by receiving much greater financial support, others have either not benefited in any way or have been left worse off. Those on benefits have accused the government of using child support to reduce expenditure on those benefits by transferring the burden of child support onto the absent parent. In some cases families became worse off because of the inefficiencies of the Child Support Agency. There is an element of compulsion on a parent with care on benefit to co-operate with a child support assessment. If he or she does not co-operate he or she runs the risk of having his or her benefit reduced by 20 per cent for the first six months and by 10 per cent for the following year. It is possible for such a parent to persuade the Child Support Agency that to provide information would lead to undue distress or harm (eg violence from the absent parent). However, this element of compulsion illustrates that the government is seeking to reduce its expenditure on benefits through the child support system. The government has tried to improve the service provided to parents with care (eg by allowing lone parents on income support to keep an extra amount of child support before losing their benefit and by trying to improve the service provided by the CSA).

The government appears to have accepted many of the criticisms from absent parents and has significantly amended the formula in the years following 1993. The latest set of reforms were made in the Child Support, Pensions and Social Security Act 2000. This introduced a much simpler formula:

a) A normal rate obliging the absent parent (called the non-resident parent or NRP) to pay 15 per cent of his net income for one qualifying child; 20 per cent for two qualifying children; and 25 per cent for three or more qualifying children.

b) Reductions if the NRP has a dependent child(ren) living with him.

c) A reduced rate of child support for NRPs on a low income.

d) Reductions if the care of the child is shared between the NRP and parent with care.

e) Allowance for 'special expenses' of the NRP (eg school fees).

f) Allowances for pre-1993 capital or property transfers.

Unfortunately the government announced a delay in implementing these reforms in 2002 because of computer problems.

The problems of applying a rigid formula have been manifold and has led to a steady stream of amendments to meet those problems. The system remains largely based on the formula so many problems may still remain even with the safety net of 'departures'. The system has had its successes. It has collected increasing amounts of child support and reduced government expenditure on benefits, as well as increasing the income of parents with care. However, it remains to be seen whether the latest set of reforms, when implemented, will meet these criticisms.

Chapter 6

The Financial Consequences of Divorce

6.1   Introduction

6.2   Key points

6.3   Key cases and statute

6.4   Questions and suggested solutions

6.1 Introduction

This is an important topic both in practice and as far as the examination is concerned. Invariably at least one question on ancillary relief is included in the examination paper each year.

The courts' powers are contained in ss23, 24, 24A, 24B–24D and 25B–25D MCA 1973 which allow the courts to make wide-ranging orders for periodical payments, lump sums, settlements, sale of property and division of proceeds, pension splitting and pension attachment orders to either spouse and/or the children. Sections 25 and 25A give guidelines to the court on how to exercise these powers. The student must demonstrate a clear knowledge and understanding of those powers and guidelines, together with the important case law in this areas. Sections 25 and 25A give guidelines to the court on how to exercise those powers. The student must demonstrate a clear knowledge and understanding of those powers and guidelines, together with the important case law in this area.

It must be remembered that maintenance orders for children are now almost solely dealt with by way of child support through the Child Support Agency (see the Child Support Act 1991). A sound knowledge of when the rules on child support apply and a general awareness of how child support is calculated is also essential for the student.

6.2 Key points

The wide powers under ss23, 24 and 24A MCA 1973

A question about ancillary relief should start with an outline of the wide powers of the court to:

a) make periodical payment orders (s23 MCA 1973);

b) make lump sum orders (s23 MCA 1973);

c) settle property on one or both spouses (s24 MCA 1973);

d) order the sale of property and division of the proceeds (s24A MCA 1973);

e) order that a pension be split between the spouses (ss24B–24D MCA 1973);

f) make a pensions attachment or earmarking order: ss25B-25D MCA 1973.

Section 25(1) 'having regard to all the circumstances' – the yardstick of equal division

The House of Lords in *White* v *White* [2000] 2 FLR 981 emphasised that the court had to be fair to both parties. Courts are advised, before reaching a firm conclusion and making ancillary relief orders, to check its tentative view against the yardstick of equal division. As a general rule equality should be departed from only if and to the extent that there is good reason to do so. The need to consider and to articulate reasons for departing from equality should avoid discrimination.

The s25 guidelines

If there are children involved their welfare is the first consideration: s25(1). This does not mean that their welfare is paramount and overrides other considerations but it will be of the first importance: see *Suter* v *Suter and Jones* [1987] 2 All ER 336.

The court will consider all the circumstances but must have regard to particular matters.

First, the income, earning capacity, property and other financial resources which each of the parties has or is likely to have in the foreseeable future, including in the case of earning capacity any increase in that capacity which it would in the opinion of the court be reasonable to expect a party to the marriage to take steps to acquire (see s25(2)(a)). This will largely be a factual matter based on the information given in the question, though the student will often be expected to highlight any earning capacity and comment on it (eg whether a non-working wife with the care of children has any earning capacity). The student may also be required to consider any interest by way of damages or under a will or by way of third parties (eg wealthy members of a spouse's family). Students will need to know such cases as *Michael* v *Michael* [1986] 2 FLR 389 (interests under a will), *Wagstaff* v *Wagstaff* [1992] 1 WLR 320 and *Thomas* v *Thomas* [1995] 2 FLR 668 (assets of third party).

Second, the financial needs, obligations and responsibilities which each of the parties to a marriage has or is likely to have in the foreseeable future have to be considered: s25(2)(b). The costs and responsibilities of bringing up any children for the parent with whom they live or are to live must be emphasised. This may be particularly important in terms of any property orders since the need for any children to be properly housed will be of the first importance. This may favour an outright transfer to the parent with the children or a *Mesher* order (though the dangers of *Mesher* orders need to be known).

The costs of any second family must also be considered (applying *Delaney v Delaney* [1990] 2 FLR 457).

Third, the student should mention the standard of living enjoyed by the parties before the breakdown of the marriage: see s25(2)(c) MCA 1973. The point which needs to be made in most cases is that there is likely to be a reduction in that standard as a a result of the breakdown of the marriage, but that the court will seek to spread such a reduction fairly between the parties. Where the spouses are wealthy the court will seek to maintain both parties to the standard they are accustomed to. Mention should also be made of the age of the parties and the duration of the marriage (see s25(2)(d) MCA 1973). The age of the parties may be more relevant when it comes to the clean break provisions and in assessing the earning capacity of either party. Where there has been a long marriage both parties are likely to be given credit for that, whereas a short marriage is likely to lead to a clean break and limited financial provision. The student will be expected to be aware that cohabitation before marriage is not normally considered to be relevant: see *H v H* (1981) 2 FLR 392, but contrast *Day v Day* [1988] 1 FLR 278. Questions do not normally disclose any physical or mental disability of either party so this consideration rarely needs mention: see s25(2)(e) MCA 1973.

An important factor is the contribution made by each of the parties to the welfare of the family, including looking after the home and/or caring for the family: see s25(2)(f) MCA 1973. This was emphasised in *White v White* where it was made clear that whatever the division of labour chosen by a husband and wife fairness required that this should not prejudice or advantage either party. If each has contributed equally in their own way then in principle it does not matter which of them earned the money and built up the assets. There can be no bias in favour of the money-earner and against the home-maker and child-carer. Exceptional contributions to a business may justify a higher award (eg *White v White* and *Cowan v Cowan* [2001] 2 FLR 192). A lack of contribution can be a minus factor.

The student should be aware of the place of conduct in assessing financial provision. Financial provision is more of a mathematical exercise than a moral one: see *Duxbury v Duxbury* [1987] 1 FLR 7. The court will only consider conduct if it is such that it would be inequitable to ignore it: see s25(2)(g) MCA 1973. The student will need to be aware of the kinds of conduct which the court has taken into account (eg financial misconduct as *Day v Day* (above)).

The importance of the loss of any pension rights remains much in vogue. The student should be aware of ss24B–24D and ss25B–25D MCA 1973 and the power of the court to make pension splitting orders and pension ear-marking or attachment orders. The student does not need to have a detailed knowledge of these provisions. In addition, there is the power to make a lump sum order to offset the loss of pension rights.

The student must then move on to deal with the clean break provisions. He/she must state that in deciding what orders to make the court has a duty to consider making orders whereby the obligations of one party towards the other will be terminated as soon after the grant of the decree as the court considers just and reasonable: see s25A(1) MCA 1973. If the court decides to make a maintenance order for a spouse it must consider whether it would be appropriate to limit the term of the maintenance for such period as to enable that spouse to adjust without undue hardship to the end of his/her financial dependence on the other party: see s25A(2) MCA 1973. The student should stress that the court does not have a duty to impose a clean break but must consider it: see *Barrett* v *Barrett* [1988] 2 FLR 516. In advising on the effect of these provisions the age of the spouses and their work experience and/or earning capacity will be important. If there are children this will not rule out a clean break but will make it less appropriate. Where one spouse is older, and has no or limited work experience, the courts have shown considerable reluctance to impose a clean break: see *M* v *M* [1987] 2 FLR 1. The clean break provisions are relevant to property orders since they favour an outright transfer or, where this would not be fair to one party, a *Martin* style order: see *Clutton* v *Clutton* [1991] 1 All ER 340. Where one of the parties is wealthy the possibility of a lump sum calculated by the *Duxbury* calculation may be relevant. However, it should be emphasised that such a calculation is only a tool to assist the court and should not supplant s25 considerations.

The statutory charge (imposed by the Legal Services Commission) may be an additional complication. Where one party is in receipt of civil legal aid the student must be able to describe the effects of the statutory charge and how to avoid or minimise its consequences. This will include advice to parties to minimise their costs and not to contest trivial issues or to unnecessarily raise matters (eg conduct) which may raise costs. It will also include advice on limiting lump sums of £2,500 and making use of the exemption on maintenance orders. It will also include advice on postponing any charge on the home or proceeds of sale used to house the spouse/children.

The relevance of state benefits may also be an important feature. This both includes the fact that the maintenance of the children will be invariably outside the court's jurisdiction and will be a matter for the Child Support Agency by way of child support. An important exception is where there are step-children which can be made the subject of court maintenance orders. Where there are only limited financial resources the fact that the courts will accept one spouse having to rely on state benefit rather than making financial provision orders which will financially cripple the other spouse needs to be highlighted: see *Delaney* v *Delaney* [1990] 2 FLR 457.

Child Support Act 1991

Although the Child Support Act (CSA) 1991 has been mentioned already a fuller outline of how child support is provided since some questions deal exclusively with this area. As from 5 April 1993 courts lost the jurisdiction to make maintenance orders for children (see s8(3) CSA 1991) with the following exceptions:

a) Only natural or adopted children are included in child support so courts can make maintenance orders for step-children who are 'children of the family'.

b) Lump sum and property orders for children may still be made by the courts.

c) In the case of wealthy parents the courts may still make child maintenance orders which exceed the maximum levels of child support.

d) Where the child is over 19 (or is between 16 and 19 and not in education) the court can make a child maintenance order.

e) Where one parent is not habitually resident in the United Kingdom the court can make a child maintenance order.

f) Where the child maintenance order is intended solely for education purposes (eg school fees) a child maintenance order may be made for such purposes.

g) Where the child is disabled and the child maintenance is to meet expenses attributable to the child's disability again a child maintenance order can be made for such purposes.

A parent with children who is in receipt of benefit is obliged to supply details of the absent parent to the Child Support Agency (CSA) should the CSA wish to make a child support assessment against the absent parent. The parent with children (called the parent with care) may be penalised if he/she does not supply this information unless he/she can show that he/she or the children would suffer undue harm or distress. The penalty is a 20 per cent reduction in the parent with care's benefit for the first six months and a 10 per cent reduction for the following year.

Child support is calculated using the following stages:

a) calculating the maintenance requirement (which is the income support allowance for each qualifying child plus the income support allowance for the caring parent plus the income support family premium plus the income support lone parent premium if the parent with care is single less the child benefit for each child – the income support allowance for the caring parent reduces as the youngest child gets older);

b) calculating the assessable incomes of the parent with care and the absent parent (which is net income less exempt income – 'exempt' income is the income support allowance for a single parent plus reasonable housing costs plus other allowances plus certain travel to work costs – allowance is given for property or capital transfers of at least £5,000 made by the absent parent before 5 April 1993);

c) calculating the deduction rate (which is 50 per cent of the combined assessable incomes of both parents – there is provision for 'top up' payments if the deduction rate is more than the maintenance requirement);

d) comparing the deduction rate with the absent parent's protected income (protected income is the income support allowance for an adult/couple plus reasonable housing costs plus other allowances plus £30 a week plus council tax plus 15 per cent of any spare income – any deduction of child support must not bring the absent parent's income below his/her protected income).

Where an absent parent has contact with his/her children for 104 nights a year there are provisions to reduce the amount of child support.

A particular source of grievance for absent parents is the consequence of child support for existing court orders, particularly clean break orders imposed by the court on the basis that the absent parent did not have any ongoing financial commitment to the former spouse and/or children. As outlined above child support includes an element for the parent with care – a kind of indirect spouse maintenance. It was confirmed in *Crozier* v *Crozier* [1994] 2 WLR 444 that a child support assessment was not a reason to set aside a clean break consent order made in full and final settlement of a spouse's claim for herself and the children. The consequences of *Crozier* have been recognised in that allowance is now given for clean break property or capital settlements of a value of £5,000 or more. The courts will take into account child support in fixing its orders for financial provision. See *Mawson* v *Mawson* [1994] 2 FLR 985 where a spouse's financial provision was varied to take into account the child support position.

The Child Support Act 1991 has proved very controversial. Its provisions have attracted much criticism as being unfair, rigid and bureaucratic. The CSA has a considerable backlog of work. As a result it has abandoned plans to take over existing court maintenance orders where the spouse in receipt of the maintenance is not in receipt of benefit.

The Child Support Act 1995 has introduced, inter alia, provision to allow for a limited right of appeal against child support assessment. The appeals are called 'departure directions' and allow a limited discretion to deal with cases where unfairness may have been caused as a result of the child support assessment

From April 2002 child support should have been calculated by the non-resident parent (NRP) paying according to a much simpler formula, namely:

a) 15 per cent of his net income for one qualifying child;

b) 20 per cent of his net income for two qualifying children;

c) 25 per cent of his net income for three or more qualifying children.

There would have been a 15 per cent reduction in his net income if the NRP has one dependent child; 20 per cent if he has two dependent children; and 25 per cent for three or more dependent children.

As with the existing system there would have been a reduced rate where the NRP has a low income with a flat rate of £5 a week where he is on benefit. There would have been a nil rate for certain NRPs (eg serving prisoners). There would have been a maximum amount of child support which can be paid.

There would also have been a reduction in what the NRP pays if care of the qualifying child(ren) is shared with the resident parent (called the parent with care – PWC). For example, if the children stay with the NRP there is a proportionate reduction. Only the net income of the NRP would have been taken into account. The income of the PWC would have been ignored.

Account would continue to have been taken of capital or property transfer orders made before April 1993. A PWC would have been able to ask for increased payments where a NRP has capital assets which suggest that he could afford to pay more than his net income suggests: see *Mawson* v *Mawson* [1994] 2 FLR 985.

However, in March 2002 the government announced that computer problems had led to implementations of the reforms being postponed indefinitely. Examiners are likely to ask whether the proposed reforms would have met the many criticisms of the existing child support system.

6.3 Key cases and statute

- *Atkinson* v *Atkinson* [1987] 3 All ER 849
  Relevance of conduct in ancillary relief

- *Barrett* v *Barrett* [1988] 2 FLR 516
  When to impose a clean break

- *Clutton* v *Clutton* [1991] 1 All ER 340
  Property orders and the clean break

- *Mesher* v *Mesher* [1980] 1 All ER 126
  Property orders for a wife and children

- *Suter* v *Suter and Jones* [1987] 2 All ER 336
  The welfare of the children and ancillary relief

- *White* v *White* [2000] 2 FLR 981
  The yardstick of equal division

- Matrimonial Causes Act 1973 – dealing with ancillary relief

6.4 Questions and suggested solutions

QUESTION ONE

Imogen and John married in 1973. They had one child, Kate, who is now 19 and studying at a drama college in London. John, who is a dentist, established a successful practice in the matrimonial home. His elderly parents, who are very wealthy, regularly supplemented his comfortable income with significant cash sums. Imogen had trained as a teacher, but she chose not to work outside the home after her marriage, preferring to act as a homemaker and mother and occasionally assisting John in his practice.

The family enjoyed a comfortable lifestyle. The matrimonial home, which John inherited from his grandmother, was refurbished more than once, the couple acquired a holiday home in Scotland and took yearly holidays abroad. To provide for their future, John invested in a valuable private pension scheme and collected twentieth-century paintings.

In 1992, John began a public affair with Laura, one of Kate's schoolfriends. Imogen was hurt and humiliated, but encouraged a reconciliation. However, the affair continued and Imogen divorced him in March 1994. Imogen and Kate now seek your advice with regard to the financial provision that they can expect from John.

Advise Imogen and Kate.

University of London LLB Examination
(for External Students) Family Law June 1994 Q4

General Comment

The question deals with the likely orders for financial relief for a wife and 'adult child' as a result of a recent divorce. It requires discussion of the wide powers of the court under ss23, 24 and 24A and the considerations in ss25 and 25A of the Matrimonial Causes Act 1973. From Imogen's point of view particular attention needs to be given to the credit she will receive for the length of the marriage, her contribution to the household and bringing up the family, the standard of living enjoyed during the marriage and possible loss of pension rights. John's behaviour may also be relevant. The significance of his wealthy family needs to be discussed. This is also relevant as far as Kate is concerned, as are her plans to attend drama college. Given her age the court is able to make orders for her despite the Child Support Act 1991.

Skeleton Solution

Wide powers to order financial provision under ss23, 24 and 24A of the Matrimonial Causes Act 1973 – general considerations under ss25 and 25A MCA 1973 – considerations for Imogen: John's financial resources including his wealthy family; Imogen's financial resources and earning capacity; the standard of living enjoyed by Imogen and John during the marriage; the age of the parties and duration of the marriage; Imogen's contribution to the family and household; John's conduct; Imogen's loss of pension rights; whether the clean break provisions are likely to be applied – considerations for Kate: Child Support Act 1991 does not apply; her financial needs and the way she expects to continue her education; John's financial resources; the duration of any maintenance order.

Suggested Solution

Imogen and Kate should be advised that the court has wide- ranging powers to make maintenance, lump sum and property orders (including transferring the ownership or ordering the sale of the matrimonial home and/or holiday home): see ss23, 24 and 24A of the Matrimonial Causes Act (MCA) 1973. In deciding whether to exercise its wide powers and, if so, in what manner, the court will have regard to all the circumstances and make such orders as it considers just and reasonable. It is bound to have regard to particular matters which will affect the likely financial provision for Imogen and Kate.

In Imogen's case the court will have regard to the income, earning capacity, property and other financial resources she and John each have and are likely to have in the foreseeable future: see s25(2)(a) MCA 1973. In the case of earning capacity the court will have regard to any increase in that capacity which it would be reasonable to expect either party to take steps to acquire. The court will consider John's successful dental practice. It will consider the financial assistance given to him by his wealthy parents. This may include his inheritance prospects but only if this is a reasonable possibility in the foreseeable future. This will depend on the age and health of his parents. If such prospects are too vague and remote the court will not consider them: see *Michael* v *Michael* [1986] 2 FLR 389. The court will take into account the matrimonial home and holiday home and John's collection of twentieth-century paintings. Imogen and Kate should be advised that the court will not be bound by strict rules of who owns what. It may distribute the property or order its sale as it sees fit. From Imogen's point of view the court will note that she has not worked full time for many years. She may have a earning capacity either as a teacher (though the world of teaching has undergone many changes in recent years) or by virtue of her experience in helping in John's practice. If she is able to make use of these skills to acquire an income the court will expect her to do all that is reasonable to take steps to acquire that income.

The court will then look at the financial needs, obligations and responsibilities which each have now and will have in the foreseeable future: see s25(2)(b) MCA 1973. This will include the need for either party to find alternative accommodation if the other party remains in the former matrimonial home. Since John's business is established there it is likely that the court will allow him to remain there so that he can carry on with his successful business. However, the court will require him to make provision whereby Imogen is rehoused in as equivalent style of housing as is reasonable. Expenses could also include any expenses either parent will have in supporting or accommodating Kate while she is at college or when she returns home to visit either parent. It could also include John's obligations towards Laura if he intends to marry or support her. The standard of living enjoyed by the family before the breakdown of the marriage will also be considered: see s25(2)(c) MCA 1973. In this case the parties enjoyed a comfortable standard of living. Now that the marriage has broken down it may not be possible to maintain this standard. However, the court will seek to ensure that any decline in that standard of living is equally shared so that, for example, John is not left with a far better standard of living than Imogen.

The court will consider the age of Imogen and John and the duration of the marriage: see s25(2)(d) MCA 1973. Both parties will be given credit for the length of the marriage. Imogen's age may be particularly relevant in terms of her earning capacity since the older she is the more difficult it may be for her to find full time employment. The court will consider any physical or mental disability of either party (see s25(2)(e) MCA 1973) and the contributions made by John and Imogen to the welfare of the family, including Imogen's contribution in looking after the home and caring for Kate as she grew up: see s25(2)(f) MCA 1973. Imogen is likely to be given considerable credit for her contribution for more than twenty years in acting as homemaker, bringing up Kate and occasionally assisting John in his practice and thereby foregoing her own chance of establishing employment as a teacher. The court will only consider the conduct of the parties if it would, in the court's opinion, be inequitable to disregard it: see s25(2)(g) MCA 1973. Normally the court considers that determining financial provision is largely a mathematical exercise rather than a moral one. It normally would wish to avoid any kind of post mortem into the breakdown of the marriage. However, in this case conduct may be in issue if it appears that John has behaved particularly badly in abandoning a 'blameless spouse', in making his affair with Laura so public and in rejecting a reasonable offer of reconciliation: see *Robinson* v *Robinson* [1983] 2 WLR 146. If the court is of this view then John may be required to make greater provision for Imogen. The court will also consider any loss of pension rights which may result from the divorce: see s25(2)(h) MCA 1973. This may be particularly important for Imogen since she may have very poor pension provision. If the marriage had continued she would have been covered by John's pension cover either as his spouse or as his widow. The court may seek to compensate her for the loss of her pension rights.

In relation to deciding what provision to make for Imogen the court is under a duty to consider whether it would be appropriate to exercise its powers so that the financial obligations between John and Imogen will be terminated as soon after the grant of the decree as the court considers just and reasonable: see s25A(1) MCA 1973. If the court decides that John should pay maintenance to Imogen the court must consider whether it would be appropriate to require those payments to be made only for such term as would in the court's opinion be sufficient to enable Imogen to adjust without undue hardship to the termination of her financial dependence on John: see s25A(2) MCA 1973. Imogen may find it difficult to attain financial independence given her age and lack of work experience. Unless a generous capital and property settlement is made in her favour the court may feel unable to impose a clean financial break between the parties. The courts have shown considerable reluctance to impose such a clean break where a late middle-aged wife is left in a situation of financial weakness and uncertainty: see for example *M* v *M* [1987] 2 FLR 1.

Financial provision for children of separated parents is mostly dealt with by the Child Support Agency: see s8 Child Support Act (CSA) 1991. However, Kate is of such an age that the divorce court would be able to deal with the question of financial provision for her (see s55 CSA 1991). Normally the court only orders financial provision in relation to children aged under 18 years, but it can make provision for children above this age who are receiving training or education: see s29(3) MCA 1973. Since Kate is going to drama school the court can consider her case. It will consider her financial needs, her income, financial resources and earning capacity (eg whether she can work during holiday periods) and the manner in which she is being, and in which John and Imogen expected her to be, educated or trained. The court will also consider the matters already discussed in relations to s25(2)(a), (b), (c) and (e) MCA 1973. Given that Kate also enjoyed a comfortable lifestyle while her parents were together, and that her parents may well have supported her wish to study at drama school, it is likely that John will be ordered to make financial provision for her while she is studying full time at the drama school.

In conclusion, given all the considerations outlined above and the court's duty to achieve a fair result having regard to all the circumstances, it is likely that John will remain in the former matrimonial home where his business has been established. The court is likely to order him to make generous financial provision for Imogen so that she can be rehoused and is able to continue to live as close as possible to the lifestyle she has become accustomed to. The provision will need to reflect Imogen's possible weak financial position having regard to her sacrifices and contribution to the welfare of the family. This may involve John in having to sell his paintings and the holiday home or transfer them to Imogen in order to increase the provision for her. That provision may also be increased having regard to John's conduct in breaking up the marriage. A clean-break settlement seems unlikely unless John can provide a sufficiently large capital settlement to give Imogen long-term financial security. Kate is also likely to receive financial provision to allow her to continue her education and the lifestyle she has enjoyed while her parents were together.

QUESTION TWO

Discuss the applications for financial relief of the following petitioners:

a) Fiona, now 40, who married Gerard in 1975. Although a qualified accountant, Fiona did not work outside the home during the marriage, but devoted herself to the care of the household and the upbringing of Harry and Imogen, the children of Gerard's dead sister and brother-in-law, who are now aged 12 and 11 respectively. During the marriage, Gerard, a merchant banker, earning over £100,000 per annum, accumulated a number of properties, including the large home that the family have lived in since 1980 which is now valued at £1,000,000. He also established a valuable private pension scheme. Gerard is now living with Jane, his former secretary who is 22, in a new flat he has acquired, while Fiona, who still has care of the children, is currently living in the former matrimonial home.

b) Kelvin, an unemployed actor, now 35, who married Lia, a barrister, now 43, in 1985. The couple have no children and Kelvin, who developed an ulcer in 1990, largely as a result of alcohol abuse which is still continuing, will be unable to work for some time. Lia earns £80,000 per annum and her assets include the former matrimonial home, which Kelvin continues to occupy, valued at £120,000 and the small flat she lives in, worth £70,000, acquired since the breakdown of the marriage.

University of London LLB Examination
(for External Students) Family Law June 1995 Q3

General Comment

The two parts of the question deal with ancillary relief after the breakdown of the marriage (and presumably as a result of divorce proceedings, though the question does not make this clear). Part (a) asks the student to evaluate the claim of a wife of some 20 years who has no work experience and who made a significant contribution to the welfare of the family. Her contribution includes caring for children who are 'children of the family'. She is likely to have a strong claim against her wealthy spouse. Her lack of pension provision and his valuable pension scheme merit special consideration. Part (b) reverses the situation in that the husband has no income and it is the wife who is in the stronger financial position. The conduct of the husband is a particular factor in these circumstances.

Skeleton Solution

a) Wide range of powers under ss23, 24 and 24A MCA 1973 to make financial provision for Fiona – welfare of children of family is first consideration (s25(1) MCA 1973) – definition of 'child of the family' and whether Harry and Imogen are children of the family – s25(2) MCA 1973 considerations, particularly in terms of respective incomes and outgoings, Fiona's contribution to the welfare of the family and the respective pension provisions of the parties – clean-break provisions under s25A MCA 1973 and whether they might apply in Fiona's case.

b) Wide range of powers under ss23, 24 and 24A MCA 1973 to make financial provision for Kelvin – s25(2) MCA 1973 considerations, particularly the respective income and outgoings of the parties, Kelvin's earning capacity and whether his conduct might be relevant.

Suggested Solution

The question does not make it clear what kind of petitions have been lodged by Fiona or Kelvin. It is assumed that they have petitioned for divorce though since the provisions for financial relief also apply to petitions for nullity or judicial separation the advice given could apply to these applications as well.

a) Fiona should be advised that the court has wide powers to make financial provision for her. It can order Gerard to pay maintenance and/or a lump sum payment to her and make orders either settling property on her or transferring it to her or ordering its sale and the division of the proceeds: see ss23, 24 and 24A of the Matrimonial Causes Act 1973 – hereinafter called MCA 1973. In deciding what provision, if any, it should order it will do what it considers just and reasonable taking into account particular factors.

First, the court must give first consideration to the welfare of any children of the family under the age of 18: see s25(1) MCA 1973. This does not mean that the welfare of such a child overrides all other considerations but it will be of first importance: see *Suter* v *Suter and Jones* [1987] 2 All ER 336. Harry and Imogen are not the natural children of Fiona and Gerard. They will nevertheless be children of the family if they have been treated by both parties as children of Fiona and Gerard's family: see s52(1) MCA 1973. The court will look at the situation objectively and ask whether both Fiona and Gerard have treated and looked after Harry and Imogen as they would have their own children: see *W v W* [1972] 2 WLR 371. Assuming that the children have been treated as children of the family the court will give first consideration to their need to be housed, maintained and looked after. Since Fiona is living with them and they remain in the former matrimonial home the court will give first consideration to making orders which preserve this situation.

Second, the court will look at the income, earning capacity, property and other financial resources which each of the parties to the marriage has or is likely to have in the foreseeable future. In the case of earning capacity the court will expect either party to take reasonable steps to increase that capacity: see s25(2)(a) MCA 1973. Fiona has no income of her own. She appears to have a very limited earning capacity since she has not worked outside during the 20 years of marriage. Though she is a qualified accountant it is likely that her skills will be significantly out of date so that she is unlikely to find well-paid accountancy work. Having said that, she should make all efforts to find employment now that the children are in full-time education. By contrast, Gerard is well paid and has various properties, including his own independent accommodation.

The court will then look at the financial needs, obligations and responsibilities the parties have now and in the foreseeable future: see s25(2)(b) MCA 1973. This will include Fiona's and the children's need to be housed and to have sufficient income to live on. It may include Gerard's obligations towards Jane if he intends to marry her or have a long-term relationship with her. In relation to the children, Gerard is likely to be required by the court to make financial provision for them, taking into account the fact that he has accepted responsibility for them (together with Fiona) over what may be a considerable period of time: see s25(3) and (4) MCA 1973. He is likely therefore to bear the financial burden of their maintenance. Fiona should be advised that the Child Support Agency cannot be involved since Harry and Imogen are not his natural children. The court will look at the standard of living enjoyed by the parties before the breakdown of the marriage: see s25(2)(c) MCA 1973. Fiona is likely to have enjoyed a high standard of living as the wife of a wealthy merchant banker and the court will seek to avoid any unnecessary drop in her standard of living. The court will look at the age of Fiona and Gerard and the duration of the marriage: see s25(2)(d) MCA 1973. Fiona's age may count against her obtaining suitably paid employment. Gerard's age is not given. Both parties will be given credit for the 20 years of marriage. No physical or mental disabilities are disclosed for the court to consider: see s25(2)(e) MCA 1973. The court will give credit to Fiona for her contribution over the 20 years of marriage in looking after the home and in looking after Harry and Imogen: see s25(2)(f) MCA 1973. Gerard will similarly be given credit for his contribution to the welfare of the family. The court will not take the conduct of either Fiona or Gerard into account unless any conduct was such as it would be inequitable to disregard it: see s25(2)(g) MCA 1973. Financial provision is treated by the courts more as a mathematical exercise than a moral one and the court is likely to want to avoid any post mortem into why the marriage broke down. It may be possible that Gerard's conduct might be relevant if the court took the view that he abandoned a blameless wife, but this is not likely unless he behaved in a particularly reprehensible manner: see *Robinson* v *Robinson* [1983] 2 WLR 146.

In the case of a divorce or nullity, the court will have regard to any pension rights Fiona may lose as a result of the end of the marriage: see s25B MCA 1973. Fiona may well lose generous pension rights under Gerard's valuable pension scheme, and the court will seek to compensate her for that, particularly in view of the fact that she is unlikely to be able to provide sufficient pension cover for herself. The court can order Gerard to pay Fiona a lump sum or make a pension attachment order or a pension-splitting order to provide Fiona with some pension provision: see ss23, 24, 24B–24D and 25B–25C MCA 1973.

The court has to consider whether to exercise its powers in such a way that the financial obligations of each party towards the other terminate as soon after the decree as the court considers just and reasonable: see s25A(1) MCA 1973. In the case of any maintenance order Gerard might have to pay for Fiona, the court will consider whether it should limit the term of the order to such term as would enable Fiona to adjust to the termination of her financial dependence on Gerard without undue hardship: see s25A(2) MCA 1973. The courts have shown themselves to be cautious in imposing a clean break after a long marriage and where a spouse has limited earning capacity: see *Morris* v *Morris* [1985] FLR 1176 and *M* v *M* [1987] 2 FLR 1.

While insufficient information is given to be more precise about what will happen to Fiona's application for financial relief, it appears that unless Gerard can provide a sufficiently large lump-sum payment which would generate sufficient income to meet Fiona's reasonable living expenses (called a *Duxbury* calculation), in addition to providing for the children he is likely to be required to pay maintenance to her. It is possible that the court will make an order that the former matrimonial home be held on trust for Fiona and the children to stay there until the children have finished their education when the house can be sold and the proceeds divided so that Fiona can find suitable accommodation: see *Mesher* v *Mesher* [1980] 1 All ER 126. An outright transfer of the home to her is unlikely, given its value. Alternatively, Gerard may be required to provide Fiona with a sufficient lump sum to allow her to rehouse herself and the children. Since the children may have lived in the same home for most of their lives this may persuade the court that they should continue to live in it for as long as they need to.

b) The same statutory provisions apply in Kelvin's case and so there is no need to repeat them. There are no children so s25(1) MCA 1973 will not apply in this context. The court will look at Kelvin's lack of income but also at his earning capacity. The condition of his ulcer suggests that he will be unable to work for some time. By contrast, Lia is a well-paid barrister. Their respective financial needs, obligations and responsibilities will be considered, as will the ages of the parties and the duration of the marriage. Credit will be given to both parties for the ten years of marriage. Lia may receive greater credit for her contribution to the welfare of the family unit since she has borne the brunt of financially maintaining Kelvin. Kelvin's physical disability will be considered. If Kelvin's disability has been largely self inflicted this may count as behaviour which it would be inequitable to disregard: see s25(2)(g) MCA 1973. In a case with similar circumstances the husband's poor financial state was considered to be largely self inflicted, in contrast to the wife's efforts to improve herself. Having said that, financial provision was still made whereby he could accommodate himself: see *K* v *K* [1990] 2 FLR 225. The clean-break provisions will also be relevant. In one case a husband had so reduced the quality of his life because of his drinking the court concluded that there would be no point in ordering the wife to pay maintenance since it would add nothing to his quality of life: see *Seaton* v *Seaton* [1986] 2 FLR 398. Kelvin's case does not seem to be in this somewhat extreme category. Following the decision in *K* v *K* the court may consider ordering the sale of the former matrimonial home and providing Kelvin with sufficient proceeds of sale to rehouse himself. This could be combined with a maintenance order whereby Lia provides financial support for Kelvin, if the court considers this just and reasonable, or a maintenance order for a limited period during which Kelvin would be expected to adjust to the end of any financial dependence on her (whereupon Kelvin would have to find work or rely on state benefits).

QUESTION THREE

Rebecca and Andrew, now aged 37 and 48 respectively, married in 1982. The matrimonial home was inherited by Andrew from his grandparents and is now worth £500,000. At the time of the marriage it was Andrew's wish that Rebecca act as a housewife and look after any children they might have and support him in his career as owner of a large newspaper chain. Rebecca, who had had a short career as a nanny prior to her marriage, was happy to agree to this plan. Rebecca was an excellent homemaker during the marriage and by virtue of her skills as a hostess, she proved to be an enormous asset to Andrew in expanding his business. Unfortunately, Rebecca and Andrew were unable to have children of their own, but in 1990 took over the care of Sabrina, Andrew's niece, who is now aged eight, whose parents, charity workers, had been killed in a car accident.

In 1992, Rebecca discovered that Andrew was having an affair with Lucy. Believing that this was a result of a short-term crisis, Rebecca was at first understanding and sought to retain the marriage. However, Andrew continued the affair and began to take Lucy, rather than Rebecca, to social functions and began to refer to her to his business associates as 'my true partner'. In early 1996, Rebecca divorced Andrew on the basis of his adultery.

Rebecca now wishes to be advised as to the likely financial provision she can expect for herself and Sabrina. As well as owning the matrimonial home, Andrew owns a country house outside Oxford, worth £200,000. The newspaper chain, which is partly owned by his sister, is worth £12 million and he draws a personal salary of £150,000 per annum. He has also invested in a number of private pension plans so that his future will be secure. Sabrina, whose parents left no assets, attends a private day school and is a promising pianist.

Advise Rebecca.

University of London LLB Examination
(for External Students) Family Law June 1996 Q4

General Comment

This is a standard question on ancillary relief after divorce. It involves a wealthy husband and a wife with no apparent means but who has made a substantial contribution to the family and helped her husband in his business. It also involves a 'child of the family' who is not the natural child of the parties. These points need to be brought out in the outline of the considerations under the Matrimonial Causes Act 1973 which the court will have regard to.

Skeleton Solution

Wide powers of the court under the MCA 1973 to make orders for financial consideration – discretion to make orders as is just and reasonable but subject to certain considerations – welfare of child of family is first consideration (s25(1) MCA 1973); definition of child of family and considerations which apply (ss23 and 52 MCA 1973) – considerations under s25(2) MCA 1973: income, property and earning capacity; outgoings; standard of living before marriage ended; age of parties and duration of marriage; contribution to welfare of family by looking after the home and child and contribution towards business; relevance of conduct; need to consider pension position – clean break provisions under s25A MCA 1973 – the *Duxbury* calculation as a basis for a clean break – conclusion: provision of accommodation for wife and child; provision for child (especially education); clean break lump sum for wife.

Suggested Solution

Rebecca asks for advice on the likely financial provision she can expect for herself and for Sabrina following her divorce from Andrew. Rebecca should first be advised that the courts have wide powers to make orders for maintenance payments, lump sum orders and for the sale or settlement of property owned by either her or Andrew: see ss23, 24 and 24A Matrimonial Causes Act 1973 – hereinafter referred to as MCA 1973. The court has a wide discretion to make such orders as it considers just and reasonable but must take into account particular considerations: see ss25 and 25A MCA 1973. Rebecca can be advised that these particular considerations will have considerable influence on the likely financial provision for herself and Sabrina.

The court will give first consideration to the welfare of Sabrina as a child of Rebecca's and Andrew's family: see s25(1) MCA 1973. This does not mean that her welfare will determine what orders are made but the need for her to be maintained and to be properly housed and educated will be of the first importance: see *Suter v Suter and Jones* [1987] 2 All ER 336. It is noted that Sabrina is not the natural child of Andrew and Rebecca. However, if she has been treated by both as a child of their family she will be a 'child of the family': see s52(1) MCA 1973. Since Sabrina appears to have been so treated from 1992 until the parties separated the court is likely to conclude that she is a child of the family. In deciding on financial provision for her, the court will take into account her financial needs and any income, earning capacity, property and other financial resources she has. It will consider the manner in which she is being educated or trained, as well as the manner in which Andrew and Rebecca expected her to be educated or trained: see s23(3) MCA 1973. This is likely to include Andrew continuing to pay for her private day school and for any piano tuition if this is what he and Rebecca provided and planned for. The court will also have regard to the extent to which he assumed responsibility for Sabrina knowing she was not his child and the liability of any other person to support her: see s23(4) MCA 1973. Andrew and Rebecca appear to have accepted sole and full responsibility for her since she is an orphan and has no assets of her own.

The court will then go on to consider the income, earning capacity, property and other financial resources which each of Rebecca and Andrew has now or is likely to have in the foreseeable future, including any increase in earning capacity which it would be reasonable to expect either party to take steps to acquire: see s25(2)(a) MCA 1973. Rebecca appears to have no income or assets of her own. She may have a limited earning capacity but appears to have been away from the world of work since her marriage in 1982. She is unlikely to have either the qualifications or work experience to have any realistic ability to get a well-paid job. Sabrina is also still quite young and at a day school, which may further limit Rebecca's employment options. However, if she has any earning capacity she will be expected to take steps to realise it. Andrew has considerable assets. He has an income of £150,000, owns the matrimonial home worth £500,000 and a country house worth £200,000. He has interests in a business worth £12 million. It is noted that this is part-owned by his sister. The court will take a realistic approach to the wealth to which he has access via the business and also to the assets he could have access to should the court make an order he could not meet from his immediate liquid assets: see *Thomas v Thomas* [1995] 2 FLR 668. He also appears to have private pension plans to secure his retirement. The court will then look at the financial needs, obligations and responsibilities which each of the parties has or is likely to have in the foreseeable future: see s25(2)(b) MCA 1973. Since Rebecca appears to be continuing to care for Sabrina, this financial obligation and responsibility will be of first importance in the court's mind. Rebecca needs to be housed appropriately and to receive an appropriate income to live on. If Andrew wishes to remarry he can argue that he will have the obligation and responsibility for maintaining Lucy. The court will also have regard to the standard of living enjoyed by the family before the breakdown of the marriage: see s25(2)(c) MCA 1973. It is assumed that Rebecca and Andrew had a rich lifestyle in keeping with Andrew's income and status. The court will seek to ensure that Rebecca is either able to maintain an equivalent lifestyle or that any drop in lifestyle is shared equitably between the parties. However, in light of Andrew's apparent wealth Rebecca should be advised that there is a possibility that the court will only make provision which maintains her to the lifestyle to which she is accustomed as opposed to any higher provision: see *Thyssen-Bornemisza v Thyssen-Bornemisza (No 2)* [1985] FLR 1069. English courts tend to order what they consider to be reasonable financial provision to meet reasonable needs rather than make higher orders in order to give a former spouse a larger share of the other spouse's wealth. The court will have regard to the age of the parties and the duration of the marriage: see s25(2)(d) MCA 1973. Rebecca is still relatively young but has a limited earning capacity. Andrew is at an age when he is likely to carry on working for another ten years or so but where retirement may be an option. Both parties will be given credit for a marriage which has lasted 14 years, particularly Rebecca who has made considerable efforts to keep the marriage going.

The court will look at the contributions which each of the parties has made or is likely to make in the foreseeable future to the welfare of the family. This will include any contribution by looking after the home or caring for the family: see s25(2)(f) MCA 1973. Rebecca can be advised that this consideration is likely to be a significant factor since she gave up work to act as a housewife and to support up Andrew in his career. The court will note that she was described as an 'excellent homemaker' during the marriage and her skills as a hostess were an 'enormous asset' to Andrew in expanding his business. She will also receive credit for taking over the care of Sabrina who was no relation to her. She is also likely to receive credit for her understanding after discovering Andrew's adultery in 1982 and trying to keep the marriage going. Her future contribution in caring for Sabrina will also be noted by the court. Rebecca can be advised that these factors are likely to increase any award for financial provision: see *Wachtel v Wachtel* [1973] 2 WLR 366 and *Vicary v Vicary* [1992] 2 FLR 271. Rebecca can be advised that the court is unlikely to consider the conduct of the parties unless that conduct is such that it would in the opinion of the court be inequitable to disregard it: see s25(2)(g) MCA 1973. The courts tend to treat financial provision as more of an arithmetical exercise than a moral one: see *Wachtel v Wachtel* and *Duxbury v Duxbury* [1987] 1 FLR 7. The court may take Rebecca's positive conduct into account in that she appears to have made considerable efforts to keep the marriage going and to help Andrew and to care for Sabrina. It may possibly consider Andrew's conduct if it considers that he abandoned a blameless spouse for no good reason: see *Robinson v Robinson* [1983] 2 WLR 146, but more recent authorities suggest a greater reluctance to take conduct into account.

The court will also consider the value of any pension rights which each party will lose as a result of the divorce: see s25B MCA 1973. Rebecca may lose any rights to any pension cover which may be included in Andrew's private pension plans. She can be advised that the loss of pension rights is a matter of considerable debate at the present time. The court is likely to be concerned that Rebecca has some kind of provision for the future given her lack of any kind of cover in her own right. This concern may be emphasised by amendments to the Matrimonial Causes Act 1973 introduced by the Pensions Act 1995 (which added ss25B–25D to the MCA 1973). The new provisions place a duty on the court to consider the pension provision of the parties and give new powers to make orders so that when Andrew's pensions come into effect provision can be made for Rebecca. In her case the court can compensate her with a lump sum payment. It may also be possible to make a pension attachment or pension splitting order: see ss24B–24D and ss25B–25C MCA 1973.

The court will also consider whether it would appropriate to make orders whereby the financial obligations of Andrew to Rebecca will terminate as soon after the divorce decree as the court considers just and reasonable: see s25A(1) MCA 1973. If the court makes a maintenance order in her favour the court must consider whether it would be appropriate to limit the term of the order to such a term as would enable Rebecca to adjust without undue hardship to the termination of her financial dependence on Andrew: see s25A(2) MCA 1973. Rebecca can be advised that the courts have shown some reluctance in imposing a clean break where a former wife is in a financially weak position, particularly where she is of an age where it is difficult to get back into the job market or to find any work with a reasonable income. However, if Andrew is able to provide a lump sum payment which will give her security then a clean break order may well be considered. Given Andrew's apparent wealth this may be a real possibility. Rebecca should be advised that one way of achieving a clean break is via the *Duxbury* calculation (named after the case of *Duxbury* v *Duxbury*). This involves calculating a lump sum which if invested (with assumptions made as to life expectancy, rates of inflation, return on investments, growth on capital and tax rates) would produce enough to meet Rebecca's needs for life. Such a figure can then be used as a guide to produce a settlement which the court considers just and reasonable (eg *Vicary* v *Vicary*).

Rebecca should be advised that the court is likely to provide her with accommodation suitable to her standard of living and suitable for Sabrina. If the former matrimonial home is considered too large and lavish for their needs the court may order that Andrew provide a lump sum to buy a suitable property (even if this means the sale of one of the properties and a division of the proceeds). It is likely to require Andrew to provide for Sabrina's education including her school fees and any expenses for her piano tuition. Normally the court cannot provide for any child maintenance since this is dealt with by the Child Support Agency. However, given Andrew's wealth this is likely to be an exceptional case in which the court could make a child maintenance order in an amount well above the maximum amount of child support which could be paid. It is also likely to require Andrew to provide a lump sum clean break settlement for Rebecca to give her security and to provide for her retirement. Such provision is likely to be generous given her substantial contribution to the home and to caring for Sabrina and her help in Andrew's business.

QUESTION FOUR

Abe and Beryl met in 1985 when she was working and he was a student. They lived together in her flat, and she supported him financially throughout the period of his training as an engineer. They married when he qualified in 1990. He soon obtained employment. She sold her flat for £70,000 and they bought a house for £100,000, which was conveyed into joint names and upon which they took a joint mortgage. After their first child was born in 1990, Beryl decided not to return to work, although Abe had said they could have afforded a nanny to look after the child, and he would have preferred Beryl to work. After their second child was born in 1994, Beryl suffered from serious post-natal depression. Abe had to spend increasing amounts of time away from work, helping in the home and caring for the children. In 1994 he was dismissed from his employment, with six months' salary in lieu of notice. Shortly afterwards he was able to find part-time work.

Later in 1994 Beryl's health improved and she took greater charge of running the home and caring for the children. Abe, however, met Enid and in 1996 left home to live with her in rented accommodation. Enid is now expecting their child, and Abe has used the lump sum of £25,000 to start his own business.

Beryl has now divorced Abe and seeks your advice on the upbringing of the children and financial and property matters. Advise her.

University of London LLB Examination
(for External Students) Family Law June 1997 Q4

General Comment

This is a standard question on ancillary relief after divorce. It involves a husband and a wife who are both of limited means and who have both made contributions to the family's welfare. The earning capacity of the respective parents is important. The involvement of the Child Support Agency is highly relevant. The questions also asks about resolving the upbringing of children following divorce.

Skeleton Solution

Wide powers of the court under the MCA 1973 to make orders for financial consideration – discretion to make orders as is just and reasonable but subject to certain considerations – welfare of child of family is first consideration (s25(1) MCA 1973) – considerations under s25(2) MCA 1973: income, property and earning capacity – outgoings; standard of living before marriage ended; age of parties and duration of marriage; contribution to welfare of family by looking after the home and child and contribution towards business; relevance of conduct; need to consider pension position; clean break provisions under s25A MCA 1973 – whether this is feasible in this case – financial support of the children – the Child Support Agency – s41 MCA 1973 and consideration of arrangements for children – orders under s8 Children Act 1989 to resolve any disputes – conclusion: provision of accommodation for wife and child –

maintenance for wife; child support for children; whether any application for residence/contact orders are needed with respect to the children.

Suggested Solution

Beryl should first be advised that the courts have wide powers to make orders for maintenance payments, lump sum orders and for the sale or settlement of property owned by either her or Abe: see ss23, 24 and 24A of the Matrimonial Causes Act 1973 – hereinafter referred to as the MCA 1973. The court has a wide discretion to make such orders as it considers just and reasonable, but must take into account particular considerations: see ss25 and 25A MCA 1973. Beryl can be advised that these particular considerations will have considerable influence on the likely financial provision for herself and their two children.

The court will give first consideration to the welfare of Beryl and Abe's two children: see s25(1) MCA 1973. This does not mean that their welfare will determine what orders are made, but the need for them to provided for, be properly housed and educated will be of the first importance: see *Suter* v *Suter and Jones* [1987] 2 All ER 336. In deciding on financial provision for them the court will take into account their financial needs and any income, earning capacity, property and other financial resources they have. It will consider the manner in which they are being educated or trained, as well as the manner in which Beryl and Abe expected them to be educated or trained: see s23(3) MCA 1973.

The court will then go on to consider the income, earning capacity, property and other financial resources which each of Beryl and Abe has now or is likely to have in the foreseeable future, including any increase in earning capacity which it would be reasonable to expect either party to take steps to acquire: see s25(2)(a) MCA 1973. It is not clear if Beryl has any income of her own. Since their youngest child is only aged three years it is assumed that she is not working. It is also not clear whether she has any earning capacity. It is assumed that she had a reasonably paid job up to 1990 since she had a flat worth £70,000. However, she has now been out of employment for some seven years so it appears unlikely that she has much of a earning capacity, particularly with two young children to bring up. If she has any earning capacity she will be expected to take steps to realise it. Abe appears to have limited means in that he has only just started his own business. His income is unlikely to be augmented by Enid if she is expecting their child. The court will have to make an assessment of the earning capacity of the business in the foreseeable future. There do not appear to be any capital assets (given Abe's spending of his lump sum) apart from the home.

The court will then look at the financial needs, obligations and responsibilities which each of the parties has or is likely to have in the foreseeable future: see s25(2)(b) MCA 1973. Since Beryl appears to be continuing to care for the two children, this financial obligation and responsibility will be of first importance in the court's mind. She needs to be housed appropriately and to receive an appropriate income to live on. Abe can argue that he will have the obligation and responsibility for maintaining Enid and any child born to them. The court will also have regard to the standard of living enjoyed by the family before the breakdown of the marriage: see s25(2)(c) MCA 1973. It is assumed that Beryl and Abe had a limited lifestyle given Beryl's problems in 1994. The court will seek to ensure that Beryl does not suffer any further drop in her lifestyle or that at any drop is shared equitably between the parties. The court will have regard to the age of the parties and the duration of the marriage: see s25(2)(d) MCA 1973. The ages of the parties are not given. They may well be relatively young if they met as students in 1985. Both parties will be given credit for a marriage which has lasted seven years. The court may also have regard to the period before the marriage when they lived together. The courts do not normally have regard to a period of cohabitation before marriage since the commitment of marriage has not been entered into. However, Beryl's contribution in housing Abe and supporting him financially while he qualified could be included as part of the overall circumstances and should strengthen Beryl's claim: see *S v S (Financial Provision) (Post-Divorce Cohabitation)* [1994] 2 FLR 228.

The court will look at the contributions which each of the parties has made or is likely to make in the foreseeable future to the welfare of the family. This will include any contribution made by looking after the home or caring for the family: see s25(2)(f) MCA 1973. Beryl can be advised that this consideration is likely to be a significant factor since she gave up work to act as a mother. The court may have to make a judgment about whether this was reasonable in light of Abe's view that she should have stayed in work. Courts appear to accept as reasonable a mother's desire to give up work in order to care for very young children. Her future contribution in caring for the two children will also be noted by the court. Beryl can be advised that these factors are likely to increase any award for financial provision: see *Wachtel v Wachtel* [1973] 2 WLR 366. Her contribution before the marriage may also be considered as outlined above. Abe's contribution in helping the family during Beryl's depression is likely to strengthen his case. His dismissal from his employment is difficult to criticise if it was as a result of him trying to help Beryl and the children. Beryl can be advised that the court is unlikely to consider the conduct of the parties unless that conduct is such that it would in the opinion of the court be inequitable to disregard it: see s25(2)(g) MCA 1973. The courts tend to treat financial provision as more of an arithmetical exercise than a moral one: see *Wachtel v Wachtel* and *Duxbury v Duxbury* [1987] 1 FLR 7. The court may take both parties' positive conduct into account in their efforts to bring up the children despite all the difficulties.

The court will also consider the value of any benefit which each party will lose as a result of the divorce: see s25B MCA 1973. The question does not make it clear whether Beryl will lose any rights in any pension Abe may have. Given Abe's interrupted work history and likely age it seems unlikely that he will have built up much in the way of pension rights. The court is likely to be concerned that Beryl has some kind of provision for the future given her lack of any kind of cover in her own right. This concern is emphasised by amendments to the Matrimonial Causes Act 1973 introduced by the Pensions Act 1995, which add ss25B–D to the MCA 1973. The provisions place a duty on the court to consider the pension provision of the parties and give powers to make orders whereby when Abe's pensions come into effect provision can be made for Beryl.

The court can also make an immediate pension splitting order: see ss24B–24D and 25B–25C MCA 1973. As already stated it does not seem likely that there will be sufficient pension cover for these provisions to have much relevance.

The court will also consider whether it would appropriate to make orders whereby the financial obligations of Abe to Beryl will terminate as soon after the divorce decree as the court considers just and reasonable: see s25A(1) MCA 1973. If the court makes a maintenance order in her favour the court must consider whether it would be appropriate to limit the term of the order to such a term as would enable Beryl to adjust without undue hardship to the termination of her financial dependence on Abe: see s25A(2) MCA 1973. Beryl can be advised that the courts have shown some reluctance in imposing a clean break where a former wife is in a financially weak position, particularly where she may find it difficult to get back into the job market or to find any work with a reasonable income.

With regard to financial provision for the two children Beryl should be advised that jurisdiction now rests with the Child Support Agency: see s8 Child Support Act 1991. As a result she will have to make a separate application to the CSA should she wish to oblige Abe to provide for their two children. The CSA would assess child support on the basis of a fixed formula. The formula includes an assessment of the children's 'maintenance requirements' (which includes an element for Beryl), a calculation of the income of both Beryl and Abe, calculating a protected income for Abe and then reaching a final figure. As Beryl may be aware, child support assessments can be high (though recent changes aim to ensure that such an assessment would be no more than 30 per cent of Abe's income). Only a limited account would be taken of Enid and the forthcoming baby in assessing Abe's disposal income. Beryl may also be aware that the CSA has a backlog of work and may not be able to respond quickly to any application she makes. It is possible for Beryl and Abe to reach an agreement between themselves as to what Abe can afford to support the children. It would then be possible to incorporate such an agreement into a court order. Abe may be willing to consider this if the alternative of a child support assessment would work against him. If agreement is not possible then Beryl must approach the CSA and await their assessment of Abe. Given that Abe's income may be limited it may be that any child support is limited. If this is the case then Beryl may claim state benefit to make the difference. If she is already on benefit she is likely to be obliged to apply for child support or suffer a reduction in her benefit.

Beryl should be advised that the court is likely to provide her with accommodation suitable to her standard of living and suitable for the children. Given her contribution towards the purchase of the family home and the factors outlined above, it is likely that the court will transfer the home into her sole name. There is insufficient information to give clear advice on what financial support Abe can provide Beryl. The financial support of the children would be a matter for the Child Support Agency and again there is insufficient information to state what child support assessment is likely to be made.

With regard to the upbringing of the children, the divorce court would have considered the arrangements made for the children and asked whether it should exercise its powers under the Children Act 1989 before granting a decree absolute of divorce: see s41 MCA 1973. No disputes or difficulties over the arrangements for the children are revealed so it is assumed that the court has already declared that there is no need to exercise its powers. Beryl should be advised that the courts are not likely to interfere with what the parents agree amongst themselves unless there is concern that such arrangements will harm the children. The courts will not make any order concerning the children unless making that order would be better for the child than making no order at all: s1(5) CA 1989. The only matter which is not clear is whether Beryl has fully recovered from her depression. Even if the arrangements for the children were such as to cause the court to consider using its powers the decree could still be made absolute if there are exceptional circumstances which make it desirable to so direct. If there was a dispute about the children's residence then the court could make a residence order determining where the children should live. If there was a dispute about Abe having contact with the children the court make a contact order determining when the children should have contact with their father. In determining any such dispute the court would consider that the welfare of the children was its paramount consideration: s1(1) CA 1989. It would also consider that any delay in resolving the dispute would be likely to be harmful to the children: s1(2) CA 1989. If an application to the court was opposed it would consider a checklist of matters in deciding how to resolve the dispute: s1(3), (4) CA 1989. In the absence of any specific disputes or problems concerning the children being identified it is not possible to give any more specific advice.

Chapter 7

Domestic Violence

7.1   Introduction

7.2   Key points

7.3   Key cases and statute

7.4   Questions and suggested solutions

7.1 Introduction

In this chapter we look at the way the law attempts to deal with the social problem of domestic violence. The emphasis here is on violence by a husband or male partner towards his wife or female partner (though violence by the wife or female partner towards the husband or male partner does occur). Child abuse is dealt with in Chapter 10. It is possible that a question combines violence towards both wife/partner and her children but the answer normally only requires a discussion of the remedies under the Family Law Act 1996 rather than local authority child protection procedures. The student has to demonstrate a knowledge of Part IV of the Family Law Act 1996 which has codified the law on matrimonial home rights, occupation orders and non-molestation orders.

7.2 Key points

Occupation and non-molestation orders under the Family Law Act 1996

To which court should application be made?

Application can be made to the High Court, county court or magistrates' court: see s57 FLA 1996. There is provision allowing magistrates' courts to transfer more difficult cases to the county court. Magistrates' courts will not be allowed to deal with any application involving disputes concerning a party's entitlement to occupy a property by virtue of a beneficial interest estate or interest or contract unless it is unnecessary to determine the question in order to deal with the application or make the order: see s59(1) FLA 1996. This is because magistrates' courts do not have the expertise to deal with such applications. The magistrates can decline to deal with applications which may be more conveniently dealt with in another court (eg a county court): see s59(2) FLA 1996.

Definition of terms

'Cohabitants' are a man and woman who, although not married to each other, are living together as husband and wife: see s62(1)(a) FLA 1996. 'Former cohabitants' is to be read accordingly but does not include cohabitants who have subsequently married each other: see s62(1)(b) FLA 1996. See also *G v G (Non-Molestation Order: Jurisdiction)* [2000] 2 FLR 532.

'Relevant child' means any child who is living with or might reasonably be expected to live with either party to the proceedings and any child in relation to whom an order under the Children Act (CA) 1989 or Adoption Act (AA) 1976 is in question in relation to the proceedings and any other child whose interests the court considers relevant: see s62(2) FLA 1996. A 'child' means a person under the age of 18 years: see s63(1) FLA 1996.

The phrase 'significant harm' carries a similar meaning as in the CA 1989: see s63(1) and (3) FLA 1996.

A person is 'associated' with another person if:

a) they are or have been married to each other;

b) they are cohabitants or former cohabitants;

c) they live or have lived in the same household otherwise than merely by reason of one of them being the other's employee, tenant, lodger or boarder;

d) they are relatives;

e) they are engaged (whether or not that engagement has been terminated);

f) they are parents of a child or have parental responsibility for the child (or are a natural parent of a child and the adoptive parents or a child who has been or is in the process of being adopted);

g) they are parties to the same family proceedings (other than proceedings under Part IV FLA 1996).

See s62(3), (4) and (5) FLA 1996.

'Relative' is defined by reference to a list (which includes fathers, mothers, stepparents, siblings, stepsiblings, grandparents and grandchildren including by virtue of that person's spouse or former spouse or cohabiting partner, brothers, sisters, uncles, aunts, nephews and nieces): see s63(1) FLA 1996.

Application for occupation orders

There are five kinds of application for occupation orders:

a) application by a person with occupation rights or with matrimonial home rights against an 'associated' person (pursuant to s33 FLA 1996);

b) application by a former spouse with no existing right to occupy against the other former spouse who has a right to occupy (pursuant to s35 FLA 1996);

c) application by a cohabitants/former cohabitants with no right to occupy against a cohabitant/former cohabitant with a right to occupy (pursuant to s36 FLA 1996);

d) application by a spouse with no right to occupy against a spouse who also has no right to occupy (pursuant to s37 FLA 1996); and

e) application by a cohabitant/former cohabitant with no right to occupy against the cohabitant/former cohabitant who also has no right to occupy (pursuant to s38 FLA 1996).

It may be important to make the right kind of application since different provisions apply depending on the kind of application to be made. Applicants may have to clarify their rights of occupation in order to determine which kind of application should be made. However, if an applicant makes an application under one section but the court considers it should have been made under another section then the court can make the order under the correct section: see s39(3) FLA 1996.

Application for an occupation order by a person with occupation rights or with matrimonial home rights (the s33 occupation order)

a) Who may apply for a s33 occupation order?

If a person is entitled to occupy a dwelling-house by virtue of a beneficial estate or interest or contract or by virtue of any enactment giving him/her the right to remain in occupation or has matrimonial home rights in relation to a dwelling-house (eg under s30(2) FLA 1996) and the dwelling-house is, or at any time has been, or is intended to be, the home of the person entitled and of another person with whom he/she is associated, then the person entitled may apply for an occupation order against that other person ('the respondent'): see s33(1) FLA 1996.

For these purposes if an agreement to marry is terminated no application can be made under s33 FLA 1996 by reference to that agreement after the end of three years beginning with the date on which it is terminated: see s33(2) FLA 1996.

b) What is a s33 occupation order?

A s33 occupation order is an order which:

i) enforces the applicant's entitlement to remain in occupation as against the respondent; or

ii) requires the respondent to permit the applicant to enter and remain in the dwelling-house or part of the dwelling-house; or

iii) regulates the occupation of the dwelling-house by either or both parties; or

iv) prohibits, suspends or restricts the exercise by the respondent of his/her rights to occupy the dwelling-house by virtue of his/her beneficial estate or interest or contract or enactment giving him/her the right to remain in occupation; or

v) if the respondent has matrimonial rights in relation to the dwelling-house and the applicant is the other spouse, restricts or terminates those rights; or

vi) requires the respondent to leave the dwelling-house or part of the dwelling-house; or

vii)excludes the respondent from a defined area in which the dwelling-house is situated.

See s33(3) FLA 1996.

A s33 occupation order may also declare that the applicant is entitled to occupy a dwelling-house or has matrimonial home rights: see s33(4) FLA 1996. If the applicant has matrimonial home rights and the respondent is the other spouse an occupation order made during the marriage may provide that those rights are not brought to an end by the death of the other spouse or the termination (otherwise than by death) of the marriage: see s33(5) FLA 1996. The court may exercise such powers in any case where it considers that in all the circumstances it is just and reasonable to do so: see s33(8) FLA 1996. Otherwise a s33 occupation order ceases to have effect on the death of either party and may not be made after the death of either party: see s33(9) FLA 1996. A s33 occupation order may be made for a specified period or until the occurrence of a specified event or until further order: see s33(10) FLA 1996.

c) What the court must consider before making a s33 occupation order

Under s33(6) FLA 1996 the court must have regard to all the circumstances including:

'(a) the housing needs and housing resources of each of the parties and of any relevant child;
(b) the financial resources of each of the parties;
(c) the likely effect of any order, or of any decision by the court not to exercise its powers under subsection (3), on the health, safety or well-being of the parties and of any relevant child;
(d) the conduct of the parties in relation to each other and otherwise.'

The court must balance the risk of significant harm – if it appears to the court that the applicant or any relevant child is likely to suffer significant harm attributable to conduct of the respondent if an occupation order is not made the court shall make the occupation order unless it appears to the court that: (i) the respondent or any relevant child is likely to suffer significant harm if the order is made; and (ii) the harm likely to be suffered by the respondent or child in that event is as great as, or greater than, the harm attributable to the conduct of the respondent which is likely to be suffered by the applicant or child if the order is not made: see s33(7) FLA 1996.

In *Chalmers* v *John* [1999] Fam Law 26 it was confirmed that s33(7) did not come into play where only minor acts of violence were involved. An occupation order was a draconian order which was not suited to the facts of that case. A non-molestation order was the more appropriate remedy. See also *B* v *B (Occupation Order)* [1999] 1 FLR 715 which also considered the balance of harm test. See *G* v *G (Occupation Order: Contact)* [2000] Fam Law 466 where again it was said that an occupation order was a draconian order and not appropriate where there was friction rather than violence.

Application by former spouse with no existing right to occupy (a s35 occupation order)

a) What is a s35 occupation order?

If one former spouse is entitled to occupy a dwelling-house by virtue of a beneficial estate or interest or contract or has a right of occupation by virtue of any enactment, and the other former spouse is not so entitled, and the dwellling-house was at any time their matrimonial home or was at any time intended by them to be their matrimonial home, then the former spouse not so entitled may apply to the court for an occupation order against the other former spouse: see s35(1) and (2) FLA 1996.

For these purposes a former spouse who has an equitable interest in the dwelling-house or in the proceeds of sale, but who has no legal interest, is treated as not being entitled to occupy the dwelling-house: see s35(11) FLA 1996.

b) Meaning of a s35 occupation order

For these purposes a s35 occupation order must include the following:

i) where the applicant is in occupation, s35(3) states that it must contain provision

'(a) giving the applicant the right not to be evicted or excluded from the dwelling-house or any part of it by the respondent for the period specified in the order; and
(b) prohibiting the respondent from evicting or excluding the applicant during that period.'

ii) where the applicant is not in occupation, s35(4) states it must contain provision

'(a) giving the applicant the right to enter into and occupy the dwelling-house for such period specified in the order; and
(b) requiring the respondent to permit the exercise of that right.'

Under s35(5) a s35 order may also:

'(a) regulate the occupation of the dwelling-house by either or both of the parties;
(b) prohibit, suspend or restrict the exercise by the respondent of his right to occupy the dwelling-house;
(c) require the respondent to leave the dwelling-house or part of the dwelling-house; or
(d) exclude the respondent from a defined area in which the dwelling-house is included.'

c) What the court must consider

In deciding whether to make an occupation order under s35(3) or (4) and, if so, in what manner, the court shall have regard to all the circumstances.

In particular the court must consider the same matters as for a s33 occupation order.

In addition the court must consider:

i) the length of time that elapsed since the parties ceased to live together;

ii) the length of time that has elapsed since the marriage was dissolved or annulled; and

iii) the existence of any pending proceedings between the parties –

- for an order under s23A or 24 MCA 1973;

- for an order under para 1(2)(d) or (e) Sch 1 of the CA 1989; or

- relating to the legal or beneficial ownership of the dwelling-house.

In deciding whether to add a s35(5) provision (eg an order excluding the respondent) and, if so, in what manner, the court shall have regard to all the circumstances including the matters mentioned in s35(6)(a)–(e) FLA 1996.

The balance of harm test (which applies to s33 occupation orders) also applies. If the balance of harm is in favour of the applicant or relevant child a s35(5) provision must be added. For example: see *S v F (Occupation Order)* [2000] 2 FCR 365.

An order may not be made under s35 after the death of either of the former spouses and ceases to have effect on the death of either of them (s35(9) FLA 1996). An order under s35 must be limited so as to have effect for a specified period not exceeding six months. It may be extended on one or more occasions for a further specified period not exceeding six months: s35(10) FLA 1996.

So long as a s35 order remains in force s30(3)–(6) apply in relation to the applicant as if he/she were the spouse entitled to occupy the dwelling-house by virtue of s30, and as if the respondent were the other spouse: s35(11) FLA 1996.

Where the applicant is an unmarried cohabitant or former cohabitant with no existing right to occupy (a s36 occupation order)

a) What is a s36 occupation order?

Where one cohabitant or former cohabitant is entitled to occupy a dwelling-house by virtue of a beneficial estate or interest or contract or by virtue of any enactment giving him/her the right to remain in occupation, and the other cohabitant or former cohabitant is not so entitled, and that dwelling-house is the home in which they live together as husband and wife or a home in which they at any time so lived together or intended so to live together, then the cohabitant or former cohabitant not so entitled may apply for an occupation order against the other cohabitant or former cohabitant (the respondent): s36(1), (2) FLA 1996.

b) Meaning of a s36 occupation order

If the applicant is in occupation a s36 order must contain provision (see s36(3) FLA 1996):

'(a) giving the applicant the right not to be evicted or excluded from the dwelling-house or any part of it by the respondent for the period specified in the order; and
(b) prohibiting the respondent from evicting or excluding the applicant during that period.'

If the applicant is not in occupation a s36 order must contain provision (see s36(4) FLA 1996):

'(a) giving the applicant the right to enter into and occupy the dwelling-house for the period specified in the order; and
(b) requiring the respondent to permit the exercise of that right.'

A s36 order may also (see s36(5) FLA 1996):

'(a) regulate the occupation of the dwelling-house by either or both of the parties;
(b) prohibit, suspend or restrict the exercise by the respondent of his/her right to occupy the dwelling-house;
(c) require the respondent to leave the dwelling-house or part of the dwelling-house; or
(d) exclude the respondent from a defined area in which the dwelling-house is included.'

For these purposes a person who has an equitable interest in the dwelling-house or in the proceeds of sale, but has no legal interest, is to be treated as not being entitled to occupy the dwelling-house: see s36(11) FLA 1996.

c) What the court must consider

In deciding whether to make a s36(3) or (4) order and, if so, in what manner, s36(6) provides that the court shall have regard to all the circumstances, including the same matters as for a s33 occupation order. In addition, under 36(6) the court must consider:

'(e) the nature of the parties' relationship;
(f) the length of time during which they lived together as husband and wife;
(g) whether there are or have been any children who are children of both parties or for whom both parties have or have had parental responsibility;
(h) the length of time that has elapsed since the parties ceased to live together; and
(i) the existence of any pending proceedings between the parties –
(i) for an order under paragraph 1(2)(d) or (e) of Schedule 1 to the Children Act 1989; or
(ii) relating to the legal or beneficial ownership of the dwelling-house.'

In deciding whether to exercise its powers to include any s36(5) provision (eg an order excluding the respondent) and, if so, in what manner, the court must have regard to all the circumstances including the matters mentioned in s36(6)(a)–(d): see s36(7)(a) FLA 1996.

The balance of harm test applies *but* if the balance is in favour of the applicant or relevant child there is *no* obligation to include a s36(5) provision – only a discretion. For example: see *Gay v Sheeran* [1999] 2 FLR 519.

In considering the nature of the parties' relationship the court must have regard to the fact that they have not given each other the commitment involved in marriage: see s41 FLA 1996.

d) Duration of the order

A s36 order must be limited so as to have effect for a specified period not exceeding 6 months, but may be extended on one occasion for a further specified period not exceeding six months: see s36(10) FLA 1996. A s36 order may not be made after the death of either of the parties and ceases to have effect on the death of either of them: see s36(9) FLA 1996.

So long as the order remains in force s30(3)–(6) apply in relation to the applicant as if he/she were a spouse entitled to occupy the dwelling-house by virtue of s30 and as if the respondent were the other spouse: see s36(13) FLA 1996.

Where neither spouse entitled to occupy (a s37 occupation order)

a) What is a s37 occupation order?

Where a spouse or former spouse and the other spouse or former spouse occupy a dwelling-house which is or was the matrimonial home but neither of them is entitled to remain in occupation, then either may apply to the court for an occupation order: see s37(1) and (2) FLA 1996.

b) Meaning of a s37 occupation order

A s37 occupation order means an order (see s37(3) FLA 1996) which may:

'(a) require the respondent to permit the applicant to enter and remain in the dwelling-house or part of the dwelling-house;
(b) regulate the occupation of the dwelling-house by either or both of the parties;
(c) require the respondent to leave the dwelling-house or part of the dwelling house; or
(d) exclude the respondent from a defined area in which the dwelling-house is included.'

c) What the court must consider

In deciding whether to exercise its powers and, if so, in what manner, the court shall have regard to all the circumstances including the same matters as for a s33 occupation order.

The balance of harm test applies as for a s33 occupation order.

d) Period of the order

A s37(3) order must be limited to have effect for a specified period not exceeding six months but may be extended on one or more occasions for a further specified period not exceeding six months: see s37(5) FLA 1996.

e) Effect of the order

The order will only operate between the parties and will not, for example, affect a third person who is entitled to occupy the property.

Where neither cohabitant nor former cohabitant is entitled to occupy (a s38 occupation order)

a) Who may apply for a s38 occupation order?

If one cohabitant or former cohabitant and the other cohabitant or former cohabitant occupy a dwelling-house which is the home in which they live or lived together as husband and wife but neither of them is entitled to remain in occupation then either of them may apply to the court for an order against the other: see s38(1) and (2) FLA 1996.

b) Meaning of a s38 occupation order

A s38 occupation order means an order (see s38(3) FLA 1996) which may:

'(a) require the respondent to permit the applicant to enter and remain in the dwelling-house or part of the dwelling-house;
(b) regulate the occupation of the dwelling-house by either or both of the parties;
(c) require the respondent to leave the dwelling-house or part of the dwelling-house; or
(d) exclude the respondent from a defined area in which the dwelling-house is included.'

c) What the court must consider

In deciding whether to exercise its powers to make a s38(3) order and, if so, in what manner the court must have regard to all the circumstances including the same matters as for a s33 occupation order.

The balance of harm test also applies *but* if the balance is in favour of the applicant or relevant child there is *no* obligation to include a s38(3) provision.

d) Period of a s38(3) order

A s38(3) order shall be limited so as to have effect for a specified period not exceeding six months but may be extended on one occasion for a further specified period not exceeding six months: see s38(6) FLA 1996.

General provisions concerning occupation orders

An occupation order under ss33, 35, 36, 37 or 38 may be made in other family proceedings or without any other family proceedings being instituted: see s39(2) FLA 1996. If an application is made for an occupation order under one of those sections and the court considers that it has no power to make the order under the section concerned, but that it has power to make an order under one of the other sections, the court may make an order under that other section: see s39(3) FLA 1996.

The fact that a person has applied for an occupation order, or that an occupation has been made, does not affect the right of any person to claim a legal or equitable interest in any property in any subsequent proceedings: see s39(4) FLA 1996.

Under s40(1) FLA 1996 the court may on, or at any time after, making an occupation order under ss33, 35 or 36 provide for the payment of rent and mortgage and for the repair of the property. It can also make orders about furniture or other contents of the dwelling-house.

Non-molestation orders

a) Meaning of non-molestation order

A non-molestation order means an order prohibiting the respondent from molesting another person who is associated with the respondent and/or prohibiting the respondent from molesting a relevant child: see s42(1) FLA 1996. The order may refer to molestation in general or to particular acts of molestation or both: see s42(6) FLA 1996.

b) Who can apply for a non-molestation order?

Application can be made by a person who is associated with another person. The definition of a person 'associated' with another person has already been given.

c) When can a non-molestation order be made?

The court may make a non-molestation order if an application for a non-molestation order has been made (whether or not in other family proceedings) by a person associated with the respondent or on the court's own motion if it is hearing family proceedings to which the respondent is a party and the court considers such an order should be made for the benefit of any other party to the proceedings or any relevant child (even though no such application has been made): see s42(2) FLA 1996.

Where an agreement to marry is terminated no application can be made for a non-molestation order by reference to that agreement after the end of the period of three years beginning with the date on which it is terminated: see s42(4) FLA 1996.

d) What the court must consider

In deciding whether to make a non-molestation order and, if so, in what manner the court must have regard to all the circumstances, including the need to secure the health, safety and well-being of the applicant (or, where the court is making the order of its own motion, the person for whose benefit the order would be made) and of any relevant child: see s42(5) FLA 1996.

In *C v C (Application for Non-Molestation Order)* [1998] 2 WLR 599 it was held that molestation meant some deliberate conduct which was aimed at a high degree of harassment of the other party so as to justify the intervention of the court. It did not include enforcing an invasion of privacy per se. In that case newspaper articles which spoke about the applicant in unflattering terms did not amount to molestation.

e) How long can a non-molestation order last?

A non-molestation order may be made for a specified period or until further order: see s42(7) FLA 1996. However, if the order is made in other family proceedings it ceases to have effect if those proceedings are withdrawn or dismissed: see s42(8) FLA 1996.

Ex parte orders

An occupation or non-molestation order can be made ex parte where the court considers that it is just and convenient to do so: see s45(1) FLA 1996.

Under s45(3) FLA 1996 the court must have regard to all the circumstances including:

'(a) any risk of significant harm to the applicant or a relevant child, attributable to conduct of the respondent, if the order is not made immediately;
(b) whether it is likely that the applicant will be deterred or prevented from pursuing the application if an order is not made immediately; and
(c) whether there is reason to believe that the respondent is aware of the proceedings but is deliberately evading service and that the applicant or a relevant child will be seriously prejudiced by the delay involved –
(i) … in effecting service of the proceedings; or
(ii) … in effecting substituted service.'

If the court makes an ex parte order it must give the respondent an opportunity to make representations relating to the order as soon as just and convenient at a full hearing (ie a hearing notice of which has been given to all the parties): see s45(3) FLA 1996. The length of an order made at a full hearing is treated as starting from the date of the ex parte order, and any extension may be made as if the ex parte order and the order made at the full hearing are one order: see s45(4) FLA 1996.

Undertakings

Instead of making an occupation or non-molestation order the court may accept an undertaking from any party to the proceedings. Such an undertaking is enforceable as a court order: see s46(1) and (4) FLA 1996. A power of arrest cannot be attached to an undertaking and an undertaking cannot be accepted where a power of arrest would be attached to an order: see s46(2) and (3) FLA 1996.

Attaching a power of arrest

If a court makes an occupation order or non-molestation order and it appears to the court that the respondent has used or threatened violence against the applicant or relevant child, it *must* attach a power of arrest to the order unless satisfied that in all the circumstances of the case the applicant or child will be adequately protected without such a power of arrest: see s46(2) FLA 1996.

A power of arrest cannot be attached to an ex parte order unless it appears to the court that the respondent has used or threatened violence against the applicant or a relevant child and that there is a risk of significant harm to the applicant or child attributable to the conduct of the respondent if the power of arrest is not attached immediately: see s46(3) FLA 1996. If the court does attach a power of arrest to an ex parte order it may provide that the power of arrest is to have effect for a shorter period than the occupation or non-molestation order: see s46(4) FLA 1996. Any such period may be extended by the court on one or more occasions on an application to vary or discharge the occupation or non-molestation order: see s46(5) FLA 1996.

Where a power of arrest is attached a constable may arrest without warrant a person whom he has reasonable cause for suspecting to be in breach of the occupation or non-molestation order: see s46(6) FLA 1996. The person must be produced before a court within 24 hours of his/her arrest (excluding Christmas Day, Good Friday or any Sunday) where he/she may be dealt with or remanded to appear before a later court: see s46(7) FLA 1996. The power to remand includes a remand for medical examination and report (whether on bail or in custody): see s48 FLA 1996.

Where no power of arrest is attached to an order the applicant may apply to the court for the issue or a warrant for the respondent's arrest if the applicant considers that the respondent has failed to comply with the order. The application must be substantiated on oath and the court must be satisfied that there are reasonable grounds for believing that the respondent has failed to comply with the order: see s46(8) and (9) FLA 1996.

Enforcement of an occupation or non-molestation order

The High Court, county court and (to a lesser extent) the magistrates' court have power to commit a respondent to prison for disobeying an occupation or non-molestation order. This committal power may be suspended for such period or on such terms and conditions as the court may specify.

7.3 Key cases and statute

- *B v B (Occupation Order)* [1999] 1 FLR 715
  Balance of harm and s33 occupation order

- C v C *(Application for Non-Molestation Order)* [1998] 1 FLR 554
  Non-molestation order – definition of molestation

- *Chalmer* v *Johns* [1999] Fam Law 26
  Consideration for s33 occupation order

- G v G *(Non-Molestation Order: Jurisdiction)* [2000] 2 FLR 532
  Jurisdiction to make non-molestation order

- G v G *(Occupation Order: Contact)* [2000] Fam Law 466
  Consideration for s33 occupation order

- *Gay* v *Sheeran* [1999] 2 FLR 519
  Consideration for a s36 occupation order

- Family Law Act 1996 – occupation of the family home

7.4 Questions and suggested solutions

QUESTION ONE

Ann and Bill began living together three years ago in a house they bought in joint names. Last year Ann's sister died and since then she and Bill have looked after her sister's two orphaned children. Bill had only reluctantly agreed to look after them, and their presence caused a rift between Ann and Bill. Their relationship deteriorated to the point where there was very little contact between them other than during day-to-day necessities. Bill developed a mental condition, one symptom of which was agoraphobia. His behaviour became very unpredictable. Ann showed no sympathy for or understanding of his condition and on one occasion, after accusing him of giving no help in running the home, she started to push him out into the street, telling him to go to the shops. He struck her several times, observed by the children, who became very upset by what they saw.

Bill entered hospital for treatment for his condition two weeks ago. He made frequent telephone calls to Ann to apologise for his behaviour. On some occasions the telephone was answered by one of the children, who became very distressed on hearing Bill's voice.

Bill is due to leave hospital in one week's time. Ann now feels that she needs breathing space to allow her and the children to recover, but if Bill's condition does not improve, she would not want him to return to the house.

Advise Ann.

University of London LLB Examination
(for External Students) Family Law June 1997 Q5

General Comment

On 1 October 1997 Part IV of the Family Law Act 1996 came into force. It codified and revised the law dealing with occupation of the family home. In particular, it laid down the framework for occupation and non-molestation orders. This question invites the student to apply the new law to its particular facts. The difficulties of mental illness and how this affects the 'balance of harm' are added ingredients.

Skeleton Solution

Application for a non-molestation order: s42 FLA 1996 – application for an occupation order under s33 FLA 1996 – consideration of: housing needs and resources of each of the parties and the children; financial resources of each of parties; effect of order or not making order on health, safety or well-being of the parties and the children; the conduct of the parties; balance of harm test – the special circumstances of mental illness – whether an application can be made ex parte and attaching a power of arrest – long term solutions for Ann.

Suggested Solution

Ann seeks advice about not allowing Bill back should his condition not have improved. Generally she would like 'breathing space' and any advice should explain how she can achieve this.

Ann can be advised that she can apply to the High Court, county court or magistrates' court for a non-molestation order prohibiting Bill from molesting either her or the children: see s42 Family Law Act (FLA) 1996. She is able to apply for such an order since she and Bill are 'associated persons' (because they are former cohabitants: s62(3)(b) FLA 1996). Ann can be advised that 'molestation' has been given a wide meaning and includes pestering or harassing behaviour: see *Vaughan* v *Vaughan* [1973] 1 WLR 1159. It can include annoying telephone calls: see *Horner* v *Horner* (1983) 4 FLR 50. It can include involuntary behaviour: see *Wooton* v *Wooton* [1984] FLR 871. In deciding whether to make a non-molestation order and, if so, in what terms, Ann can be advised that the court will have regard to all the circumstances, including the need to secure the health, safety and well-being of both Ann and the children. The children, though not the natural children of either Ann or Bill, are 'relevant children' because they are living with Ann: see ss62(2) and 63(1) FLA 1996. Bill's unpredictable behaviour, his assault on Ann in sight of the children and his phone calls which upset the children, are likely to amount to molestation of both Ann and the children. As a result, the court is likely to grant an order prohibiting him from molesting both Ann and the children in order to secure their health, safety and well-being. The order can prevent molestation in general or refer to particular acts of molestation or to both (eg be directed specifically at the telephone calls). It is likely that the court will limit the term of any non-molestation order. In the past a period of three months was the starting point: see *Practice Direction (Injunction: Domestic Violence)* [1978] 1 WLR 1123.

Such an order may provide Ann with the protection and breathing space she needs. However, if she wishes to prevent Bill from returning to the home she should make application for an occupation order at the same time as applying for the non-molestation order. Since she is the joint owner of the property she has a legal right to occupy and can apply for a non-molestation order: see s33 FLA 1996. She can make application against Bill since he is an 'associated person' (as already outlined). Such an occupation order could exclude Bill from the home and from a defined area in which the home is included: see s33(3) FLA 1996. In deciding whether to make such an order the court will have regard to all the circumstances including particular matters: see s33(6) FLA 1996. The court will consider Ann's and the children's housing needs and resources and take into account Ann's financial resources. It will compare these with Bill's housing needs and resources. There is no information about either Ann's or Bill's finances. Bill's finances may be limited as a result of his illness and hospital admission. It is assumed that Ann has greater housing needs compared to Bill since she has the children to look after. However, Bill may find it difficult to find alternative accommodation due to his mental illness. The availability of local authority or housing association accommodation may be important: see *Thurley* v *Smith* [1985] Fam Law 31.The court will then look at the likely effect of an occupation order on the health, safety and well-being of Bill, and will compare it with the likely effect on the health, safety and well-being of Ann and the children if an order is not made. The court will also look at the conduct of Bill and Ann in relation to each other and otherwise. The court may have to make a value judgment on how reasonably or unreasonably the parties have acted. Bill's behaviour appears to be upsetting the children. His assault on Ann is likely to be viewed as a serious matter. His telephone calls may be unreasonable if they are both too frequent and clearly unwelcome. However, Ann's behaviour may not escape criticism if the court finds that she has been unsympathetic or lacking in understanding. In another context the courts have said a spouse would be expected to share the burden imposed upon the family as a result of mental illness but that there was a limit to what was reasonable for a spouse to put up with: see *Katz* v *Katz* [1972] 1 WLR 955 and *Thurlow* v *Thurlow* [1975] 3 WLR 161. Though Ann and Bill are not married the court may apply a similar test. Ann should be advised that the needs of the children are not paramount when the court is considering making an occupation order. The fact that an occupation order is in their interests does not oblige the court to make the order: see *Richards* v *Richards* [1983] 3 WLR 173. However the interests of the children and the affect on them of Bill's behaviour is likely to be important in balancing the above considerations: see *Phillips* v *Phillips* [1973] 1 WLR 615.

The court will apply a 'balance of harm' test: see s33(7) FLA 1996. If it appears to the court that either Ann or the children is likely to suffer significant harm as a result of Bill's behaviour if an occupation order is not made then the court must make the occupation order, unless Bill is likely to suffer significant harm if the order is made and the harm he is likely to suffer is as great or greater than the harm Ann or the children are likely to suffer as a result of Bill's conduct. 'Harm' is given a wide meaning and includes in the case of Ann ill-treatment or impairment of health and in the case of the children (assuming they are under 18) ill-treatment or impairment of health or development: see s63(1) FLA 1996. 'Significant harm' has been defined as any harm which the court should take into account in considering the injured party's future: see *Humberside County Council v B* [1993] 1 FLR 257. In this case the court will have to balance the likely harm caused if Bill returns home 'uncured' against the harm which could be caused to Bill if he has no other suitable address to go to. It is difficult to advise Ann on how the court will apply the balance of harm test without more information on Bill's behaviour while he has been in hospital and his prognosis on release from hospital. If the balance of harm test is resolved in Ann's and the children's favour the occupation order must be made. If it is not, then the court could still make the order but is not obliged to do so.

If the occupation order is made the court could make orders against Bill to pay any mortgage or any other outgoings affecting the home or be responsible for its repair and maintenance: see s40 FLA 1996. In the absence of more information it is difficult to advise further on this point.

It is possible for Ann to apply for both the non-molestation and occupation order ex parte (ie without notifying Bill): see s45 FLA 1996. The court will only allow this if it considers it just and convenient to do so having regard to all the circumstances and in particular certain matters: see s45(2) FLA 1996. The court will assess any risk of significant harm to Ann or the children attributable to Bill's conduct if the order is not made immediately, whether Ann will be deterred or prevented from pursuing the application if an order is not made immediately or whether Bill would deliberately evade service. The court is unlikely to allow an application to be made ex parte since Bill is presently in hospital. He can be served with an application while he is in hospital for a hearing either while he is still in hospital or just after his release. Ann and the children do not appear to be in immediate risk from Bill, with the exception of the telephone calls. This could be dealt with by a change of telephone number if Ann so wished.

If an occupation or non-molestation order is made and it appears to the court that Bill has used or threatened violence against Ann or the children then it must attach a power of arrest unless satisfied that in all the circumstances Ann or the children will be adequately protected without a power of arrest: see s47 FLA 1996. Since Bill has used violence against Ann the court will be obliged to attach a power of arrest unless it is so satisfied. Since Bill has mental health problems this may increase the need for Ann to be protected by a power of arrest. If a power of arrest is attached, then any breach of an occupation or non-molestation order can be dealt with by a police officer arresting Bill forthwith and bringing him before a court within 24 hours. The court can then deal with Bill for breaching the court order by way of contempt.

As an alternative to an order the court can accept an undertaking from Bill that he will not molest Ann or the children and/or will leave the home: see s46 FLA 1996. This will depend on whether Bill would give such an undertaking and whether Bill is in a mental state to provide such an undertaking. In addition, the court cannot accept an undertaking where a power of arrest would be attached to an order. No power of arrest can be attached to any undertaking. As a result the court would have to be satisfied that Ann and the children would be adequately safeguarded by such an undertaking without an order with a power of arrest.

Ann should be advised that any occupation or non-molestation order is likely to be granted only for a limited period since the court will be concerned to provide a 'first aid' solution. Ann will need to look for a long term solution. This could include Ann applying to the county court or High Court for an order transferring the home to her sole name for the benefit of the children. She could only so apply if she is a guardian of the children or has a residence order for them in her favour: see s15 and Sch 1 CA 1989. Otherwise she could seek to buy out Bill's interest in the house so that she and the children can remain in the house and Bill would have to find alternative accommodation.

QUESTION TWO

'While Part IV of the Family Law Act 1996 has rationalised the law relating to domestic violence, the continued distinction between married and unmarried couples is unjustified and represents a privileging of property rights over personal safety.'

Do you agree?

University of London LLB Examination
(for External Students) Family Law June 2000 Q4

General Comment

This question invites a discussion of the various powers to make occupation orders and non-molestation orders under the Family Law Act 1996 and to draw distinctions between how they apply to married and unmarried couples. It also invites a more general discussion about property rights generally between the two kinds of couple. An analysis of the distinctions and an explanation of the justifications given for the distinctions is also called for. Finally, the student is required to give a personal view with reasons on the state of the law both in relation to domestic violence and property rights in the family home and whether there is indeed 'a privileging of property rights over personal safety'.

Skeleton Solution

Law relating to occupation orders and non-molestation orders: s33 occupation orders – s36 occupation orders – s37 occupation orders – s38 occupation orders (Family Law Act 1996 – distinction between married and unmarried couples and justifications); non-molestation orders; property rights of married and unmarried couples: matrimonial home rights under Family Law Act 1996 – rights of married couples under Matrimonial

Causes Act 1973 – rights of unmarried couples under property law; distinctions and justifications; conclusion as to the state of the law in relation to both domestic violence and property rights in the family home and whether there is 'a privileging of property rights over personal safety'.

Suggested Solution

The question invites a discussion on the distinction between married and unmarried couples in relation to personal safety and property rights. Once any distinctions have been identified then any justifications for the distinctions needs to be discussed and conclusions drawn.

Following the Family Law Act 1996 the distinction between married and unmarried couples in relation to occupation rights has been reduced. The Act consolidated a number of statutes and established a code for occupation rights in the family home. This code generally makes little distinction between married and unmarried couples. However, there are some distinctions which need to be highlighted.

There remains a clear distinction in relation to what are called 'matrimonial home rights'. A married spouse with no right to occupy the matrimonial home is able to claim 'matrimonial home rights' under s30 Family Law Act (FLA) 1996. These rights provide the spouse with no right to occupy the family home a right of occupation of the family home against the other spouse or a third party, subject to court order. For example, the spouse with no right to occupy can pay the mortgage or rent and the payments must be accepted by the lender or landlord in terms of continued occupation of the home: see s30(3) and (5) FLA 1996. The matrimonial home rights continue for as long as the marriage subsists. This matrimonial home right can be registered in order to make them binding on third parties: see s31 FLA 1996. Matrimonial home rights are not available to an unmarried partner. An unmarried partner's right of occupation would have to be established by court order through an occupation order (see below). Occupation order rights only bind the other partner and not third parties. Third parties can only be bound if the unmarried partner has a beneficial interest under property law and is in actual occupation whereby an 'overriding interest' is created under ss3 and 70 Law of Property Act 1925: see *Williams and Glyn's Bank* v *Boland* [1980] 2 All ER 408. The difficulties in establishing a beneficial interest are discussed below. There can also be difficulties in establishing actual occupation: see for example *Lloyds Bank* v *Rosset* [1990] 2 WLR 867. As a result it is far more difficult for unmarried persons to protect their right of occupation against third parties.

There is less of a distinction in terms of applying to the court for occupation orders (namely orders regulating who should occupy and who should be excluded from the matrimonial home). An unmarried partner with the right to occupy the home can apply for an occupation order in the same way as a married partner with the right to occupy the home: see s33 FLA 1996. Precisely the same criteria apply as to whether the court will or will not grant the occupation order. The only distinction is that a married person with no right to occupy, but who has matrimonial home rights, could make application whereas an unmarried partner could not have matrimonial home rights. An unmarried cohabitant with no right to occupy can also apply for an occupation order: see s36 FLA 1996. The considerations for a s33 order and a s36 order are similar. However, there important distinctions. Under s33(7) there is a balance of harm test whereby the court has to balance the risk of significant harm to the applicant and any child if the order is not granted against any significant harm the respondent and any child would suffer if the order was granted. If the balance of harm is equal or in favour of the applicant then the occupation order must be made. There is a similar balance of harm test under s36(7) but the outcome of that balance does not oblige the court to make an order. The court is also obliged to look at the quality of the unmarried relationship (see s36(6)) and have regard to the fact that unmarried partners have not given each other the same commitment as marriage: s41 FLA 1996. It is tempting to say that this latter provision was a political concession to those MPs who wished to emphasise the importance of marriage. The period of a s33 order can be unlimited, whereas a s36 order can only be for up to six months (with one extension for up to six months). Long-term occupation orders are rare. Occupation orders are meant to be short-term protection measures pending longer term solutions: see *Practice Direction (Injunction: Domestic Violence)* [1978] 1 WLR 1123 which recommended order of up to three months. In reality these distinctions are unlikely to prevent a court from acting to protect an unmarried partner who is the victim of domestic violence in much the same way as it protects a married partner when faced with the same level of violence. To this extent there is no privileging of property rights over personal safety.

There are similar provisions allowing a spouse with no right to occupy to apply for an occupation order against a spouse with no right to occupy (see s37 FLA 1996) and for a cohabitant with no right to occupy to apply against a cohabitant with no right to occupy: see s38 FLA 1996. Similar distinctions apply as between a s33 order and a s36 order. The balance of harm test is obligatory in considering whether to make a s37 order while it is not for a s38 order. Otherwise the criteria for the court to consider are similar, as are the provisions concerning the duration of the order.

There is no distinction in protecting married or unmarried partners from molestation through non-molestation orders: see s42 FLA 1996. Application is made against an 'associated person'. An 'associated person' includes spouses or cohabitants: see s62 FLA 1996. The provisions on powers of arrest apply equally to married or unmarried applicants: see 46 FLA 1996.

In relation to property rights the distinction between married and unmarried couples is more stark. When a married couple separates and divorces either spouse can apply for lump sum and/or property orders and/or pension orders under the Matrimonial Causes Act 1973. The court can make such orders as it considers fair in all the circumstances and taking into account particular considerations: see ss25(1), (2) and 25A MCA 1973. The House of Lords in *White v White* [2000] 2 FLR 981 encouraged the courts to apply a yardstick of equality in looking at matrimonial assets, strengthening the position of a non-working and financially vulnerable spouse. As a result a non-earning spouse in a long marriage who has brought up the children and looked after the household can receive a substantial contribution via lump sum orders, property orders and pension orders for his/her future maintenance. The clean break provisions discourage spouse maintenance orders but the courts have applied the clean break cautiously in terms of spouses in a weak financial position: see for example *Barrett* v *Barrett* [1988] 2 FLR 516. However, when unmarried couples separate there is no such generous scope for making fair provision. The court applies strict property law principles based on who owns property according to the conveyance, any evidence in writing and the law on resulting, implied and constructive trusts: see *Gissing* v *Gissing* [1970] 3 WLR 255. An unmarried partner can find it extremely difficult to establish property rights unless he/she has made direct financial contributions to the purchase of the home or there is a specific agreement that he/she have a share of the property: see *Lloyds Bank* v *Rosset*. The mere fact of a long-standing relationship does not in itself give rise to property rights. This was graphically illustrated in the case of *Burns* v *Burns* [1984] 2 WLR 582 where an unmarried partner of 19 years was left with no rights in the home when the relationship ended. The difficulties faced by an unmarried partner in establishing property rights have been highlighted on many occasion by the courts: see for example *Hammond* v *Mitchell* [1991] 1 WLR 1127. The courts have consistently declined to give unmarried couples greater property rights and have left it to Parliament to act. There is no provision allowing a court to award an unmarried partner pension rights. Provisions to allow a spouse to claim an interest in the home based on substantial home improvements he/she has contributed to in money or money's worth do not apply to an unmarried partner: see s37 Matrimonial Proceedings and Property Act 1970. Alternative ways of protecting property rights or rights of occupation in the case of an unmarried partner include contractual licence and proprietary estoppel. Again both are not easy to establish.

Similarly, the rights of a spouse when his/her spouse is made bankrupt are given some protection against the trustee in bankruptcy (acting for the creditors): see s335A Insolvency Act 1986. This limited protection does not apply to an unmarried partner.

A spouse has the right to claim maintenance for him/herself against the other spouse – for example, through s23 MCA 1973. An unmarried partner has no similar right.

Parliament has moved some way to recognising the property rights of an unmarried partner in terms of provision on the death of the partner. From 1996 a new s1(1)(ba) and (1A) were added to the Inheritance (Provision for Family and Dependants) Act 1975 to allow an unmarried partner of the deceased to claim from the estate provided he/she lived with the deceased as husband and wife during the whole of the period of two years ending with the death.

Therefore, in relation to property rights there is a clear inequality. This is not linked to personal safety but to establishing rights in property. It is justified on the basis of nineteenth- and twentieth-century concepts of the importance of marriage and in the late twentieth century the need to protect the rights of a spouse in a weak financial position compared to the other spouse. The Law Commission has long been considering the property rights of cohabitees but a report is still awaited. The government continues to express a preference for the institution of marriage. This is illustrated by the distinctions drawn between married and unmarried applicants for occupation orders under the Family Law Act 1996. The original Family Law Bill contained no distinction between married and unmarried couples. The government allowed amendments as a concession to MPs who wished to preserve a distinction between married and unmarried couples. Though these distinctions can be described as 'cosmetic', and probably make little difference in practice, they do demonstrate a commitment to maintaining a difference in treatment. Having said that, it is difficult to say that personal safety takes second place to property rights in terms of occupation orders under the Family Law Act 1996. Where the marked difference lies is not so much in personal safety but in terms of property rights in general. Now that the European Convention on Human Rights applies to English and Welsh law through the Human Rights Act 1998 it may become more difficult to justify such distinctions and differences. More and more couples are choosing to live in unmarried relationships. There is likely to put greater pressure on the government to act to change the law to allow unmarried partners greater rights over property.

QUESTION THREE

Tom and Rose met six years ago. She was living with her sister Sarah in the house left to them by their parents when they died. Sarah had the daunting task of bringing up her three-year-old autistic daughter Dawn. Five years ago Tom moved into their house and within a year he and Rose had a child, Fred. A year later their relationship deteriorated when Sarah, who was very persuasive, and Tom, who was naturally compliant, started having a sexual relationship. By that time Tom and Rose were hardly talking to one another. Sarah had become very hostile towards Rose who became worried about the effect the situation was having on Fred, who seemed to be very easily affected by Sarah's behaviour. Three weeks ago Rose decided to move out of the house temporarily and live with her brother and his wife. Sarah and Tom then started a campaign to convince her brother that she was not fit to look after Fred. They telephoned and sent letters telling him about how she neglected Fred and they continue to do so.

Rose wants to move back into the house, but not while Tom and Sarah are living there. She wants 'an end to all the aggression and intimidation'. Tom and Sarah have told Rose's brother that they are setting up home together there and that they intend to have Fred living with them.

Can Rose's needs be met? What action might Tom and Sarah take? Would your advice to Rose be different if she and Tom had married four years ago?

University of London LLB Examination
(for External Students) Family Law June 1999 Q2

General Comment

The question focuses on remedies under the Family Law Act 1996 in relation to non-molestation and occupation orders. The issue of non-molestation appears straightforward, given that the parties are associated persons and can make application against each other. The issue for the court will be whether the respective behaviour of the parties amounts to molestation. The issues surrounding occupation orders are more complicated on these particular facts. First, it appears that Rose can make application against Tom and Sarah under s33 Family Law Act (FLA) 1996 (since she appears to be a joint owner of the property). Second, Sarah can apply to prevent Rose from returning again under s33 FLA 1996 (also being a joint owner). Tom can apply to prevent Rose from returning under s36 FLA 1996 (as a former cohabitant with no right to occupy the home). The question requires the student to demonstrate a knowledge of the factors affecting ss33 and 36, in particular the balance of harm test, and how it differs between the two sections. If Tom and Rose had been married Tom would have gained matrimonial home rights and any application made by him to exclude Rose would have been easier to make.

Skeleton Solution

Application for a non-molestation order under s42 FLA 1996: associated persons – meaning of non-molestation; application by Rose against Tom and Sarah for an occupation order under s33 FLA 1996/application by Sarah for an occupation order against Rose under s33 FLA 1996: respective housing needs and resources – respective financial resources – likely effect on health, safety or well-being of the parties and the children – the conduct of the parties in relation to each other – the balance of harm test and the obligation on the court; application by Tom against Rose for an occupation order under 36 FLA 1996: the same factors as for a s33 application – the nature and length of the parties relationship – the child of the relationship – the lapse of time since they ceased to live together – the balance of harm test; advice on ex parte orders, powers of arrest and undertakings.

Suggested Solution

Rose wants 'an end to all the aggression and intimidation'. She can be advised that she can make application against Tom and Sarah for a non-molestation order under s42 Family Law Act (FLA) 1996. She can make such an application provided she is 'associated' with Tom and Sarah. She is 'associated' with Tom since they are former cohabitants and have lived together in the same household. She is 'associated' with Sarah since they are relatives (namely siblings) and have lived together in the same household: see ss62–63 FLA 1996. A non-molestation order means an order prohibiting Tom and Sarah from molesting Rose or her child, Fred. Though the facts of the question are not entirely clear it is assumed that Fred is living with Rose in Rose's brother's and sister-in-law's house. Rose can be advised that 'molestation' has a wide meaning which includes pestering or harassing: see *Vaughan* v *Vaughan* [1973] 1 WLR 1159 and *C* v *C*

(Application for Non-molestation Order) [1998] 1 FLR 554. It can include unwelcome visits and annoying telephone calls: see *Horner* v *Horner* (1983) 4 FLR 50. Whether or not the court will grant a non-molestation order in favour of Rose depends on the nature of Tom and Sarah's campaign against Rose through her brother. This behaviour may amount to indirect molestation which may be sufficient for Rose to succeed in obtaining a non-molestation order. The effect on Fred would also be relevant to the court's considerations.

Her brother is 'associated' with Sarah (being her brother as well as brother to Rose) so he could bring an application for a non-molestation order against her if he is being pestered or harassed by the campaign. The brother is not 'associated' with Tom so could not make application against him. It may be advisable for Rose and her brother to make application at the same time since their applications would be mutually supportive and more likely to be successful.

Rose wishes to move back into the house but not while Tom and Sarah are living there. Rose can be advised that she can make application against Tom and Sarah for an occupation order under s33 FLA 1996. It is assumed that Rose has 'occupation rights', namely the right to occupy the house left to her and Sarah by her parents. She can apply for an occupation order against an 'associated person'. As has already been discussed Rose is 'associated' with Tom and Sarah. An occupation order could require Sarah and Tom to permit Rose to enter into and remain in the home, prohibit Sarah's and Tom's right of occupation of the home and require them to leave: see s33(3) FLA 1996. It is noted that Tom and Sarah may wish to take action themselves. In this respect Sarah could apply for an occupation order against Rose also under s33 FLA 1996 since she also is assumed to have occupation rights and is 'associated' with Rose. Advice will therefore cover both scenarios.

In deciding whether to grant an occupation order the court will have regard to particular factors: see s33(6) FLA 1996. First, the court will have regard to the parties' respective housing needs and resources. Further information is required in order to advise on this point. If Rose and Fred are living in unsatisfactory conditions with her brother and sister-in-law compared to Sarah, Tom and Dawn, then this will count in her favour. The ability of the parties to find alternative accommodation, eg council housing, will also be considered. Second, the court will look at the parties' respective financial resources. Again further information is required. If Rose has limited means compared to Tom, Sarah and Dawn then again this will count in her favour. If the financial balance is the other way round then this will count in Sarah and Tom's favour. Third, the court will look at the likely effect on the health, safety or well-being of the parties and the children if no occupation order was made. This will require the court, in particular, to compare the consequences on Fred if no occupation order is made and the consequences for Dawn if an occupation order is made. Both children are young. The fact that Dawn is autistic is likely to make Sarah and Tom's position stronger in this respect. The parties should be aware that the interests of the children are not paramount and the court will not make an occupation order simply because this is in the interests of either child. The court will then look at the conduct of the parties in relation to each other. Again more information is required. On the facts given it appears that Tom and Sarah have acted unreasonably so this is likely to weigh against them and in Rose's favour. Continuous campaigns of molestation, short of violence, have persuaded courts to grant occupation orders: see *Scott* v *Scott* [1992] 1 FLR 529 and *Brown* v *Brown* [1994] 1 FLR 223.

Finally, the court must balance the risk of significant harm: see s33(7) FLA 1996. If it appears to the court that Rose or Fred is likely to suffer significant harm, attributable to conduct by Sarah and Tom, if an occupation order is not made then the court must make the order unless it appears to the court that Sarah, Tom or Dawn are likely to suffer significant harm and that harm is as great as or greater than the harm likely to be suffered by Rose or Fred. Section 33(7) only comes into play if there is a risk of 'significant' harm: see *Chalmers* v *Johns* [1999] Fam Law 26. Again more information is required on the harm Fred has suffered or is likely to suffer if obliged to carry on living at Rose's brother and sister-in-law's house and the harm Dawn would suffer if forced to move. Dawn's autism may mean that the balance of harm is in favour of Sarah and Tom.

A s33 occupation order could last for a period specified by the court or until further order: see s33(10). Under previous law the courts limited the period of an occupation order, eg to three months: see *Practice Direction (Injunction: Domestic Violence)* [1978] 1 WLR 1123. The courts would then expect the parties to reach a long-term solution, eg by Rose and Sarah agreeing to sell the house and dividing the proceeds so that each could rehouse themselves or one party buying the other party's interest.

It would be possible for Tom, as a former cohabitant with Rose, to make application against her, as a former cohabitant with the right to occupy the home in which Tom and Sarah are now living, for an occupation order restricting Sarah's right of occupation of that home: see 36 FLA 1996. The court would apply the same factors as for a s33 application made by Rose against Sarah and Tom or by Sarah against Rose. The court would also consider the nature and length of Rose and Tom's relationship, Fred as the the child of the relationship and the lapse of time since they ceased to live together. The court would have regard to the fact that Tom and Rose have not given each other the commitment involved in marriage: see s41 FLA 1996. In relation to the balance of harm test the court would apply the same test but the court is not obliged to make an occupation order even if the balance of harm is in Tom and Sarah's favour: see s36(7) and (8). Any order would be limited in time to a maximum of six months, though could be renewed for a further six months: see s36(10). In the circumstances it would seem that Sarah would have a stronger claim in applying for a s33 occupation order as opposed to Tom applying for a s36 occupation order.

The parties should be aware that it is possible for application for a non-molestation order and/or an occupation order to be made ex parte (ie with informing the other side). The facts suggest that a court would be unlikely to allow an application to be made ex parte. Ex parte applications are normally only permitted where the circumstances are such that there is such a risk of significant harm that an order should be made immediately and the applicant would otherwise be deterred or prevented from making an application and the respondent(s) may try to avoid service: see s45(2) FLA 1996. None of these factors appear to be present. The court must also attach a power of arrest to a non-molestation or occupation order if actual violence has been used or threatened unless satisfied that the applicant and any child could be otherwise adequately protected: see s46(2) FL A 1996. Again the facts in the question do not suggest any violence or threat of violence so attaching a power of arrest appears unlikely. The parties should also be aware that any application could be settled by the respondent giving undertakings: see s46(1) and (4) FLA 1996. Any undertakings would have the force of a court order and could be a convenient way of settling any disputes without the necessity of a contested court hearing.

Finally, would the advice to Rose be different if she and Tom had married four years ago? The answer is yes in that Tom's position would be strengthened. He would have gained matrimonial home rights in the house in which he lived with Rose: see s30 FLA 1996. Matrimonial home rights are granted to a spouse with no right to occupy the matrimonial home where the other spouse is entitled to occupy the home. The matrimonial home rights include the right not to excluded from the home save with the leave of the court and a right to occupy the home even against the will of the other spouse (subject to any court order). Tom could get his matrimonial home rights registered as a charge or interest to further protect his rights: see s31 FLA 1996. In addition, if Tom has matrimonial home rights, he is able to apply for an occupation order under s33 FLA 1996 rather than s36 FLA 1996 which is likely to put him in a stronger position along with Sarah.

Chapter 8

Parental Disputes Concerning Children

8.1   Introduction

8.2   Key points

8.3   Key cases and statutes

8.4   Questions and suggested solutions

8.1 Introduction

Disputes between parents concerning their children are resolved through orders available under the Children Act (CA) 1989. The student needs to know the range of orders available under the CA 1989 and the principles to be applied by a court in determining whether to make an order.

8.2 Key points

Parental responsibility

What is parental responsibility?

'All the rights, duties powers, responsibilities and authority which by law a parent of a child has in relation to the child and his property': s3(1) CA 1989.

Parental wishes give way to the exercise of choice by the child according to that child's age, maturity and understanding. See *Hewer v Bryant* [1970] 1 QB 357, quoted with approval in *Gillick v West Norfolk and Wisbech Area Health Authority* [1985] 3 All ER 402 – 'parental rights to control a child do not exist for the benefit of the parent. They exist for the benefit of the child and they are justified only insofar as they enable the parent to perform his duties towards the child': per Lord Fraser of Tullybelton in *Gillick*.

Incidents of parental responsibility

a) Determining the child's surname

Where both parents have parental responsibility both must agree to a change in the child's surname or obtain a court order in the event of a dispute (see *Practice Direction (Child: Change of Surname)* [1995] 1 WLR 365 and *Re PC (Change of Surname)* [1997] 2 FLR 730. Similarly, where a residence order is in force no one can change the child's surname without the written consent of each person with parental responsibility or the leave of the court: see s13(1) CA 1989. Where the parents are unmarried and only the mother has parental responsibility the mother can unilaterally change the child's surname but the father can seek to prevent this by a prohibited steps or specific issues order: see *Dawson* v *Wearmouth* [1997] 2 FLR 629. and *Re W; Re A; Re B (Change of Name)* [1999] 2 FLR 390.

In deciding whether to allow a change of surname the child's welfare is paramount. Courts treat a change of surname as a serious matter, particularly in relation to the link it may provide with the father. The welfare checklist applies: see *Re C (A Minor) (Change of Surname)* [1998] 2 FLR 656.

b) Leaving the jurisdiction

Where a residence order is in force no one can remove the child from the jurisdiction without the written consent of every person who has parental responsibility or with the leave of the court: see s13(1) CA 1989. This does not prevent the child from being removed for a period of up to one month (eg for a foreign holiday).

The Court of Appeal laid down the general approach in *Re H (Application to Remove from Jurisdiction)* [1998] 1 FLR 848 which followed the decision in *Poel* v *Poel* [1970] 1 WLR 1469. The first question is whether the proposed move is a reasonable one from the point of view of the adults involved? Had it been properly thought out and planned? If the answer was 'yes' then leave should only be refused if it is clearly shown beyond any doubt that the interests of the child and the residential parent were incompatible. The court would not interfere with the reasonable decision of the residential parent. Otherwise the bitterness or disappointment of the applicant may harm the child. See also *Payne* v *Payne* [2001] Fam Law 346 which considered that the European Convention on Human Rights did not add to the factors to be considered.

c) Education of the child

Parents have a duty to ensure that their children aged between five and 16 receive a full time education: see s36 Education Act 1944. Failure to do so amounts to an offence.

d) Consent to marriage

The consent of the parents with parental responsibility is required to the marriage of child between the age of 16 and 18: see s3 Marriage Act 1949. The child can apply to a court for consent which replaces parental consent. If no consent has been given the marriage will not be void in any event.

e) Medical treatment

A child over the age of 16 may validly consent to medical treatment: see s8(3) Family Law Reform Act 1969. Under that age the parent may give consent on the child's behalf or the child may give consent him/herself provided the child is of sufficient maturity and understanding to make an informed decisionsee *Gillick* v *West Norfolk and Wisbech Area Health Authority* (above) – this gives rise to the phrase '*Gillick* competent' child.

The court retains the power to override the wishes of a child where a particular child lacks sufficient maturity and understanding to make an informed decision about his/her medical treatment, ie is not *Gillick* competent: see *Re R (A Minor) (Wardship: Medical Treatment)* [1991] 4 All ER 177.

The court retains the power to override the wishes of the child's parents where the court considers that the parents' decision is not in the child's best interests. See *Re E (A Minor) (Wardship: Medical Treatment)* [1993] 1 FLR 179 where a court overruled the wishes of 15-year-old boy and his parents in authorising a blood transfusion which was required to save his life.

Who has parental responsibility?

Where a child's parents are married to each other at the time of birth they each have parental responsibility: s2(1) CA 1989.

Where a child's parents are not married to each other at the time of birth the mother has sole parental responsibility for the child: s2(2)(a) CA 1989.

The unmarried father can only acquire parental responsibility through:

a) a parental responsibility agreement signed by him and the mother and witnessed (eg by a magistrate) (see s2(2)(b) and s4(1)(b) CA 1989 and Parental Responsibility Agreement Regulations 1991); or

b) an order from the court giving him parental responsibility: see s2(2)(b) and s4(1)(a) CA 1989.

A court in deciding whether to make a parental responsibility order must consider:

a) the degree of commitment shown by the father towards his child;

b) the degree of attachment between the father and his child; and

c) whether or not he is motivated by a concern for the welfare of the child in asking the court to make a parental responsibility application.

See *Re C (Minors)* [1992] 2 All ER 86 and *Re G (A Minor)(Parental Responsibility Order)* [1994] 1 FLR 504.

If an unmarried father is able to satisfy these three criteria then he is entitled to a parental responsibility order unless there are clear reasons not to do so. The fact that he has no contact with the child, or that the mother will not allow him to be involved in decisions affecting the child, are not reasons for not making the order. The order confers a status on the father which may be important in the future: see *Re P (A Minor) (Parental Responsibility Order)* [1994] 1 FLR 578 and *Re S (Parental Responsibility)* [1995] 2 FLR 648. A parental responsibility order does not entitle the father to interfere with the day-to-day management of the child's life but he should be involved in important decisions: see *Re P*.

For an example of a case in which an unmarried father, who had shown commitment to his daughter over the whole of her childhood, was attached to her and was motivated to want the legal status of parental responsibility, being refused parental responsibility see *Re M (Contact: Parental Responsibility)* [2001] 2 FLR 342. In the case relations between the father and the mother and her husband were very strained. The three factors of commitment, attachment and motivation were not the only factors. The predicted misuse of parental responsibility by the father would stress the mother and undermine her ability to care for the child (who was severely disabled).

In the consultation paper 'Procedures for the Determination of Paternity and the Law on Parental Responsibility for Unmarried Fathers' (Lord Chancellor's Department, 1998) a range of options were discussed:

a) all biological parents to have parental responsibility;

b) parental responsibility extended to unmarried fathers who:

    i)   registered the child jointly with the mother;

    ii) lived with the mother at the time of birth;

    iii) had a declaration of parentage in their favour;

    iv) paid child support;

    v)   some combination of the above.

The Adoption and Children Bill 2001, clause 91 (by amending s4 CA 1989) proposes that an unmarried father should gain parental responsibility if he registers the birth of the child jointly with the mother (or they both re-register the birth). Clause 92 proposes to extend parental responsibility to a married step-parent via agreement by the parent(s) with parental responsibility or by court order.

A person in whose favour a residence order is made shall acquire parental responsibility for the child: see s12(2) CA 1989.

A person with parental responsibility does not lose it because some one else acquires parental responsibility (eg a local authority acquiring parental responsibility when a care order is made), but shares it with that other person (though subject to not being able to act in a way incompatible with any court order): see s2(6) and (8) CA 1989.

A person without parental responsibility may do what is reasonable in all the circumstances to safeguard or promote the child's welfare: see s3(5) CA 1989.

Determining disputes concerning a child

Section 8 orders

There are four main types of order available to a court when deciding on a dispute between parents (or other persons) concerning a child: see s8 CA 1989. These are:

a) The residence order (determining with whom a child should reside).

b) The contact order (requiring the person with whom a child lives, or is to live, to allow the child to visit or stay with the person named in the order or for that person and the child to otherwise have contact with each other).

c) The prohibited steps order (whereby a specified act of a kind which could be taken by a parent in meeting his/her parental responsibility for a child shall not be taken by any person without the consent of the court).

d) The specific issues order (determining a specific question which has arisen or may arise in connection with any aspect of a parental responsibility for a child).

The court can make a shared residence order whereby the child lives with one parent for part of the time and with the other parent for the rest of the time. There is no need to show exceptional circumstances or that such an order would be of positive benefit to the child: see *Re D (Children) (Shared Residence Orders)* [2001] 1 FLR 495. It is sufficient that a shared residence order is in the child's best interests.

In deciding whether to make any of the above orders that court must take into account particular considerations:

a) The welfare of the child is paramount

In determining any question concerning the upbringing of a child, the child's welfare shall be the paramount consideration: see s1(1) CA 1989. This means that the child's welfare determines the course to be followed: see *J* v *C* [1969] 2 WLR 540.

b) Delay is assumed to be harmful to the child's welfare

The court must assume that any delay in making its decision is likely to harm the child's welfare: see s1(2) CA 1989. To this end the court will make directions as to the conduct of the case in order to avoid delay.

c) The no order principle

The court cannot make any order unless it is satisfied that making the order is better than making no order at all, ie the order will positively benefit the child: see s1(5) CA 1989.

d) The welfare checklist

If the making of a s8 order is opposed the court must consider a number of particular factors – these are known as the welfare checklist (see s1(3) and (4) CA 1989):

i) The ascertainable wishes and feelings of the child considered the light of his/her age and understanding: s1(3)(a).

ii) The child's physical, emotional and educational needs: s1(3)(b).

iii) The likely effect on the child on any change in his/her circumstances: s1(3)(c).

iv) The child's age, sex, background and other relevant characteristics: s1(3)(d).

v) Any harm the child has suffered or is at risk of suffering: s1(3)(e).

vi) How capable each of his parents and any other relevant person is of meeting the child's needs: s1(3)(f).

vii)The court's full range of powers: s1(3)(g).

Case law can assist in applying the checklist:

i) The views of children aged nine years or more tend to be regarded as important – the older the more important (see *M v M (A Minor: Custody Appeal)* [1987] 1 WLR 404).

ii) There is no longer any presumption that mothers should look after young children – each parent must be carefully assessed: see *Re S (A Minor)(Custody)* [1991] 2 FLR 388 and *Re A (A Minor)(Custody)* [1991] 2 FLR 394.

iii) There may be advantages in keeping siblings together since they can given themselves emotional support after a family has split up: see *C v C (Minors: Custody)* [1988] 2 FLR 291.

iv) The court recognises that stability is important in a child's life – if a child has been in the care of one parent for a long time the court may be slow the change the child's residence given the upset this may cause: see *Stephenson v Stephenson* [1985] FLR 1140.

v) The court also recognises the importance of a child being looked after continuously by one adult rather than a child being looked after in a fragmented way by a succession of adults: see *Re K (Minors) (Children: Care and Control)* [1977] 2 WLR 3.

vi) Though the court is not bound by the recommendation in the CAFCASS report (CAFCASS is the Children and Family Court Advisory and Support Service who provide 'welfare' reports to the courts), the court should give reasons if it is departing from that recommendation: see *Stephenson v Stephenson* (above).

In relation to contact orders the courts assume that the emotional needs of a child are best met by continued contact with both parents: see *Re H (Minors)(Access)* [1992] 1 FLR 148 and *Re M (Contact: Welfare Test)* [1995] 1 FLR 274. The court is likely to ask whether that fundamental emotional need is outweighed by any harm which may befall the child and taking into account the child's wishes and feelings.

Who can apply for a s8 order?

Applications can be made in the context of family proceedings or an application. A parent or guardian or person in whose favour a residence order has been made can apply for any s8 order.

A person who is a party to the marriage in respect of a child of the marriage who is a child of the family (ie a step-parent), or a person with whom the child has lived for at least three years, or a person with the consent of those with parental responsibility, can apply for a residence or contact order.

Other persons have to obtain the leave of the court to apply. An example would be grandparents applying for leave to apply for a residence or contact order. In deciding whether to grant leave under s10(9) CA 1989 the court must have particular regard to:

a) the nature of the proposed application;

b) the applicant's connection with the child;

c) any risk there might be of the proposed application disrupting the child's life to such an extent that he/she would be harmed by it; and

d) where the child is being looked after by a local authority, the authority's plans for the child's future and the wishes and feelings of the child's parents.

The welfare of the child is not paramount in deciding on leave: see *Re A (Minors)(Residence Orders: Leave to Apply)* [1992] 3 WLR 422. The prospect of success of the intended application is a relevant factor: see *G v Kirklees MBC* [1993] 1 FLR 805.

A child can apply for leave to make an application of a s8 order in his/her own right. The court must be satisfied that the child has sufficient understanding to make the application. The child's welfare is important but not paramount. The court has to be cautious and balance two considerations. Firstly, a child is an individual with wishes and feelings which should command serious attention. Secondly, a child may be vulnerable and impressionable, may lack maturity and be unable to weigh the long term against the short term. If a child was given party status he/she would be present when parents gave evidence and were cross-examined and may hear things it would be better for the child not to hear. The child could be cross-examined: see *Re C (Residence: Child's Application for Leave)* [1995] 1 FLR 927. An application by a child for leave to apply for a s8 order should be transferred to the High Court because of the difficult issues raised: see *Practice Direction* [1993] 1 All ER 820.

Resolving disputes over the paternity of a child

Questions involving disputes over a child can include disputes over the paternity or parentage of a child and the student must demonstrate a knowledge of how such disputes can be resolved.

Presumption of legitimacy

A child conceived by or born to a mother who is married at the time of the conception or birth is presumed at common law to be the child of the mother and her husband. This presumption applies even if the marriage is dissolved after the child has been conceived but before the child is born.

Rebutting the presumption of legitimacy

The presumption may be rebutted on a balance of probabilities (see s26 Family Law Reform Act 1969). However, the courts have considered the status of a child to be a grave matter and the standard of proof is more than a narrow balance of probabilities: see *W v K (Proof of Paternity)* [1988] 1 FLR 86; *Serio v Serio* [1983] 4 FLR 756.

Examples of how to rebut the presumption include:

a) The sterility of the husband: see *W v K* (above).

b) The absence of the husband at the time of conception – the court will apply the present-day standards of medical science in deciding the possible dates of conception, taking into account the nature of the pregnancy and when the child was born: see *Preston-Jones v Preston-Jones* [1951] 1 All ER 124.

c) Registration of the name of the father on the birth certificate under the Births and Deaths Registration Act 1953.

d) Scientific tests (see below).

Scientific tests

The court may direct that scientific tests be carried out to ascertain the parentage of the child: see s20 Family Law Reform Act 1969. In most cases the scientific tests will involve mouth swabs or blood samples which are then subject to DNA testing. The courts assume that DNA tests are virtually conclusive and so generally will determine whether a particular man is the father of a child.

Scientific tests are directed. There is no power to order a person to provide a scientific sample. A person (and in the case of a child aged under 16, the child's parent) has to consent to a scientific sample being taken: see s21(1) and (3) FLRA 1969. If a person fails to take any steps required of him/her to comply with a scientific test direction then the court may draw such inferences from that failure as appear proper in the circumstances: see s23(1) FLRA 1969. In the case of DNA tests a failure by a putative father to comply is likely to lead to the inference that he is the father because any man unsure of paternity could put his doubts at rest by submitting to a test: see *Re A (A Minor) (Paternity: Refusal of Blood Test)* [1994] 2 FLR 463. In the case of a parent with the care of the child the court can direct that a scientific sample can be taken from the child even if the parent refuses to give consent.

Where there is a dispute as to whether there should be scientific tests the general view is that the child's welfare requires that the truth as to the child's parentage be clarified. If scientific tests can resolve any reasonable doubt the courts will direct that they be carried out. A child has the right to know the truth unless his/her welfare clearly justifies the truth being covered up. A child should grow up knowing that he/she may have two fathers – one, his psychological father who lived with him and his mother, and the second, his biologicial father – rather than having a time-bomb ticking away: see *Re H (A Minor) (Blood Tests: Parental Rights)* [1996] 3 WLR 506. In *Re T (Paternity: Ordering Blood Tests)* [2001] Fam Law 738 the European Convention on Human Rights was considered. In balancing the various rights of the child and of the adult parties under art 8 of the European Convention the child's interests in having the possibility of knowing, perhaps with certainty, his true roots and identity carried the most weight. Any interference with the parents' right to a private and family life was proportionate to the legitimate aim of providing such knowledge to the child.

For a case in which a party successfully persuaded a court not to order scientific tests: see *O v L (Blood Tests)* [1995] 2 FLR 930. A child was born to married parents who separated when the child was aged three years. The husband applied for contact. The wife claimed that the child's father was another man. The court refused to direct scientific tests since the child and her father had a good relationship. Tests might jeopardise the contact with the man whose status as her father had not been questioned until the marriage broke down. The court should take into account the prospects of success in any proceedings brought by a person saying he is the parent of the child. Any gain to the child from knowing who his/her parent is may be outweighed by the disturbance to the child's security.

8.3 Key cases and statutes

- *Re C (Minors)* [1992] 2 All ER 86
  When to make a parental responsibility order

- *Re D (Children) (Shared Residence Orders)* [2001] 1 FLR 495
  Shared residence orders

- *Dawson v Wearmouth* [1997] 2 FLR 629
  Changing a child's name

- *Gillick v West Norfolk and Wisbech Area Health Authority* [1985] 3 All ER 402
  Extent of parental rights over children

- *Re M (Contact: Welfare Test)* [1995] 1 FLR 274
  When to make a contact order

- *Payne v Payne* [2001] Fam Law 346
  Removing a child from the jurisdiction

- *Re T (Paternity: Ordering Blood Tests)* [2001] Fam Law 738
  Ordering scientific tests to establish parentage

- Children Act 1989 – parental responsibility and children's rights
- Family Law Reform Act 1969 – establishing a child's parentage

8.4 Questions and suggested solutions

QUESTION ONE

Ursula and Vernon began living together in 1985. In 1987, they had a son, William. In December 1993 after fertility treatment at a clinic licensed under the Human Fertilisation and Embryology Act 1990, Ursula gave birth to a girl, Xanthe, who [was] registered as Vernon's child.

In December 1994, Ursula left Vernon, taking the children with her and went to live with Zack, a 20-year-old musician with whom she has been having an affair since January 1993. Ursula has refused to allow Vernon to see the children. She has told him that Xanthe is Zack's child and, although she will never allow Xanthe to be tested for the purposes of establishing her paternity, she will swear that Zack is her father in any legal proceedings. Ursula has also told Vernon that she intends to change the children's surname to that of Zack and to start a new life with him where Vernon will be unable to find them.

Advise Vernon.

University of London LLB Examination
(for External Students) Family Law June 1995 Q6

General Comment

The question deals with the status of children. The student is required to display knowledge of the legal status of an unmarried father in relation first to a child born naturally, and second to a child born after artificial insemination within an unmarried relationship. The student also has to show how an unmarried father can acquire legal rights over such children, and how a court can resolve a dispute over the parentage of a child. Finally, the legal position relating to a child's surname needs to be outlined together with advice on how a dispute over contact with the children can be resolved.

Skeleton Solution

Status of William: child of unmarried parents; father lacks parental responsibility (s2(2) Children Act 1989); application for parental responsibility (s4(1)(a) CA 1989) – status of Xanthe: licensed fertility treatment to Ursula while she was living with Vernon; Vernon is the legal father by s28(3) Human Fertilisation and Embryology Act 1990 (HFEA 1990) – dispute as to parentage of Xanthe: power to direct blood tests (s29 Family Law Reform Act 1969); consequences of failure to comply with blood test direction (s23 FLRA 1969) – application for contact with children and principles to be applied (ss1, 8 and 10 CA 1989) – change of surname and move away – prohibited steps and specific issues order (ss1, 8 and 10 CA 1989) – case law on change of surname.

Suggested Solution

Vernon asks for advice in relation to his two children, William and Xanthe. The question suggests that he wishes to have contact with them, that he would like to confirm his status as their father and that he would wish to prevent Ursula changing the children's surname and taking them away from him in order to start a new life with Zack.

Ursula and Vernon lived together from 1985 to December 1994, namely for nine years. They did not marry. William was born in 1987 and lived with Ursula and Vernon for seven years until he left with his mother to live with Zack. Xanthe was born in December 1993 so only lived with Ursula and Vernon for a year before she left with her mother and brother to live with Zack. Vernon should first be advised about his legal status in relation to William. There appears to be no dispute that Vernon is his father. However Vernon, as an unmarried father, does not have parental responsibility for him: s2(2)(a) Children Act 1989 – hereinafter referred to as the CA 1989. Parental responsibility is entirely vested in Ursula. Parental responsibility means all the rights, duties, powers, responsibilities and authority which by law a parent of a child has in relation to that child and his or her property: see s3(1) CA 1989. It would include the right to be consulted on major decisions concerning William (eg, about his health or his schooling) though it would not give Vernon the right to interfere in day-to-day decisions: see *Re P (A Minor) (Parental Responsibility Order)* [1994] 1 FLR 578. Vernon should take action to acquire parental responsibility by way of an application to the court for a parental responsibility order: see s4(1)(a) CA 1989. It is possible for him to sign a parental responsibility agreement with Ursula, giving him parental responsibility, but given her present stance this does not appear to be a viable option: see s4(1)(b) CA 1989. In order to succeed in an application for parental responsibility he must satisfy the court of various matters. He must demonstrate to the court that he has shown commitment to William and that he has a good relationship with him. He must also show that his application is motivated by a concern for William's welfare and to be involved in his life (and is not motivated by malice against Ursula and with a wish to use William to interfere with her life): see *Re C (Minors)* [1992] 2 All ER 86. Given the fact that William lived with Vernon for some seven years, this appears to demonstrate that Vernon is committed to William's welfare, that they have a relationship and that he does wish to be involved in important decisions in relation to William's life. Vernon appears to have a strong case should he apply for parental responsibility.

In relation to Xanthe, she appears to have been conceived as a result of fertility treatment at a clinic licensed under the Human Fertilisation and Embryology Act 1990 (hereinafter referred to as the HFEA 1990). It is assumed that this was with Vernon's consent and support since Vernon was registered as Xanthe's father. If Vernon's sperm was used in the treatment he will be treated as the biological and legal father. If his sperm was not used, but the treatment can be said to have been provided for Ursula and Vernon together, then Vernon is treated as being the legal father of Xanthe: see s28(3) HFEA 1990. No other man can then be treated as Xanthe's father: see s28(4) HFEA 1990. In particular, if Ursula was inseminated by sperm from an anonymous donor then that donor is specifically excluded from being Xanthe's father: see s28(6) HFEA 1990. Vernon would have the status of an unmarried father in relation to Xanthe so all the comments in relation to parental responsibility for William and how it can be acquired apply equally to her as they do to William. Vernon appears to have a weaker case if he applies to the court for parental responsibility in relation to Xanthe since she only lived with him and Ursula for a year before Ursula left with her. However, he may still be able to demonstrate sufficient commitment and a sufficient relationship to be successful in such an application.

Ursula now states that Xanthe was conceived as a result of an affair with Zack which started in January 1993. As has been outlined above, Vernon appears to have the legal status of father in relation to Xanthe. If he applies for a parental responsibility order (and for contact and a prohibited steps order) in relation to his two children no doubt she will challenge his status in relation to Xanthe. The court may then be called upon to make a declaration as to Xanthe's parentage before proceeding with the applications. Whether the court will give any credence to Ursula's claim will depend on the circumstances. If she and Vernon received fertility treatment as a result of problems with her ability to conceive a child then any claim that these difficulties suddenly ceased when she started her affair with Zack may lack any credibility. If the treatment was provided as a result of Vernon being unable to provide suitable sperm then her claim may have more validity. More information is required on the nature of Vernon's and Ursula's problems in conceiving a child and in relation to the treatment they received. The fact that she presumably agreed to register Vernon as Xanthe's father will weaken her claim. If the court does give credence to Ursula's claim it may direct of its own motion (or at Vernon's request) that blood tests be carried out to establish Xanthe's paternity: see s20 Family Law Reform Act 1969 – hereinafter referred to as the FLRA 1969. The court is likely to direct that DNA tests be carried out since these conclusively establish paternity. Blood samples would be required from Xanthe (with her mother's consent), from Ursula, from Vernon (unless it is accepted that he cannot be the biological father because of the nature of the fertility treatment) and from Zack. The DNA from these samples would analysed to show conclusively whether Zack is or is not the father of Xanthe (and if appropriate to show that Vernon is Xanthe's biological father). The taking of blood samples is voluntary so Ursula could refuse to allow samples to be taken from her and from Xanthe. However, the court could then draw such inferences from that refusal as appear proper in the circumstances: see s23(1) FLRA 1969. Such an inference could be that Ursula knows that Zack is not Xanthe's biological father and is afraid that the truth will be revealed by the tests: see *McVeigh v Beattie* [1988] 2 All ER 500 and *Re A (A Minor) (Paternity: Refusal of Blood Test)* [1994] 2 FLR 463. The courts have held that it is in the child's best interests for the truth of his/her parentage to be established, so Ursula is unlikely to be able to persuade a court that there is good reason for her failure to comply with any blood test direction.

As the children's father (with or without parental responsibility) Vernon can apply to the court for a contact order, namely an order requiring Ursula to allow the children to visit or stay with him or for Vernon and the children to otherwise have contact with each other: see ss8(1) and s10 CA 1989. He can also apply for a prohibited steps order prohibiting the children from being known by a different surname and prohibiting Ursula from moving without notifying Vernon, so that he knows where the children are: see ss8(1) and 10 CA 1989. He can make these applications at the same time as any applications for parental responsibility. In deciding whether to grant the applications the court will treat the welfare of William and Xanthe as paramount: see s1(1) CA 1989. This means that their welfare will determine the decision to be made, as opposed to what either parent may consider fair or just: see *J v C* [1969] 1 All ER 788. The court will also assume that any delay in deciding on the issues affecting the children is likely to prejudice their welfare. As a result, the court is likely to lay down a timetable for hearing the applications before it and ensure that the parties stick to the timetable: see ss1(2) and 11 CA 1989. The court can also not make any order relating to the children unless it is satisfied that making that order would be better for the children than making no order at all: see s1(5) CA 1989. Vernon must show that any orders he seeks will positively benefit the children.

In relation to the applications for contact or prohibited steps, assuming that Ursula opposes them, the court will have regard to particular considerations: see s1(3),(4) CA 1989. The court will consider the ascertainable wishes and feelings of each child considered in the light of his or her age and understanding: see s1(3)(a) CA 1989. Xanthe is too young to express her wishes and feelings. William is aged seven or eight years and may well be old and mature enough to make his views clear. Though he is too young for his views to be decisive with the court, they are likely to carry great weight. If he wishes to keep in touch with his father and wishes to retain his surname then this will greatly strengthen Vernon's case. The court is likely to order that a welfare report be prepared by a welfare officer so that he or she can independently ascertain William's views rather than rely on whatever Ursula or Vernon say William's wishes and feelings are. The court will consider the children's physical, emotional and educational needs: see s1(3)(b) CA 1989. This will include each child's emotional need to know their father. The court will also consider the likely effect on each child of a change in his or her circumstances: see s1(3)(c) CA 1989. The court may ask whether Ursula's planned change of surname and breaking off of contact between the children and their father is likely to harm them. The court will also consider the age, sex, background and characteristics of the children aswell as any harm they have suffered or are at risk of suffering (eg by a loss of contact with their father and/or a change of surname): see s1(3)(d) and (e) CA 1989. The court will also consider how capable Vernon and Ursula (and, if appropriate, Zack) are of meeting the children's needs as well as its full range of powers: see s1(3)(f) and (g) CA 1989.

In relation to Vernon's application for contact, it has been stated that no court should deprive a child of contact with either parent unless it is wholly satisfied that it is in the child's interests that there should be no contact. This is a conclusion which courts are generally extremely slow to arrive at. The courts have recognised the long-term advantages of a child keeping in touch with the absent parent after a family breakdown. To deprive a child of contact with such a parent may deprive the child of an important contribution to his/her emotional welfare: see *Re H (Minors) (Access)* [1992] 1 FLR 148 and *Re M (Contact: Welfare Test)* [1995] 1 FLR 274. Unless Ursula can demonstrate that the children will be harmed by contact with Vernon, he is likely to have a strong case for the making of a contact order and for a prohibited steps order preventing Ursula from moving without telling him.

In relation to the children's surname, Vernon should be advised that the existing case law is not always consistent and was mostly decided before the Children Act 1989 came into force. However, the weight of the authorities suggest that if Vernon has played and will continue to play an important part in the lives of the children then the court will not permit a change in surname: see *L* v *F* (1978) The Times 1 August, *W* v *A* [1981] 1 All ER 100 and *Re F* [1994] Fam Law 12. The use of Vernon's surname will preserve the link with him. This may outweigh any embarrassment which may be caused should Ursula and Zack marry or otherwise by Ursula taking a different surname.

QUESTION TWO

Linda and Matt have lived together for 16 years but they never married. They have two children: Nat who is 15 and Olivia who is 14.

Nat has been unhappy at home for two years because he thinks his parents are too strict with him (Linda believes in corporal punishment but Matt does not). Nat has read that children can 'divorce' their parents and wishes to know how he can divorce Linda and Matt. He wants to live with his 15-year-old girlfriend Kate and her parents, who have agreed that he can share Kate's self-contained apartment built on to their house. Nat knows that his parents will object.

Olivia has recently become pregnant. She wishes to have an abortion but Matt, who is an active member of a pro-life movement, refuses to allow an abortion. Linda thinks that Olivia should decide.

Advise Nat and Olivia.

University of London LLB Examination
(for External Students) Family Law June 1997 Q6

General Comment

This question approaches private law applications under the Children Act 1989 from the interesting perspective of children seeking orders. First, the considerations involved in a child applying for a residence order need to be outlined, and second the difficult area of the medical treatment of a child against the wishes of a parent needs to be discussed.

Skeleton Solution

A child applying for a residence order: s8 CA 1989; requirement of leave; s10 CA 1989; likely approach of the High Court – application by third parent for a residence order on behalf of a child: requirement of leave; s10 CA 1989 – no order principle, delay principle and application of welfare checklist, in particular: wishes and feelings of child; likely effect on child of a change in his circumstances; any harm the child has suffered or is at risk of suffering; the capabilities of the child's parents and of his girlfriend's parents – the medical treatment of a child – child's capacity to consent to medical treatment – *Gillick* competency – the extent of the parental veto – application for a specific issue order/prohibited steps order – no order principle, delay principle and application of welfare checklist.

Suggested Solution

Nat requires advice on his wish to 'divorce' his parents, Linda and Matt, and his wish to live with his girlfriend and her parents. Olivia requires advice on whether she can have an abortion.

Nat's situation will be dealt with firstly. He should be advised that it is not accurate to say that he can 'divorce' his parents. More accurately he can apply to the court for an order allowing him to live apart from his parents, namely he seek to apply for a residence order under s8 Children Act (CA) 1989. Nat should be advised that he cannot apply for a residence order as of right. He must obtain the leave of the court: see s10(1)(a)(ii) CA 1989. The court may only grant Nat leave to make such an application if it is satisfied that he has sufficient understanding to make an application for a residence order: see s10(8) CA 1989. The court will have to make an assessment of Nat's maturity and degree of understanding. For these purposes Nat should be advised that his welfare is not paramount (as it is if the application proceeds to a full hearing). If it considers that Nat is not sufficiently mature and lacks an appropriate degree of understanding of the application and its consequences the court will refuse leave. If it is so satisfied it has a discretion whether or not to grant leave. It will balance the need to give Nat's wishes serious attention against any harm which may befall him should his application be contested. For example, he could have to listen to his parents opposing his application and he could be cross-examined on their behalf: see *Re C (Residence: Child's Application for Leave)* [1995] 1 FLR 927. As a result of the difficult issues in such an application he would have to apply to the High Court: see *Practice Direction* [1993] 1 All ER 820.

Alternatively he could ask Kate's parents to ask for leave to apply for a residence order on his behalf. They could only apply for an order as of right with the consent of each person who has parental responsibility for Nat: see s10(5)(c)(iii) CA 1989. Linda appears to have sole parental responsibility for Nat: see s4(2)(a) CA 1989. Matt, as an unmarried father, will not have parental responsibility for Nat unless he has made a parental responsibility agreement with Linda or has obtained a parental responsibility order from the court: see s4(1) CA 1989. It is assumed that in any event Linda would not consent to Kate's parents applying for a residence order. They could also apply as of right if Nat had been living with them for three years: see s10(5)(b) CA 1989. This does not appear to be the case. As a result Kate's parents would have to obtain the court's leave to make the application. In deciding whether to grant them leave to make the application the court would consider the nature of the proposed application, their connection with Nat and any risk there might be that the proposed application would disrupt Nat's life to such an extent that he would be harmed by it: see s10(9) CA 1989. Again Nat's welfare would not be the paramount consideration: see *Re A and Others (Minors) (Residence Order)* [1992] 3 WLR 422.

The court could consider the question of leave ex parte (ie without informing Nat's parents), but is more likely to direct that they have the opportunity to make representations as to whether leave should be granted.

Assuming that leave was granted to either Nat or to Kate's parents to apply for a residence order on his behalf then the court would consider the circumstances of his application. Nat's welfare would be the paramount consideration: see s1(1) CA 1989. The court would also endeavour to determine the application without delay since it has to assume that any delay is likely to prejudice Nat's welfare: see s1(2) CA 1989. To this end it is likely to lay down a timetable which the parties must comply with in order to prepare for the hearing. It will not make any order unless it considers that doing so would be better for Nat than making no order at all: see s1(5) CA 1989. In other words it must be satisfied that any order it makes would have some positive benefit for him. If the application is contested, as seems likely, the court must have regard to particular matters: see s1(3),(4) CA 1989. It will consider Nat's wishes and feelings considered in the light of his age and understanding: see s1(3)(a) CA 1989. Since Nat is aged 15 his wishes and feelings are likely to carry considerable weight. Nat should be advised that once he reaches the age of 16 the court would not normally be allowed to make any order since a child of that age can 'vote with his feet': see s9(7) CA 1989. Indeed if the court does make an order then that order cannot extend beyond his 16th birthday, unless there are exceptional circumstances: see s9(6) CA 1989. The court will consider Nat's physical, emotional and educational needs and the likely affect on him of any change in his circumstances: see s1(3)(b) and (c) CA 1989. The court will have to assess how any move to live with Kate and her parents would affect him. The court will consider his age, sex, background and any relevant characteristics: see s1(3)(d) CA 1989. The court will also consider any harm which he has suffered or is at risk of suffering and the capabilities of his parents and of Kate's parents in meeting his needs: see s1(3)(e) and (f) CA 1989. These two considerations are likely to crucial to Nat's case. If the court finds that his parents have harmed his welfare and have demonstrated that they are not capable of meeting his needs, while Kate's parents can meet his needs, then his application is likely to be a strong one. However, if the court finds that his parents are capable and have not harmed Nat or are unlikely to do so then it may decide that his wishes to live with Kate and her parents lack sufficient substance. At present English law allows parents to reasonably chastise their children. Without more specific information about how strict Nat's parents are it is difficult to advise in more detail.

One difficulty is that both Nat and his girlfriend are 15 years of age, below the age of consent for sexual intercourse. If they have sexual intercourse then Nat may fall foul of the criminal law: see s6 Sexual Offences Act 1956. Though prosecutions in these circumstances are rare the court may not feel able to sanction a situation in which Nat shares Kate's self-contained apartment. However, even if Nat's case is not a strong one, whether on this ground or another, once he reaches the age of 16 he can 'vote with his feet'. As already outlined the court is unlikely to grant any application by his parents to prevent him living where he wishes.

Olivia wishes to be advised on whether she can have an abortion given Matt's refusal to consent to this. As already outlined Matt, as an unmarried father, does not have parental responsibility for Olivia. This may limit his ability to prevent Olivia from having an abortion. If Linda has sole parental responsibility for Olivia then she can consent to the abortion. It is also possible for Olivia to determine her own treatment. Generally once a child reaches the age of 16 she can effectively consent to medical treatment without parental consent: see s8 Family Law Reform Act 1969. Where a child is under 16 the question of whether a child's consent would be effective to protect a doctor against legal action for infringement of parental rights will depend on the child's maturity and understanding and the nature of the treatment: see *Gillick* v *West Norfolk and Wisbech Area Health Authority* [1985] 3 All ER 402. If the court determines that Olivia has the maturity and understanding to make an informed decision about having an abortion then it could allow the operation without parental consent. The objection of Matt could be considered but would not prevent an abortion which the court considered was in her best interests: see *Re P (A Minor)* [1986] 1 FLR 272.

As Olivia's father Matt could apply for a prohibited steps order to prevent the abortion even though he lacks parental responsibility: see ss8 and 10(4) CA 1989. If he did make such an application and it was opposed by Linda and Olivia then the court would apply similar considerations as with the residence application concerning Nat. Olivia's welfare would be paramount. Her wishes and feelings would be likely to carry considerable weight because of her age, assuming she is mature and understanding. Any likely harm to her of having a baby she does not want would be considered. Having a baby against her will may in particular harm her education and other aspects of her development. In all these circumstances it is likely that any application by Matt for a prohibited steps order is unlikely to succeed.

Matt could endeavour to obtain parental responsibility, either by agreement with Linda or by court order. If he applies for a court order under s4(1)(a) CA 1989 the court is likely to grant his application since he is likely to have shown commitment towards his children, have a relationship with them and be motivated in their interests: see *Re P (A Minor)(Parental Responsibility Order)* [1994] 1 FLR 578. However, even with this status if Linda gives her consent and/or Olivia is *Gillick* competent then the abortion can take place without his consent. Where more than one parent has parental responsibility for a child each of them may act alone in meeting that responsibility: see s2(7) CA 1989. This further strengthens the case for Olivia.

QUESTION THREE

Jennifer and Tom, who have never married, have two children, Ian and Harriet, now aged 13 and 11. Ian dislikes school and claims that he is being bullied and wants to attend a school some miles away. Harriet has decided that she is quite old enough to have her tongue and nose pierced. In 1999, Jennifer met and fell in love with Winston who has told her that he would like her and the children to come and live with him and ultimately to emigrate to South Africa.

Advise Jennifer, Tom, Ian and Harriet as to their respective legal rights in relation to choice of school and cosmetic treatment and the long-term residence of the children.

University of London LLB Examination
(for External Students) Family Law June 2000 Q5

General Comment

This question focused on the rights of unmarried parents in relation to their two children. It focuses on four aspects of parental responsibility: education, medical treatment, residence and removal of children from the jurisdiction. The latter area will also include the right of the children to contact with their father. The student needs to demonstrate a sound knowledge of the relevant parts of the Children Act 1989 and the applicable case law. In particular, the welfare checklist requires discussion. This includes taking into account the wishes and feelings of children of an age whereby their wishes and feelings could be an important factor in the court's considerations. There is also the possibility of the children applying to the court for leave to make their own applications to the court.

Skeleton Solution

Rights of married mother – sole parental responsibility; rights of unmarried father – how he can apply for a parental responsibility order; application for specific issue order or prohibited steps order concerning: education – medical treatment; applying the welfare checklist, the delay principle and the no order principle; law on consent for medical treatment from parent and/or child – the concept of *Gillick* competence; application for a residence order and orders relating to removal of children from the residence order; applying the welfare checklist, the delay principle and the no order principle; application by children direct to the court for leave to make application for s8 orders.

Suggested Solution

Jennifer, Tom, Ian and Harriet ask for advice on their respective legal rights in relation to the choice of school for Ian, the cosmetic treatment for Harriet and the long-term residence for the children and their possible removal to South Africa by Jennifer and Winston.

Firstly Jennifer and Tom are unmarried parents. Jennifer as the unmarried mother has sole parental responsibility for Ian and Harriet: see s2(2)(a) Children Act (CA) 1989. She therefore has the sole right to determine the children's future, subject to the intervention of the court. Tom as an unmarried father has no parental responsibility for the children unless he acquires it by agreement with Jennifer or by court order: see ss2(2)(b) and 4 CA 1989. If Jennifer will not enter into a parental responsibility agreement with Tom (pursuant to s4(1)(b) CA 1989), Tom is advised to apply to the court for a parental responsibility order in order to give him equal status with Jennifer in terms of being involved in determining the children's future. Tom can be advised that he must show to the court that he has a relationship with his children, is committed to them and is motivated out of a concern for their welfare (as opposed to, for example, trying to harass Jennifer through the children): see *Re C (Minors)* [1992] 2 All ER 86. On the brief facts given he appears to have been involved in bringing up the children for virtually all of their lives. This is likely to persuade a court that he has shown the required commitment and has the required relationship with his children whereby he should be granted a parental responsibility order.

In relation to the choice of school and the tongue and nose piercing either Jennifer or Tom (whether or not he has parental responsibility) can apply to the court for a specific issues order or prohibited steps order to resolve any dispute between each other or with the children: see ss8 and 10(4) CA 1989. They are encouraged to try to reach agreement rather than resort to court proceedings. The court will not make an order unless that order will be of positive benefit to the child – otherwise it must make no order: see s1(5) CA 1989. If agreement cannot be reached and the matter cannot otherwise be resolved, then the no order principle is unlikely to apply and application can be made by either parent to the court for a s8 order. In determining an application for a s8 order the court will have treat the welfare of each child as paramount: see s1(1) CA 1989. This means that the court will make the decision which is in the best interests of each child and that the views of the parents or individual child may not be followed if they are inconsistent with the child's welfare. The court will also assume that any delay in determining any question is likely to be harmful to each child: see s1(2) CA 1989. Assuming that any application is opposed the court will have particular regard to a number of matters, called the welfare checklist: see s1(3) and (4) CA 1989. The court will have regard to the ascertainable wishes and feelings of each child having regard to their age and understanding: see s1(3)(a) CA 1989. The children are old enough for their views to carry weight with the court. The degree of weight will depend on each child's maturity and understanding of the issues involved. For example, if Harriet is found by the court to be immature and lacking in understanding of the consequences of tongue and nose piercing then her views will carry limited weight. Alternatively, if Ian has a mature and well considered objection to his present school his views will be of considerable importance. The court will consider each child's physical, educational and emotional needs: see s1(3)(b) CA 1989. Harriet's physical safety and emotional well-being will be considered as will Ian's educational needs and, if he is being bullied, his physical and emotional well-being. The court will consider the likely effect on each child of a change in his/her circumstances: see s1(3)(c) CA 1989. For example, a change in Ian's schooling may be of benefit to him. Alternatively, it may be damaging to his education if the disruption of the move is not outweighed by the benefits of moving schools. The court will consider the consequences for Harriet of the piercing. The court will consider each child's age, sex, background and any relevant characteristics: see s1(3)(d) CA 1989. It will consider any harm each child is suffering or is likely to suffer: see s1(3)(e) CA 1989. This will require the court to assess, in Ian's case, any harm he has suffered as a result of his present schooling and, in Harriet's case, any harm she is likely to suffer as a result of the piercing. The court will also consider how capable Jennifer and Tom are of meeting each child's needs and, if Jennifer wishes to care for the children with Winston, how capable he is of meeting each child needs: see s1(3)(f) CA 1989. Finally, the court will consider its full range of powers: see s1(3)(g) CA 1989.

Turning now to the specific matters in dispute, in relation to Ian's schooling, the court will assess the actual harm Ian is suffering or is likely to suffer at his present school. Since he is aged 11 he may only have just moved to a new school and may not have had sufficient time to settle in. If the court finds that he has not suffered any real harm, that his dislike of the school is not well founded and that a move of school is likely to do more harm than good it is likely to overrule his wishes and feelings and may make an order whereby he stays at his present school. If the court finds that he has suffered real harm, that his dislike of the school is well founded and that a move of school will improve his education then it is likely to follow his wishes and feelings and make an order moving his schooling (provided the new school agrees to take him): see for example *Re P (A Minor) (Education)* [1992] 1 FLR 316.

In relation to Harriet's wish to have her tongue and nose pierced it is not clear whether this amounts to 'medical treatment', an area the court is used to dealing with in terms of disputes. Body piercing is not normally included in the term 'medical treatment'. However, Harriet can be advised that any piercing of her body would amount to an assault on her without the appropriate consent. Generally speaking, since she is aged 13 years, a parent with parental responsibility must consent to the piercing before it can be lawfully given. It may be possible for the court to allow Harriet to give her own consent if she is deemed *Gillick* competent: see *Gillick v West Norfolk and Wisbech Area Health Authority* [1985] 3 All ER 402. The courts have ruled that parental control of a child exists for the benefit of the child. In most instances the parents are the best persons to control any treatment their child receives. However, in certain circumstances a child of sufficient age and understanding as to the issues involved could give a valid consent to such treatment. In this case the court is unlikely to find that Harriet is *Gillick* competent on the issue of piercing. She is young. The 'treatment' appears to be for fashionable, cosmetic purposes. The consequences of piercing her nose and tongue include the risk to health of the piercing and the risk of having jewellery in her mouth and nose. It is not clear how her peers or other adults would react. The chances of the court holding that Harriet's wish is less than mature and without full understanding of the consequences seem quite high. In these circumstances the court is likely to hold that Jennifer, as the mother with parental responsibility, must consent to the piercing to make it lawful. Tom, if opposing the piercing, could apply for a prohibited steps order to stop it (as could Jennifer if she is such a view but cannot otherwise prevent Harriet from getting the piercing done). The court would then apply the welfare checklist. If Harriet's wish is found to be immature and the piercing carries with it a significant risk to her well-being then the court is likely to overrule her wishes and feelings and prevent the piercing. If Harriet's wish is well thought out, will enhance her well-being and carries no risks the court could allow the piercing to be carried out. Jennifer, Tom and Harriet should be aware that the court retains the power to override all of them if it considers that is in the best interests of the child.

In relation to the possible move to South Africa, if a residence order is in force with respect to the children, then they cannot be removed from the United Kingdom without either the written consent of each person with parental responsibility or the leave of the court (see s13(1) CA 1989) – unless the children are being taken abroad for less than a month. If there is no residence order in force then Tom would have to apply for a prohibited steps order to prevent the children's removal. In considering whether to grant leave or to make such an order the welfare of each child is paramount. This will include the importance of maintaining a link with Tom which may be lost if they live abroad. The court will place great importance on any realistic and well thought out plans of Jennifer and would be reluctant to frustrate those plans unless they were clearly not in the children's best interests: see *Re H (Application to Remove from Jurisdiction)* [1998] 1 FLR 848. Again the court would apply the welfare checklist. The key issue is likely to be the relationship between the children and Tom. If they have a good relationship which they will lose if they go to live in South Africa it is unlikely that the court would allow them to leave. If they can go to South Africa but maintain a relationship with Tom then the court may allow them to leave, subject to undertakings or orders that they return to the United Kingdom to see him. Article 8 of the European Convention of Human Rights (the right to family life) is now an important factor in English and Welsh law via the Human Rights Act 1998. Article 8 serves to emphasise the court balancing the competing rights to family life and making a reasoned judgment: see *Re A (Permission to Remove Child from Jurisdiction: Human Rights)* [2000] 2 FLR 225.

In relation to the long-term welfare of the children either parent may apply for residence orders to settle with whom the children should live. Again the court would apply the welfare checklist. There is insufficient information to advise on the prospects of success for either party. It would depend on, for example, the wishes and feelings of the children and the capabilities of both parents (and Winston). If Tom was not successful in getting a residence order he could apply for a contact order whereby he visits the children or vice versa and/or they come and stay with him. Tom can be advised that contact is the right of each child. The court will ask whether the fundamental emotional need of each child to have an enduring relationship with both parents (s1(3)(b) of the welfare checklist) is outweighed by any harm which would be caused by contact (s1(3)(e) of the checklist) taking account of each child's wishes and feelings: see *Re M (Contact: Welfare Test)* [1995] 1 FLR 274. In the absence of any evidence of the children being harmed by their continued relationship with Tom it is likely that he would have a strong chance of success in obtaining a contact order.

Finally, Harriet and Ian may wish to be advised on whether they can make their own application to the court for s8 orders. They can be advised that they have no right to make such application but can apply for leave to make application: see s10(1) CA 1989. The court would consider the nature of the application and any risk that the application might disrupt and harm the child's life: see s10(9) CA 1989. The court must also be satisfied that the child has sufficient understanding to make the application: see s10(8) CA 1989. Such applications are rare, raise difficult issues and have to be made to the High Court: see *Practice Direction* [1993] 1 All ER 820. Again, more information is required but it would seem difficult for either child to make application in their own right. Their views would be put across by the children and family reporter appointed by the court to prepare a welfare report in a contested case. As a result the court would have a method of obtaining the children's wishes and feelings from an independent source without the need for them having to apply to the court themselves.

QUESTION FOUR

Gina and Harry began living together in 1990 in Harry's house. In 1991, she had a son, John. In 1993, after fertility treatment (to which Harry consented) at a clinic, licensed under the Human Fertilisation and Embryology Act 1990, Gina gave birth to a daughter, Fiona.

After eight years of what appeared to be a happy family life, Gina left Harry, taking the children with her and went to live with Ed, with whom she had been having a relationship since 1992. She refused to allow Harry to see the children. John has said that he wants to live with 'my dad' but Fiona wishes to be with 'my mum'. Gina has now told Harry that Fiona was not born as a result of the treatment but is Ed's child and that, as she and Harry were not married, he has 'no rights over either of the children'. She has also told him that she plans to change the children's surnames to that of Ed and to move abroad where Harry will be unable to find them.

Harry wants the children to live with him, or failing that, to prevent Gina from carrying out her plans.

Consider:

a) Harry's legal relationship with the children and whether the relationship has any bearing upon any steps he might take;

b) what steps he can take regarding the children's future.

University of London LLB Examination
(for External Students) Family Law June 1999 Q4

General Comment

This is an intriguing question dealing with the parentage of children, including a child conceived through fertility treatment. This is an area of law of growing importance as medical advances increase the chances of successful fertility treatment and more children are born by such methods. The question then deals with the rights of an unmarried father in relation to residence and contact. The question also invites discussion on removing the children from the jurisdiction and on changing a child's surname. This latter area has been subject to much case law recently with which the student will be expected to be familiar. The suggested solution takes account of the law up to August 2001. This includes the new provisions on scientific tests to establish parentage and involves discussion of the European Convention on Human Rights (incorporated into English and Welsh law in October 2000 by the Human Rights Act 1998).

Skeleton Solution

Legal relationship between Harry and John: status of unmarried father under the Children Act 1989 and art 8 ECHR – acquiring parental responsibility through application for parental responsibility (s4 Children Act (CA) 1989); legal relationship between Harry and Fiona: provisions of Human Fertilisation and Embryology Act 1990 which deal with parentage of child conceived through fertilisation treatment – scientific tests to determine parentage of Fiona – status of Harry in relation to Fiona if found to be her unmarried father and status if found not to be her father; application for residence, contact and prohibited steps orders under the CA 1989 to gain residence and determine the children's future with regard to contact between Harry and the children, their surnames and whether Gina will be permitted to take them abroad: welfare of children being paramount – applying the welfare checklist – applying the no order and delay principles.

Suggested Solution

First, consideration must be given to Harry's legal relationship with the children and whether that relationship has any bearing upon any steps he might take.

In relation to the child, John, there appears to be no dispute as to parentage. Harry has the status of an unmarried father. Harry can be advised that Gina is partly correct in stating that he has no rights over John. Harry lacks parental responsibility for John as an unmarried father: see s2(2)(a) Children Act (CA) 1989. This means that he lacks legal status in relation to John. For example, he may not be consulted by outside bodies such as John's school or doctor in relation to important aspects of John's life. Harry can be advised that art 8 of the European Convention on Human Rights provides some protection for his right to a family life with John. However, he is strongly advised to make application for a parental responsibility order with respect to John: see s4(1)(a) CA 1989. He can seek to make a parental responsibility agreement with Gina under s4(1)(b) CA 1989, but given Gina's views it appears that she is unlikely to sign such an agreement. Harry can be advised that if he applies for parental responsibility for John the court will consider three criteria: the degree of commitment he has shown John; the degree of attachment between him and John; and the reasons why he wants parental responsibility for John: see *Re H (Minors) (Parental Responsibility)* [1993] 1 FLR 484. Applying these three criteria Harry appears to have a strong case for gaining parental responsibility for John. He has been his father and helped bring him up for eight years before Gina left. He appears to have a good relationship with John since John wishes to live with his Dad. Harry appears to be motivated out of concern for his children, rather than motivated to unreasonably interfere with Gina's life. In these circumstances he is likely to gain parental responsibility for John and gain a full legal status as his father.

In relation to the child, Fiona, Harry can be advised that, first, Gina is treated in law as Fiona's mother. Second, Harry is treated as Fiona's father if Gina received fertility treatment at a licensed clinic together with Harry even if Harry is not the genetic father: see s28(3) Human Fertilisation and Embryology Act 1990. The facts seem to suggest that s28(3) does apply so Harry would be treated as Fiona's unmarried father. The same advice about him applying for parental responsibility would then apply. Applying the three criteria he again appears to have a strong case for gaining parental responsibility. He has been Fiona's father for five years up until Gina left. His relationship with Fiona is less clear since she wants to live with her Mum. However, it is assumed that he has had a normal, loving relationship with his daughter. Harry's motivation in applying for parental responsibility for Fiona is assumed to be the same as his application for parental responsibility for John. In such circumstances it appears likely that he would gain parental responsibility for Fiona and gain a full legal status as her father.

Despite the above advice Gina may be able to argue a sufficient case whereby Fiona's parentage is in doubt. In such circumstances the court may direct that scientific tests be carried out to ascertain whether Harry or Ed is Fiona's father: see ss20–23 Family Law Reform Act 1969. Harry, Gina or Ed could make a free-standing application for a declaration of parentage (see s55A Family Law Act 1986) or the court could make directions for tests as part of an existing application (eg an application by Harry for parental responsibility and residence). The court is likely to direct DNA testing which is virtually conclusive as to parentage. Even if Gina objects the court can direct testing provided this is in Fiona's interests.

For the purposes of the next part of this answer it is assumed that Harry is found to be Fiona's father. He can take steps regarding the children's future by applying for orders under the Children Act 1989, namely residence orders to settle with whom the children should reside, contact orders to oblige Gina to allow him contact should the children continue to live with her and prohibited steps orders to prevent Gina from changing the children's surname and from taking them abroad. For all of these applications the children's welfare will be treated by the court as paramount: see s1(1) CA 1989. This means the court will make the decisions which most promote the children's welfare even if this involves some perceived unfairness to either Harry or Gina: see *J v C* [1969]

2 WLR 540. The court will also assume that any delay in resolving a dispute over the future of the children is likely to harm their welfare: see s1(2) CA 1989. The court will aim to resolve any dispute with the minimum of delay. The court will not be able to make any of the above orders unless it considers that making the order would be better for each child than making no order at all: see s1(5) CA 1989. Since important matters are in dispute there clearly is a need for orders to resolve those disputes. Finally, if the applications are contested, the court must have regard to particular matters. These matters will now be discussed in relation to any applications for residence, contact and prohibited steps order.

The court will have regard to the ascertainable wishes and feelings of each child considered in the light of each child's age and understanding: see s1(3)(a) CA 1989. It is noted that John, aged eight years, says he wishes to live with his Dad. Further information is required on John's maturity and understanding. If he is a mature eight-year-old his wishes and feelings will carry weight with the court: eg *M v M (A Minor: Custody Appeal)* [1987] 1 WLR 404 in which a court gave great weight to the wishes of a nine-year-old. The court may be more cautious with regard to Fiona's wishes and feelings. A six-year-old's wishes and feelings carry far less maturity and understanding. The court will have regard to each child's physical, emotional and educational needs: s1(3)(b) CA 1989. Harry can be advised that the courts do not assume that a mother should bring up young children: see *Re A (A Minor) (Custody)* [1991] 2 FLR 394 in which the father was given residence of a ten-year-old boy and six-year-old girl because he would be the better parent compared to the mother. The court will also take into account the advantages of keeping siblings together. This can provide a brother and sister with mutual support and comfort. If the court decides that John should reside with his father then it may decide that Fiona should also live with her father so that she can stay living with her brother. This feature is not so strong if while the children are living with separate parents they enjoy frequent contact with each other and with the other parent. If Harry is unsuccessful in gaining residence of either child the children's emotional needs are likely to include keeping in touch with their father. This emotional need will support any application for contact he brings. Contact is the right of the children and not the right of, for example, Gina to deny as she wishes. The court would ask whether the fundamental emotional need of each child to have an enduring relationship with both parents was outweighed by any harm the child would be at risk of suffering if contact were ordered: see *Re M (Contact: Welfare Test)* [1995] 1 FLR 274. There does not appear to be any feature on the facts disclosed to suggest that contact should not be ordered. The court will also have regard to the likely effect on each child of any change in his or her circumstances: see s1(3)(c) CA 1989. This factor may support Gina's case since the children are currently living with her and Ed and changing with whom they live may be disruptive to their lives. The court will ask whether upsetting the status quo is in the children's long-term interests. If it is then the court will order that one or both children live with Harry. The court will also have regard to each child's age, sex, background and relevant characteristics and any harm each child has suffered or is at risk of suffering: see s1(3)(d) and (e) CA 1989. The court will also consider how capable Harry and Gina are of looking after the children and how capable Ed is of looking after the children if either or both are to live with Gina and Ed: see s1(3)(f) CA 1989. In this context Gina's apparent opposition to the children having contact with Harry may be important. The court will take a dim view of a parent who unreasonably refuses to allow a child to have contact with the other parent when it is clearly in the child's interests to have such contact. The court will look at its full range of powers: see s1(3)(g) CA 1989.

In relation to the proposed change of surname Harry can apply for a prohibited steps order to prevent Gina from changing their surnames. Harry should be advised that until he obtains parental responsibility Gina can act unilaterally to change the children's surnames. Harry will have to act through a court order to prevent such a change. The court will apply the welfare checklist. The courts treat a change of surname as a profound matter whatever the age of the child, particularly in relation to the link it holds with Harry. The courts have tended to refuse to allow a change of surname which severs this important link unless there is very good reason: see *Dawson* v *Wearmouth* [1997] 2 FLR 629. It is difficult to see what the children would gain from using Ed's surname. In relation to Gina taking the children abroad the court will apply similar principles. The children's welfare is paramount. This will include the importance of maintaining their link with their father. If Gina's plans are realistic and well thought out the court will give them great importance. However, if they are unrealistic and potentially harmful to the children in terms of disrupting their lives and severing their links with their father the court is likely to refuse to allow the children to leave the country: see *Re H (Application to Remove from Jurisdiction)* [1998] 1 FLR 848.

If Fiona is found not to be Harry's child then he does not lose the right to apply for residence or contact orders for her. Fiona appears to have lived with him and Gina from 1993 to 1999 which means that Harry has the right to make application even though he is not her natural father: see s10(5)(b) CA 1989. He would have to apply for leave to make a prohibited steps application: see s10(1)(a) CA 1989. In deciding whether to grant leave the court would have regard to the nature of the application (eg to prevent her surname from being changed and/or her from being taken abroad), Harry's long connection with Fiona and any risk that his application might disrupt her life to the extent of harming it: see s10(9) CA 1989. Given Fiona's long connection with Harry it is likely that leave would be granted. If Harry is not Fiona's natural father this will weaken Harry's case. However, the courts will recognise that Fiona may look to Harry as her father regardless of the biological truth and/or have such a strong bond with him that he is virtually in the position of being her natural father.

Chapter 9

Adoption

9.1   Introduction

9.2   Key points

9.3   Key cases and statute

9.4   Questions and suggested solutions

9.1 Introduction

Adoption was introduced in 1926. It is now governed by the Adoption Act (AA) 1976 which came into force in 1988 (and replaced previous provisions in the Children Act 1975 and the Adoption Act 1958). An adoption order ends the legal relationship between a child and his or her natural parents and creates a new and exclusive relationship between the child and the adopters. It gives the applicants parental responsibility for the child and extinguishes the parental responsibility of the birth parents: see s12(1) and (3) AA 1976.

Applications for adoption have fallen dramatically in recent years. In 1974 there were 22,500 applications compared to only 7,000 in recent years (many of which are applications made by a natural parent and step-parent).

9.2 Key points

Who can apply for an adoption order?

A married couple may apply for an adoption order. Each partner should be at least 21 years of age but if the husband or wife is the father or mother of the child and is at least 18 years of age and his or her spouse is at least 21 years of age then application can be made: see s14(1) and (1A) AA 1976.

Under s15(1) AA 1976 a single person may apply for an adoption order if he or she is at least 21 years of age. He or she must be unmarried or if he or she is married the court must be satisfied that:

a) his or her spouse cannot be found; or

b) that they have separated and are living apart and the separation is likely to be permanent; or

c) the spouse is incapable of making an application for an adoption by reason of physical or mental ill-health.

Under s15(3) AA 1976 if the single applicant is the mother or father of the child the court cannot make an adoption order unless it is satisfied that:

a) the other parent is dead or cannot be found; or

b) there is some other reason justifying the exclusion of the other natural parent. This provision was considered by the House of Lords in *Re B (Adoption: Natural Parent)* [2002] 1 FLR 196 which allowed a father to adopt a child to the exclusion of the mother who had given the child up for adoption and consented to the father's application.

These provisions do not allow an unmarried couple to apply for an adoption order. However, it is possible for one partner to apply for adoption and, if an adoption order is made, for a joint residence order to be made whereby the other partner acquires parental responsibility for the child: see *Re AB (Adoption: Joint Residence)* [1996] 1 FLR 27.

The child must live with the applicant(s) before the making of the application

If the applicant, or one of the applicants is a parent, step-parent or relative of the child (or the child was placed with the applicants by an adoption agency or by the High Court) the child must be at least 19 weeks old and must have had his or her home with the applicant(s) or one of them for at least 13 weeks preceding the making of the application: see s13(1) AA 1976.

If the applicant or one of the applicants is not so related to the child, the child must be at least twelve months old and have had his or her home with the applicant(s) or one of them for at least the 12 months preceding the making of the application: see s13(2) AA 1976.

The applicant(s) must notify the local authority of the application. The local authority prepares a report (called a 'Schedule II' report) which assists the court in making its decision.

What the court must consider

In reaching any decision relating to the adoption of a child the court must have regard to all the circumstances, first consideration being given to the need to safeguard and promote the welfare of the child throughout his/her childhood and shall give due consideration to the child's wishes and feelings having regard to his/her age and understanding: see s6 AA 1976. It is important to note that this is not the same test as that applied in s1(1) Children Act 1989. 'All the circumstances' include the interests of the natural parents. While the welfare of the child is the single most important factor it does necessarily outweigh all other circumstances such as the wish of the natural parents to retain links with their child: see *Re W (An Infant)* [1971] 2 WLR 1011.

The delay principle in s1(2) CA 1989 applies so the court must assume that any delay in deciding upon the adoption is likely to prejudice the child's welfare.

The need for parental consent

An adoption order cannot be made unless the child has been freed for adoption, or in the case of each parent or guardian of the child the court is satisfied that the parent or guardian freely and with full understanding of what is involved agrees unconditionally to the making of an adoption order or that agreement has been dispensed with: see s16(1) and (2) AA 1976.

The mother cannot give agreement until at least six weeks after the child's birth (to avoid any immediate post-natal depression which might influence a mother's wishes): see s16(4) AA 1976.

A parent for these purposes does not include an unmarried father unless he has obtained parental responsibility for the child under s4 Children Act 1989, or has a residence order in his favour: see s72 AA 1976 and *Re C (Adoption: Parties)* [1995] 2 FLR 483.

However, the courts will respect the rights of an unmarried father and, where appropriate, give him the opportunity to be involved in the adoption process. See *Re H (A Child) (Adoption: Disclosure); Re G (A Child) (Adoption: Disclosure)* [2000] All ER (D) 2946 where it was held that as a matter of general practice natural fathers should be informed of adoption proceedings unless it was inappropriate to do so for good reason. A mother's wish for confidentiality ought not to deprive the father of his right to be informed and consulted about his child in the majority of cases. In the first case the father had a family life with the elder child and shown commitment to him. He was entitled to respect for a family life with H under art 8 of the European Convention on Human Rights. To place the child for adoption without notifying him would breach art 6 of the Convention. He should be identified and consulted as to the adoption. In the second case the facts were less strong. The parents had never cohabited and their relationship did not have sufficient constancy to show de facto family ties. Their relationship did not fall within the concept of family life within the meaning of art 8 and the father had no right to respect for family life. He need not be identified or notified as to the adoption. This was followed in *Re R (Adoption: Father's Involvement)* [2001] 1 FLR 302, *Re B (A Child) (Sole Adoption by Unmarried Father)* [2001] 1 FLR 589, *Re M (Adoption: Rights of Natural Father)* [2001] 1 FLR 745 and *Re B (Adoption Order)* [2001] 2 FLR 26.

An adoption question is likely to focus on the grounds for dispensing with consent:

a) Has persistently failed without reasonable cause to discharge his/her parental responsibility for the child: s16(2)(c).

b) Has abandoned or neglected the child: s16(2)(d).

c) Has persistently ill-treated the child or has seriously ill-treated the child (and because of that ill-treatment or for other reasons the rehabilitation of the child within the household of the parent is unlikely): see s16(2)(e) and (f) and s16(5).

d) Is withholding agreement unreasonably: see s16(2)(b).

Students will be expected to be aware of the main cases dealing with these grounds. These cases include:

a) *Re D (Minors) (Adoption by Parent)* [1973] 3 WLR 595 on the s16(2)(c) ground where it was said that the failure had not only to be culpable to a high degree but also so grave and complete that the child would derive no advantage from maintaining contact with the natural parent – a temporary withdrawal or drifting apart would not suffice.

b) *Watson v Nickolaisen* [1955] 2 WLR 1187 on the s16(2)(d) ground where it was held that abandoning a child had to be wilful or in a manner likely to cause suffering – a mother who placed her child in the hands of a couple in whom she had confidence could not be said to have abandoned the child.

The most difficult of the grounds is that of withholding agreement unreasonably. Leading cases on this ground include:

a) *Re W (An Infant)* [1971] 2 WLR 1011 where it was held that the court judged the situation as at the date of the hearing, and applied the test objectively – namely would a reasonable parent withhold agreement in all the circumstances? The welfare of the child was not paramount. The parent has legitimate rights to veto the adoption – adoption could not be granted simply because the child's welfare suggested it. In judging reasonableness a reasonable parent gives great weight to what is better for the child and does not ignore any risk or ill likely to be avoided by the adoption or the loss of some appreciable benefit likely to be gained by an adoption order. There is no need to establish culpability on the parent's behalf.

b) *Re H(B) (An Infant) and W(N) (An Infant)* (1983) 4 FLR 614 – there was room for reasonable withholding of consent; even those responsible for the child's welfare held an acceptable view that the child's welfare demanded adoption. Where the natural parent presented him/herself at the time of the hearing as someone capable of caring for the child that was a relevant factor. Where there was an inherent defect in the parent which was likely to persist that was also important. But where the unsuitability only related to past history unless the past history was likely to influence the future position then it should carry little weight in the mind of the hypothetical reasonable parent. The chances of a successful reintroduction to, or continuation of contact with, the natural parent was a critical factor.

Orders which can be made

If an adoption order is made it may contain such terms and conditions as the court thinks fit: see s12(6) AA 1976. In particular, an adoption order can include a condition allowing contact between the child and his/her natural family. In normal circumstances such a condition is not appropriate because it is desirable that there be a complete break with the natural family on adoption. If the applicants agree to contact, and this is in the interests of the child, then a condition of contact can be made. There would have to be exceptional circumstances before a court would impose such a condition without the agreement of the adoptive parents: see *Re C (A Minor)(Adoption: Conditions)* [1988] 1 All ER 705.

Adoptions have come to be classified as 'closed adoptions' (where there is no contact between the child and his/her natural family) and 'open adoptions' (where members of the child's natural family continue to have contact after the adoption order has been made). 'Open adoptions' are only practicable if the adoptive parents agree to it: see *Re C* (above), *Re GR (Adoption: Access)* [1985] FLR 643 and *Re T (Adoption: Contact)* [1995] 2 FLR 251. If the adoptive parents agree to contact, but then renege on that agreement, a member of the child's natural family could then apply for leave to apply for a contact order: see *Re T (Minors) (Adopted Children: Contact)* [1995] 3 WLR 793.

It is rare for any other kind of condition to be attached to an adoption order. The court disapproved of a condition obliging adoptive parents (who were Jehovah's Witnesses) to co-operate with a blood transfusion if the child required one. Since there were established procedures to deal with such a situation there was no need for such a condition: see *Re S (A Minor) (Blood Transfusion: Adoption Order: Condition)* [1995] 2 All ER 122.

Adoption proceedings are family proceedings: see s8(4) CA 1989. The court can therefore make a s8 order on application or of its own motion. The court could make a residence order and contact order instead of an adoption order. Third parties (eg grandparents) could apply for leave to intervene in the proceedings. The court has the flexibility in finding an alternative to adoption if that is appropriate.

Prohibition on private placements and payments for adoption

A person other than an adoption agency shall not make arrangements for the adoption of a child or place a child for adoption unless the proposed adopter is a relative of the child or he/she is acting in pursuance of an order of the High Court: see s11(1) AA 1976. Contravention of this provision is a criminal offence.

It is also unlawful to make or give to any person any payment or reward for or in consideration of the adoption by that person of a child, including payment to obtain agreement or consent to the adoption: see s57(1) AA 1976. Again contravention of this provision is a criminal offence.

The s57(1) prohibition does not apply to payments of reasonable expenses of an adoption agency or to payment authorised by the court to which the adoption application is made: see s57(3) AA 1976. Such authorisation can be done retrospectively, thus allowing an adoption preceded by an unauthorised payment to be granted: see *Re Adoption Application (Surrogacy)* [1987] 2 All ER 826.

Contravention of the ss11 and 57 prohibitions does not prevent an adoption order being made if this is clearly in the child's interests: see *Re ZHH (Adoption Application)* [1993] 1 FLR 83 and *Re MW (Adoption: Surrogacy)* [1995] 2 FLR 759.

9.3 Key cases and statute

- *Re H (A Child) (Adoption: Disclosure); Re G (A Child) (Adoption: Disclosure)* [2000] All ER (D) 2946
  Role of unmarried father in adoption proceedings

- *Re H (B) (An Infant) and W(N) (An Infant)* (1983) 4 FLR 614
  Withholding consent unreasonably to an adoption

- *Re W (An Infant)* [1971] 2 WLR 1011
  Welfare of child in adoption proceedings

- Adoption Act 1976 – applying for adoption

9.4 Questions and suggested solutions

QUESTION ONE

Maria and Nicholas began cohabiting in 1986 and have two children, Oliver and Pam, who are now four and two. Shortly after Pam was born, Maria and Nicholas separated. The children remained with Maria, but the couple agreed that Nicholas would have extensive contact with them. In May 1993, Maria married Quentin, a man Nicholas dislikes. Since that time, Nicholas has had little contact with Oliver and Pam, although he has sent them cards and presents through the post. The children have little memory of Nicholas and regard Quentin as their father. Maria and Quentin have decided that they would like to adopt Oliver and Pam in order to provide them with a sense of security.

Nicholas, who is opposed to the plans for adoption and would like his contact with the children formalised, seeks your advice. He also tells you that his mother, Ruth, would like to be able to see Oliver and Pam.

Advise Nicholas and Ruth.

> University of London LLB Examination
> (for External Students) Family Law June 1994 Q6

General Comment

This question deals with the relationship between an unmarried father and his two children from whom he is separated. There is a possibility of adoption by the children's mother and her new husband. How an unmarried father can oppose such an adoption application needs to be outlined. He has not had contact with his children. How he could apply for contact and the considerations the court would take into account under the Children Act 1989 need to be discussed. The children's paternal grandmother also wishes to apply for contact. She will need to obtain leave to make such an application and the provisions relating to obtaining leave need to be described.

Skeleton Solution

Application for adoption order by Maria and Quentin: the need for parental consent; the position of an unmarried father; dispensing with parental consent (Adoption Act 1976) – application by Nicholas for a contact order under s8 of the Children Act 1989; considerations under s1 and case law in deciding how his application would be determined – application for leave by grandparent to apply for contact; provisions governing leave under s10(9) of the Children Act 1989.

Suggested Solution

Nicholas is opposed to the plans by Maria and Quentin to adopt his two children. If Maria and Quentin are successful in their application to adopt Oliver and Pam then they will acquire sole parental responsibility for the two children to the exclusion of Nicholas and in effect end his status as the children's parent: see s12 Adoption Act (AA) 1976. An adoption order also would extinguish any order made for contact under the Children Act (CA) 1989. In effect Nicholas would be deprived of any right to have contact with his children. It would be most unusual for him to be able to apply for contact after the making of an adoption order: see *Re C (A Minor) (Adopted Child: Contact)* [1993] 3 All ER 259. An adoption order can contain a condition allowing contact but given Maria and Quentin's opposition to Nicholas having contact such a condition would be unlikely to be made: see *Re C (A Minor) (Adoption: Conditions)* [1988] 1 All ER 705.

How could Nicholas oppose an application by Maria and Quentin for adoption? Nicholas has the status of an unmarried father in relation to his children. This means that he does not have parental responsibility for them and that Maria has sole parental responsibility for them: see s2(2) CA 1989. This means that though he would be informed of the adoption application and be able to make representations about it he would be in a weak legal position to prevent the adoption. Before an adoption order can be made the parents of the children must freely and with full understanding agree unconditionally to the making of the adoption order or have their consent dispensed with: see s16(1) AA 1976. A parent for these purposes is a parent with parental responsibility: see s72 AA 1976. Therefore Nicholas's consent to the adoption would not be required unless he obtained parental responsibility. In order to obtain parental responsibility he would either have to enter into a parental responsibility agreement with Maria (which is unlikely given her views) or apply to the court for a parental responsibility order under s4 CA 1989. If he does apply for a parental responsibility order the welfare of the two children will be treated as paramount: see s1(1) CA 1989. The court will have regard to the degree of commitment he has shown to his children, the degree of attachment between him and his children and the reason(s) he wants parental responsibility for them: see *Re C (Minors)* [1992] 2 All ER 86. In this case

Nicholas helped bring up Oliver for two years. After the separation he had extensive contact with both children up until a year ago. Even after contact ceased he displayed commitment to them by sending cards and presents in the post. His application for parental responsibility would be motivated by concern for the children rather than interfering with their lives. Even though the children may have little memory of Nicholas, and even though Maria and Nicholas would be opposed to such an application and prevent any contact, the courts have stated that parental responsibility should be conferred in similar circumstances. This gives the father a status and 'rights in waiting' which may become relevant should there be an adoption application or should something happen to Maria or Quentin: see *Re H (Minors) (Parental Responsibility)* [1993] 1 FLR 484 and *Re A (Minors) (Parental Responsibility)* [1993] Fam Law 464.

Assuming Nicholas obtains parental responsibility his consent would then be required for the adoption unless his consent was dispensed with by the court. A court could only dispense with his agreement on certain grounds: see s16(2) AA 1976. There appear to be only two grounds which could be applied in these circumstances – namely, that Nicholas has persistently failed without reasonable cause to discharge his parental responsibility for the children; or that he is withholding his consent unreasonably: see s16(2)(b) and (c) AA 1976. It would be difficult for the first ground to be made out since he appears to have made every effort to discharge his parental responsibilities despite Maria and Quentin's opposition. In relation to whether he could be said to be withholding his consent unreasonably the court would apply an objective test – would a reasonable parent in these circumstances withhold agreement? A reasonable parent would give great weight to what is best for the children. A reasonable parent would not ignore any risk or ill likely to be avoided by adoption or some appreciable benefit likely to accrue from adoption. In deciding whether to dispense with consent the welfare of the children would not be paramount since Nicholas has legitimate rights which would be extinguished by adoption and so has a right to veto it. The children would not be adopted simply because their welfare suggests it: see *Re W (An Infant)* [1971] 2 WLR 1011. In these circumstances Nicholas appears to have a strong case in arguing that his consent should not be dispensed with. He appears to have good reasons to maintain his legal status with regard to his children which should not be extinguished by adoption.

Assuming the children are not adopted Nicholas could apply for a contact order to formalise contact arrangements with his children: see s8 CA 1989. He could apply for such an order whether or not he had parental responsibility for them. In deciding whether or not to grant his application the welfare of Oliver and Pam would be paramount: see s1(1) CA 1989. This means their welfare would outweigh the wishes of Nicholas or of Maria and Quentin. The court would assume that any delay in hearing the application would be harmful to the children so would wish to proceed with the application quickly: see s1(2) CA 1989. Assuming that the application was opposed the court would have regard to a number of particular considerations: see ss1(3),(4) CA 1989. It would take into account the ascertainable wishes and feelings of each child considered in the light of their age and understanding. Oliver and Pam are too young for their wishes and feelings to carry great weight with a court. It would consider their physical, emotional and educational needs and the likely effect on them of any change in their circumstances. This could include any harm or benefits of being reintroduced to their father. Their age, sex, background and any other relevant characteristics would be considered as would any harm they have suffered or would be at risk of suffering. The capability of Nicholas and of Maria and Quentin in meeting each child's needs would be considered. For example, if Maria and Quentin are opposed to Nicholas having contact more because of their feelings towards him rather than what they know is best for the children this will stand against them. The court will also consider its full range of powers. The court will not make any order unless the order will bring positive benefits for the children: see s1(5) CA 1989. In considering applications by fathers for contact it has been held that a court should not deprive any child of contact with either parent unless it was wholly satisfied that it was in the interests of the child that there should be no contact. This is a conclusion at which courts are extremely slow to arrive because of the long-term benefits of children keeping in contact with both parents. Save in exceptional cases to deprive a child of contact was to deprive a child of an important contribution to the child's emotional and material growing up in the long term: see *Re H (Minors) (Access)* [1992] 1 FLR 148. Unless Maria and Quentin can show that the children will be harmed by contact, or that contact will so destabilise Maria and Quentin's family as to outweigh the benefits of contact, then Nicholas is likely to have a strong case. If contact is ordered it may be in the form of direct contact such as visits to or by the children and/or indirect contact by letters or telephone calls.

Since Ruth is not a parent of Pam and Oliver she cannot apply as of right for contact. She must apply for leave in order to make an application: see s10(9) CA 1989. In considering whether to grant leave the court will consider the nature of her application, her connection with the children and any risk there might be of her proposed application disrupting each child's life to such an extent that the child would be harmed by it. The welfare of the children would not be paramount in considering whether to grant leave: see *Re A and Others (Minors) (Residence Order)* [1992] 3 WLR 422. Whether leave would be granted will depend on Ruth's previous relationship with her grandchildren and their relationship with her. The court will be concerned to stop Ruth's application if it appears to unwarranted interference in the children's lives. If leave is granted then the court would apply similar considerations as in Nicholas's case, though there would not be the same presumption in favour of contact as there is for a parent seeking contact.

QUESTION TWO

Paula and Quentin began living together in 1992. In August 1993, Paula discovered that she was pregnant. Both Paula and Quentin were pleased that they were going to have a child and, although they talked of marriage, decided that the child would be sufficient evidence of commitment between them. In May 1994, Paula gave birth to Rebecca. It was a difficult birth and Paula suffered a long and serious period of post-natal depression, during which time she was unable to look after Rebecca. Quentin took leave from his job as a university lecturer to care for Paula and Rebecca and developed a close bond with the child. Paula's depression continued into 1995 and Quentin, deciding that the relationship had no future, left her to live with Silvia, one of his students. At the suggestion of Paula's psychiatrist, Rebecca was placed in the care of the local authority with a view to adoption in 1995. The local authority placed Rebecca with Mr and Mrs Tomkins, professionals in their late twenties, who wished to adopt her.

In May 1995, Mr and Mrs Tomkins, with the support of the local authority applied to adopt Rebecca. Paula, although still ill, decided that she wanted to have an opportunity to care for her daughter and wishes to oppose the adoption. Quentin, who has now married Silvia, considers that Rebecca should live with him or, if that is not possible, he should be able to maintain close contact with her.

Advise Paula and Quentin.

University of London LLB Examination
(for External Students) Family Law June 1995 Q7

General Comment

The question deals with the rights of a mother to oppose an adoption and the possible grounds for dispensing with her consent. In particular, the authorities concerning whether she is withholding her consent 'unreasonably' need to be discussed. The position of an unmarried father then needs to be outlined in relation to the adoption and in relation to his rights to apply for orders concerning his daughter. The interplay between applications under the Adoption Act 1976 and the Children Act 1989 is a particular feature of this question. The student is asked to demonstrate a sound knowledge of the different principles which apply to each type of application.

Skeleton Solution

Position of mother in relation to proposed adoption; need for her consent (s16 Adoption Act 1976) – status of child with local authority; right of mother to ask for her return (s20 Children Act 1989) – dispensing with her consent (s16(2) AA 1976); the relevant grounds; in particular whether she is withholding her consent unreasonably – position of unmarried father in relation to adoption; his lack of status (s72 AA 1976) – right of unmarried father to apply for a residence order and principles to be applied (ss1, 8 and 10 CA 1989).

Suggested Solution

Paula should first be advised that at present she appears to have sole parental responsibility for Rebecca: see s2(2) Children Act 1989 – hereinafter referred to as the CA 1989. She has asked the local authority to look after her daughter. It is not clear on what basis Rebecca is in the care of the local authority. If the local authority have obtained a care order then it shares parental responsibility for Rebecca with Paula but can prevent Rebecca from being returned to her: see s33 CA 1989. If Rebecca is accommodated by the local authority purely on a voluntary basis (eg, because Paula cannot cope) she has the right to require Rebecca to be returned to her at any time: see s20(8) CA 1989. Therefore, she may be able to prevent the adoption by asking that Rebecca be returned to her. However, this may not be appropriate if Paula is still ill. If she asks for Rebecca to be returned to her the local authority is liable to take immediate action to prevent this by applying for an emergency protection order and starting care proceedings so that Rebecca is placed compulsorily in their care: see ss31 and 44 CA 1989. The court would grant an emergency protection order if it was satisfied that there is reasonable cause to believe that Rebecca is likely to suffer significant harm if removed from Mr and Mrs Tomkins: see s44(1)(a) CA 1989. If such an order were granted then it would last for up to eight days but could be extended by a further seven days. Only one day's notice would be required to be given to Paula. At the same time, the local authority is likely to start care proceedings and ask the court to make an interim care order. The court could only make such an order if it was satisfied that there were reasonable grounds to believe that Rebecca is likely to suffer significant harm if removed by Paula, as a result of the lack of reasonable care given to her by Paula: see s38(2) CA 1989. Such an order if granted could last up to eight weeks and could be renewed at up to four weekly intervals until either the care proceedings were heard or the court made an adoption order.

In order to obtain an adoption order Mr and Mrs Tomkins must satisfy the court of certain requirements. At least one of them must be over 21 years of age and they must be married: see ss14 and 14A AA 1976. Rebecca must be at least 12 months old and have had her home with Mr and Mrs Tomkins for at least 12 months preceding the application: see s13(2) AA 1976. Assuming that these criteria have been satisfied the court will apply a two-fold test in deciding whether an adoption order should be made in Mr and Mrs Tomkins' favour. First, the court must give first consideration to the need to safeguard and promote Rebecca's welfare throughout her childhood: see s6 AA 1976. It must have regard to her wishes and feelings regarding the decision in light of her age and understanding. Given her age, this will not be practicable. The court must be satisfied that an adoption order would be in Rebecca's best long-term interests. Second, the court must be satisfied that either Paula consents to the adoption or that her consent can be dispensed with: see s16(1) AA 1976. Since Paula does not agree to the adoption then she will need to be advised as to the grounds on which her consent can be dispensed with.

First, the court can dispense with her consent on the basis that she is incapable of giving agreement: see s16(2)(a) AA 1976. Her illness does not suggest that she is incapable of making a rational decision so this ground does not appear to apply. Second the court can dispense with her consent on the ground that she is withholding her agreement unreasonably: see s16(2)(b) AA 1976. If Mr and Mrs Tomkins ask the court to dispense with Paula's agreement on this ground the court will make its decision on the available information and evidence at the date of the hearing. It will apply an objective test, namely, would a reasonable parent, knowing all the circumstances, withhold her agreement? In applying this test Rebecca's welfare is not paramount. Paula has a legitimate right of veto which must be respected even if the adoption might be the best decision in Rebecca's interests. A reasonable parent would take into account the welfare of her child and would place great weight on what is best for that child. Such a parent would not ignore any risk or ill which might be avoided by the adoption or any appreciable benefit which might be provided by the adoption. The court would understand Paula's anguish in refusing to give consent but would ask itself what a reasonable parent in her place would do in all the circumstances: see *Re W (An Infant)* [1971] 2 WLR 1011. The court will ask what kind of future Paula can offer Rebecca should the adoption not be granted. This will depend on the extent of her illness and whether she has any relationship with her daughter or can re-establish such a relationship. If the court decides that there are serious doubts that she could cope with her daughter and that her refusal to consent is motivated by feelings of guilt and/or sentimentality then it is likely her consent would be dispensed with, particularly if Rebecca has settled well with Mr and Mrs Tomkins. If the court decides that she is well enough to provide a good home for Rebecca then it may refuse to dispense with her consent: see *Re PA (An Infant)* [1971] 1 WLR 1530 and *Re H(B) and W(N)* (1983) 4 FLR 614.

Another ground for dispensing with Paula's consent would be that she has persistently failed without reasonable cause to discharge her parental responsibility for Rebecca: see s16(2)(c) AA 1976. This ground may be difficult to satisfy since Paula appears to have acted quite responsibly in giving up the care of her daughter given her illness, particularly if she has also made efforts to keep in touch with Rebecca: *see Re D (Minors) (Adoption by Parent)* [1973] 3 WLR 595. Similarly, she can hardly be said to have abandoned the child (another ground for dispensing with consent) if she took steps to ensure that Rebecca was properly looked after when she could not cope: see s16(2)(d) AA 1976 and *Watson v Nikolaisen* [1955] 2 WLR 1187. Since there is no suggestion that she has ill-treated the child then none of the other grounds for dispensing with her consent will apply.

If the court grants the adoption then Paula's parental responsibility for Rebecca is extinguished and vests entirely with Mr and Mrs Tomkins: see s12 AA 1976. If the court refuses to make an adoption order it may make a residence order instead whereby Rebecca lives with Mr and Mrs Tomkins. Paula would retain her parental responsibility and share it with Mr and Mrs Tomkins, though she could not remove Rebecca in breach of the residence order: see s2(5), (7) and (8) CA 1989. It would also be possible for the court to make a residence order whereby Rebecca lives with Paula. This does not seem a likely option given her illness. However, the criteria for making such an order are outlined in the advice given to Quentin which equally applies should Rebecca apply for a residence order or the court consider making such an order of its own motion.

Quentin did not marry Paula so has the status of an unmarried father in relation to Rebecca. He therefore has no parental responsibility for her unless he takes action to acquire it: see s2(2) CA 1989. Since he does not have parental responsibility his consent is not required for the adoption and indeed he would not even be a party to the adoption application: see s72 AA 1976 – meaning of 'parent'. He wishes to either have Rebecca with him or maintain close contact with her. He may make application to the court for a number of orders to achieve these wishes. First. he may apply to the court for a parental responsibility order giving him parental responsibility for Rebecca: see s4(1)(a) CA 1989. In order to obtain such an order he would have to show that he has demonstrated commitment towards her, has established a close relationship with her and that his application is motivated out of genuine concern for her welfare rather than as a way of getting at either Paula or Mr. and Mrs. Tomkins: see *Re C (Minors)* [1992] 2 All ER 86. Since Quentin took leave from his work to look after Rebecca and developed a close bond with her he appears to have a good case. It is not clear whether he has kept in close touch with her after he left Paula. If he did this will further strengthen his case. If he does obtain parental responsibility he will then become a party to the adoption, and his consent must be given for the adoption, or his consent dispensed with on one or more of the same grounds already discussed in relation to Paula. It is also possible for him to obtain parental responsibility by signing a written parental responsibility agreement with Paula: see s4(1)(b) CA 1989. This would be an easier way of obtaining parental responsibility, if Paula would agree to such a course.

In addition he may apply to the court for a residence order or a contact order: see ss8 and 10 CA 1989. A residence order would be an order that Rebecca live with him. A contact order would be an order requiring whomever Rebecca was living with to allow Rebecca to visit her father or to otherwise have contact with him. If a residence order was made in his favour the court would be obliged to make a parental responsibility order at the same time: see s12(1) CA 1989. In considering applications for parental responsibility, residence or contact the court would have regard to a number of principles. First, it would treat Rebecca's welfare as the paramount consideration (see s1(1) CA 1989). This means that her welfare would determine the course to be followed, as opposed to what any of the adults thought was fair or just: see *J v C* [1969] 1 All ER 788. Second, the court would try to deal with any application as quickly as possible since it must assume that any delay in making a decision is likely to be prejudicial to Rebecca's welfare: see s1(2) CA 1989. The court would lay down a timetable for the application(s) and ensure that the parties stuck to it: see s11 CA 1989. Third, the court would not make any order unless it would be better for Rebecca than making no order at all: see s1(5) CA 1989. Quentin would have to demonstrate that any order he seeks would provide a positive benefit for Rebecca. Fourth, in considering any applications for a residence or contact order which was opposed the court would have regard to certain matters: see s1(3), (4) CA 1989.

The court would first have regard to Rebecca's ascertainable wishes and feelings in light of her age and understanding: see s1(3)(a) CA 1989. Since she is so young these are not likely to be ascertainable. The court would then consider her physical, educational and emotional needs as well as her age, sex and characteristics: see s1(3)(b) and (d) CA 1989. Rebecca will have the needs of a one-year-old baby. She needs security and safety. She requires good housing and sustenance. She needs a good emotional bond with her carers. The court will consider the likely effect on her of any change in her circumstances: see s1(3)(c) CA 1989. If she has been living with Mr and Mrs Tomkins for a year, would she be harmed if she was moved to live with Paula or with Quentin and his wife? If either Quentin or Paula have kept in touch with Rebecca any change may be less upsetting than if they have become strangers to her. The court would consider any harm which Rebecca has suffered or is at risk of suffering, as well as the capabilities of Paula, of Quentin and Silvia and of Mr and Mrs Tomkins in meeting her needs: see s1(3)(e) and (f) CA 1989. Paula's illness will be relevant here insofar as it affects her ability to care for her daughter. The court is likely to favour whomever can provide full-time care for Rebecca, as opposed to the use of babysitters while the adults are at work. Finally, the court would consider its full range of powers: see s1(3)(g) CA 1989.

Much will depend on the court's decision in relation to the adoption. If the adoption is granted Paula and Quentin (if he has acquired parental responsibility) will lose their parental responsibility. They will lose any rights in relation to Rebecca, including the right to see her. While it is possible for an adoption order to contain a condition that Mr and Mrs Tomkins allow either or both parents to see Rebecca, such a condition is unlikely to be imposed unless Mr and Mrs Tomkins agree to it and if the court finds exceptional circumstances to justify it: see *Re C (A Minor) (Adoption: Conditions)* [1988] 1 All ER 705. If the adoption application fails (eg, because the court refuses to dispense with parental consent) then the court could make a residence order in favour of the Tomkins with or without contact orders in favour of Quentin and Paula. Alternatively, a residence order could be made in Quentin and Sylvia's favour with contact to Paula (and Mr and Mrs Tomkins, if the court considered that appropriate). There is also the possibility of a residence order in Paula's favour with contact orders for Quentin (and Mr and Mrs Tomkins). This will depend on how the court balances the strengths and weaknesses of the competing claims. Both Paula and Quentin should be advised that the court will be assisted in its deliberations by a report prepared by the local authority concerning the adoption and also by a report prepared by a guardian ad litem. The guardian ad litem would be an independent person who, where an adoption is contested, investigates the case from the child's point of view. Such reports carry weight with the court so Paula and Quentin are advised to co-operate in its preparation.

QUESTION THREE

At the age of 16, and with the support of her parents, Alison had a baby. Alison continued her education and the baby, Jason, was looked after by Alison's parents, Mr and Mrs Smith, until she left school. Unknown to her parents, Alison had applied for and been offered a place at university far from home. When Alison told her parents, she also announced that she wanted to have Jason adopted by strangers, since in the long term she had no intention of caring for him and thought they were too old to bear the responsibility. Her parents were heartbroken when in 1999 Alison insisted that Jason move to another family with a view to adoption.

In her first university year, Alison again became pregnant. Unwilling to have an abortion, Alison left university and again turned to her parents for help. She also decided that she wanted Jason back. Meanwhile Jason has been living with Mr and Mrs Brown, who are keen to adopt Jason and have the support of the local authority.

Advise Alison, Mr and Mrs Smith and Mr and Mrs Brown as to their respective legal rights and the likely outcome of legal proceedings to adopt Jason.

University of London LLB Examination
(for External Students) Family Law June 2000 Q8

General Comment

This question deals with the law on adoption and the rights of grandparents. It requires advice to be given on the right of a mother to change her mind about adoption and get her child returned to her, the right of grandparents to apply for residence or contact with their grandchild and the right of prospective adopters to obtain an adoption. There is a complication with a possible unlawful placement for adoption and the consequences of this need investigation.

Skeleton Solution

Placement for adoption: placement with non-relatives – legality and consequences; application for adoption: requirement for mother's consent – grounds for dispensing with her consent – likely outcome of adoption application; application by mother for return of child through a residence order – relevant factors if opposed; application by grandparents for return of child through application for leave to apply for a residence order – relevant factors if opposed.

Suggested Solution

The question asks for advice for Alison, Mr and Mrs Smith and for Mr and Mrs Brown as to their respective legal rights and the likely outcome of legal proceedings to adopt Jason.

First, all the parties should be advised that the placement of Jason with Mr and Mrs Brown by Alison appears be unlawful. There is a prohibition on the placement (other than through an adoption agency) of a child for adoption with a non-relative save through court order: see s11(1) Adoption Act (AA) 1976. This is a criminal offence punishable with a fine or imprisonment. Contravention of this prohibition would not prevent an adoption order being made. A court would take the contravention into account and consider whether public policy required the adoption to be refused. The court could nevertheless grant the adoption if it was in the child's interests, bearing in mind that Jason's welfare is the first consideration: see s6 AA 1976 and *Re ZHH (Adoption Application)* [1993] 1 FLR 83. Since the placement does not appear to be a deliberate example of 'baby selling' for adoption it seems unlikely that this in itself prevent the adoption application from being heard.

It is assumed that Mr and Mrs Brown are married and are both at least 21 years of age otherwise they would not be eligible to adopt Jason: see s14(1) AA 1976. It is also assumed that Jason has been in the care of Mr and Mrs Brown for at least 12 months, otherwise an adoption order could not be made: see 13(2) AA 1976. The question does not make this clear and further information is required to confirm the position. In addition, the adoption could not proceed unless Mr and Mrs Brown had allowed the local authority access to Jason in order to prepare the required court report: see s13(3) and Sch 2 AA 1976. This is assumed to be the case in light of the local authority support for the application or potential application. If Mr and Mrs Brown have made an application for an adoption order there is also a potential restriction on Jason being removed from their care if Alison has given her agreement to the making of the adoption order. Alison appears to have initially agreed to the adoption and then changed her mind so it is not clear whether this restriction applies. In any event Jason may be removed with the leave of the court: see s27(1) AA 1976. If he is removed contrary to the restriction this could amount to a criminal offence punishable with a fine and/or imprisonment: see s27(3) AA 1976. If no adoption application has been made then the only person with parental responsibility for Jason is Alison because she is an unmarried mother: see s2(1) Children Act 1989. This would mean that she could remove Jason without notice. Mr and Mrs Brown are therefore advised to make application for adoption if they have not already done so to preserve their position and possibly avoid Jason being taken away from them.

Once the adoption application has validly been made all the parties should be advised that the court will treat Jason's welfare as the first consideration: see s6 AA 1976. Mr and Mrs Brown should note that Jason's welfare is not paramount. The rights of Alison cannot be ignored. Furthermore, an adoption order cannot be granted unless either Alison consents to the adoption or her consent is dispensed with: see s16 AA 1976. No reference is made to Jason's father having to consent since as an unmarried father his consent is not required: see s72 AA 1976. He appears to have had no involvement with Jason so need not even be identified or notified of the application: see *Re H, Re G* [2001] Fam Law 175. Alison has indicated that she will not give consent, so Mr and Mrs Brown's application will only succeed if they can persuade the court to dispense with her consent on one or more of a number of grounds.

First, they could argue that she is withholding her consent unreasonably: see s16(2)(b) AA 1976. The court will apply the test at the time of the hearing. It will apply an objective test, namely would a reasonable parent withhold consent. In judging reasonableness the parent will be assumed to give great weight to the welfare of the child. A reasonable parent would not ignore or disregard any risk or ill likely to be avoided by the adoption or some appreciable benefit likely to accrue if the child is adopted. Alison should be advised that in order to show unreasonableness there is no need to show culpability on her part: see *Re W (An Infant)* [1971] 2 WLR 1011. Alison can further be advised that the court will consider whether she can take reasonable care of Jason if he is returned to her. Further information is required on this point. If the court is satisfied that Alison can provide reasonable care for Jason then it is likely to consider that any upset in moving him from Mr and Mrs Brown would be temporary and that he would benefit from the love and care of his natural mother: see *Re PA (An Infant)* [1971] 1 WLR 1530. If, by contrast, the court is faced with Alison as young, single and inexperienced mother with an uncertain future balanced against a secure and warm relationship established between Mr and Mrs Brown then it could hold that she is withholding her consent unreasonably: see *Re P (An Infant) (Adoption: Parental Consent)* [1976] 3 WLR 924. The key is whether Alison can demonstrate, at the hearing, that she is someone capable to caring for Jason. The court places some importance on a child being brought up by his natural parent where she is able to do so. If Alison is able to demonstrate an ability to properly look after Jason the court is unlikely to dispense with her consent on this ground.

The court could also be asked to dispense with her consent on the basis that she has persistently failed without reasonable cause to discharge her parental responsibility to the child: see s16(2)(c) AA 1976. Alison can be advised that this ground is a matter of fact and degree. Mr and Mrs Brown have to show that the failure was not only culpable to a high degree but also that the failure was so grave and complete that the child would derive no advantage from maintaining contact with his mother. Persistent failure means 'permanent failure': see *Re D (Minors) (Adoption by Parent)* [1973] 3 WLR 595. It would appear that Mr and Mrs Brown would have difficulty in establishing the ground. Though Alison can be criticised for placing Jason with Mr and Mrs Brown and leaving him with them for a year or more it seems difficult to say that her failure is permanent or that Jason could not gain benefit from being reunited with his mother or maintaining contact with her. The court could also be asked to dispense with Alison's consent on the ground that she has abandoned or neglected Jason: see s16(2)(d) AA 1976. Mr and Mrs Brown can be advised that again they would have difficulty in establishing this ground. In the not dissimilar case of *Watson v Nickolaisen* [1955] 2 WLR 1187 a mother left her child in the hands of people in whom she had confidence. She initially gave her consent and then changed her mind. The court held that 'abandoned' meant leaving the child to her fate, abandoning the child in a criminal sense in a manner likely to cause the child suffering. It did not mean leaving her in the hands of people who would care for her. The remaining grounds for dispensing with consent do not apply.

In these circumstances the parties can be advised that an adoption application would not be likely to succeed, because of the difficulties in dispensing with Alison's consent, a pre-requisite to the adoption succeeding.

Alison can be advised that she can firstly ask for Jason's return. Since she is the only person with parental responsibility for Jason she has the right to determine with whom he should live (subject any restriction in removing Jason as a result of any adoption proceedings). If Mr and Mrs Brown refuse to return Jason she would be advised to apply for a residence order in order to enforce his return. In theory she could try to enforce his return, for example with the help of the police, but is likely that the authorities would prefer a court to resolve any dispute. Mr and Mrs Brown can be advised that they can apply to the court for leave to apply for a residence order in order to preserve their position. Mr and Mrs Smith can be advised that they can apply to the court for leave to apply for either a residence order or for a contact order as a way of preserving their relationship with Jason. In considering whether to grant leave to Mr and Mrs Brown to apply for a residence order the court will consider the nature of the proposed application, their connection with Jason and any risk there might be of the proposed application disrupting Jason's life to such an extent that he would be harmed by it: see s10(9) CA 1989. Similar provisions apply if Mr and Mrs Smith apply for leave to apply for residence or contact orders though, if Alison consents to their application, they would not need leave and can apply to the court direct: see s10(5) CA 1989.

In considering such applications the court would consider the welfare of the child as paramount, not just the first consideration as for adoption: see s1(1) CA 1989. It would assume that any delay in dealing with the applications is likely to be harmful to Jason and so will set down a timetable to enable the case to be dealt with as quickly as possible: see s1(2) CA 1989. The court will also consider the no order principle, namely it will not make any order unless it will positively benefit the child: see s1(5) CA 1989. Given the importance of settling Jason's future the no order principle is unlikely to apply in relation to residence. It may apply in relation to any application by Mr and Mrs Smith for contact if Alison gains residence and agrees to them having contact. If the applications are contested the court will apply the welfare checklist: see s1(3) and (4) CA 1989. This will include the ascertainable wishes and feelings of Jason, which should be considered in the light of his age and understanding: see s1(3)(a). He is too young to express his wishes and feelings. The court will consider his physical, emotional and educational needs: see s1(3)(b). This will include the importance the court attaches to a child being brought up by his natural mother. This may also be importance in Jason being brought up with his sibling or half-sibling. This will assist Alison's case. The court will consider the likely effect on Jason of any change in his circumstances: see s1(3)(c). The court will balance the dangers of moving Jason from Mr and Mrs Brown with whom he may have settled and any long term advantages of him returning to live with his mother or with his grandparents. The court will consider his sex, age, background and any special characteristics: see s1(3)(d). The court will consider any harm Jason has suffered or any harm he is at risk of suffering: see s1(3)(e). The court will look at how capable Alison is of meeting Jason's needs and the capabilities of Mr and Mrs Brown and of Mr and Mrs Smith: see s1(3)(f). Finally, the court will consider its full range of powers: see s1(3)(g). There is insufficient information to assess the likelihood of success of applications for residence and/or contact orders. Mr and Mrs Brown can be advised that because of the importance the courts attach to a child being brought up by his natural mother, where possible, unless they can demonstrate that Alison would be an unfit mother and would harm Jason, then they are unlikely to gain a residence order. The same would apply to Mr and Mrs Smith if they wished to have the residence of Jason against the wishes of Alison.

QUESTION FOUR

In 1997 Melanie, who is aged 18 and not married, gave birth to Tom, who is now 19 months old. Melanie is unemployed and lived with her parents until a year ago when they told her that she and the baby would have to leave.

Melanie's friends, David and Emily, are a married couple who have been married for ten years but unable to have children. When they heard that Melanie and Tom were homeless, David and Emily suggested that they move in with them. For a while the arrangement worked well. However, in December 1998 Melanie met and fell in love with Peter, an older man who does not like children. Emily suggested that Melanie should leave Tom in their care while Melanie organised her new life, and gave Melanie £5,000 towards the cost of a 'fresh start'. Melanie accepted the gift and went to live with Peter.

Last month, Melanie was horrified to receive a visit from the local authority and to be told that David and Emily had sought advice about adopting Tom. The social worker also told Melanie that she would support David and Emily's application, which was to be heard in the courts in the very near future.

Melanie has now decided that she wants Tom back and that if necessary she will leave Peter. Advise Melanie as to her rights under adoption law, and as to the possible outcome of the adoption application.

University of London LLB Examination
(for External Students) Family Law June 1999 Q5

General Comment

This is a standard question on adoption. The suggested answer includes reference to art 8 of the European Convention on Human Rights and the affect this will have in terms of applying English law. The questions invites discussion on the grounds for dispensing with consent. In particular the ground of withholding consent unreasonably requires discussion. Complicating features include the payment of money as a possible incentive for the adoption and the possible private placement for adoption. The law on these two areas must be dealt with.

Skeleton Solution

Application by married couple for adoption (s14 AA 1976); prohibition on private placement and payment for adoption (ss11 and 57 AA 1976); grounds for dispensing with the consent of the mother: persistent failure to discharge parental responsibility for child – abandoned or neglected the child – withholding consent unreasonably (s16 AA 1976).

Suggested Solution

Melanie can first be advised that David and Emily can apply to adopt Tom as a married couple provided both are over 21 years of age: see s14(1) Adoption Act (AA) 1976. Since David and Emily are not related to Tom then Tom must be at least 12 months old and have lived with them for 12 months: see s13 AA 1976. The facts in the question are not entirely clear but it appears that Tom has lived with them for the required period. On this basis they can apply to adopt Tom. They are required to notify the local authority of their intention to apply for an adoption order which may explain the visit to Melanie by the social worker.

Melanie can then be advised that if an application for an adoption order has been made the court cannot make an adoption order unless she gives consent to an adoption order or her consent is dispensed with: see s16(1) AA 1976. There is no mention of who the father of Tom is. Since the father is an unmarried father his consent is not required (unless he has obtained parental responsibility for Tom): see s72 AA 1976 and *Re C (Adoption: Parties)* [1995] 2 FLR 483. Now that the European Convention on Human Rights (ECHR) is part of English law through the Human Rights Act 1998 the court is likely to want to know who Tom's father is and make some enquiry as to whether his right to a family life under art 8 ECHR needs to be protected by the courts. It is assumed that the father has shared no family life with Tom and will not be involved in the adoption proceedings.

The crucial question for Melanie is whether a court is likely to dispense with her consent and allow David and Emily to adopt Tom against her will. The court can only dispense with her consent on one or more specific grounds: see s16(2) AA 1976. The first ground relates to Melanie not being found or being incapable of giving agreement: see s16(2)(a) AA 1976. This does not appear to apply given the facts in this case. The second ground is that Melanie is withholding her consent unreasonably: see s16(2)(b) AA 1976. Melanie can be advised that this is not an easy ground to apply. The court will ask the question about whether Melanie is withholding her consent unreasonably at the date of the court hearing. It will apply an objective test, namely would a reasonable parent withhold consent. Tom's welfare is not treated as paramount in determining the question. The court will recognise that Melanie has legitimate rights which would be extinguished by the making of an adoption order and so has the right to veto the adoption. The adoption will not be granted simply because Tom's welfare suggests it. In judging reasonableness the court will take into account the welfare of the child. A reasonable mother gives great weight to what is better for the child. A reasonable parent does not ignore or disregard any risk of harm likely to be avoided by adoption or some appreciable benefit which the child will gain if adopted. There is no requirement to show culpability on Melanie's part or callousness or self-indulgent indifference. The test is reasonableness in the totality of the circumstances. A parent's anguish in considering whether to give consent is understandable, but the court must nevertheless see what a reasonable parent in her place would do in all the circumstances of the case: see *Re W (An Infant)* [1971] 2 WLR 1011. If Melanie is able to offer a safe home to her son the court is unlikely to be able to find sufficiently strong reasons for dispensing with her consent: see *O'Connor v A and B* [1971] 1 WLR 1227. Any upset in moving Tom back into her care is likely to be temporary compared to the benefits of being brought up by his natural mother: see *Re PA (An Infant)* [1971] 1 WLR 1530. This will depend on the bond between Melanie and her son and that between Tom and David and Emily. In the absence of information suggesting that Melanie has harmed, or would harm, Tom and cannot provide him with a home (with or without Peter) it is difficult to advise as how likely the court would apply this ground in dispensing with her consent. If she is not a risk to Tom and can provide him with a home then it is unlikely that her consent will be dispensed with. Her case is further strengthened by art 8 ECHR which emphasises the court's duty to respect Melanie's right to a family life with Tom unless it is proportionate and necessary to restrict that right.

The third ground is that Melanie has persistently failed without reasonable cause to discharge her parental responsibility for Tom: see s16(2)(c) AA 1976. Parental responsibility includes the obligation to support the child and to show affection, care and interest in the child: see *Re P (Infants)* [1962] 1 WLR 1296. Whether this ground can be made out will depend on how long Tom has been left in the care of David and Emily, and whether Melanie maintained contact with Tom and showed interest in him and over what period. The court is likely to have to find a high degree of culpability and that the failure was so grave and complete that Tom would derive no advantage in keeping a relationship with Melanie. 'Persistent' is defined as meaning 'permanent'. Even spasmodic visits and presents may show a continued interest which falls short of persistent failure: see *Re D (Minors) (Adoption by Parent)* [1973] 3 WLR 595. More information is required. However, on the brief facts disclosed it does not appear that Melanie and Tom have been apart for a sufficient period for David and Emily to succeed in persuading the court of 'persistent failure' on Melanie's part towards Tom.

The fourth ground is that Melanie has abandoned or neglected Tom: see s16(2)(d) AA 1976. Melanie can be advised that if she left Tom in the care of people she trusted then she would not be held to have abandoned or neglected Tom. A parent is treated as abandoning a child if the child was abandoned in a way which amounted to a criminal offence (whereby the child would suffer harm): see *Watson v Nickolaisen* [1955] 2 WLR 1187. It therefore appears unlikely that this ground for dispensing with Melanie's consent would be made out.

The final two grounds relate to Melanie persistently or seriously ill-treating Tom: see s16(2)(e) and (f) AA 1976. The facts in the question do not substantiate either of these two grounds.

Melanie should be advised that there is a prohibition on any person making arrangements for a child to be adopted unless the proposed adopter is a relative of the child: see s11(1) AA 1976. Contravention of this prohibition is a criminal offence. Similarly, there is a prohibition on the payment of money with a view to arranging an adoption or to persuading a parent to consent to an adoption or to transferring the custody of a child with a view to adoption: see s57 AA 1976. Again contravention of this prohibition is a criminal offence. The court can retrospectively authorise any payment. It appears that both these prohibitions have been breached, whether deliberately or unintentionally. This may count against any adoption application by David and Emily. Such breaches, however, would not prevent an adoption order being made: see *Re ZHH (Adoption Application)* [1993] 1 FLR 83. The more deliberate the breaches the more likely the court will treat the application with great caution and may refuse the adoption application: see *Re C (A Minor) (Adoption Application)* [1993] 1 FLR 87. The court will not countenance the sale of a child.

Melanie should be advised that the procedure for a contested adoption includes the appointment of a children's guardian who would provide an independent investigation of the application on behalf of Tom. This may provide her with some reassurance if she considers that the social worker is biased against her.

In addition, in deciding whether to grant an adoption Tom's welfare is only the first consideration (see s6 AA 1976) and not paramount. Even if David and Emily can show that they can provide more material benefits for Tom this will not lead to an adoption.

On the limited facts disclosed it appears that an adoption order would be unlikely to be granted.

Chapter 10

Local Authority Powers to Protect Children

10.1 Introduction

During the last 30 years the state, through local authorities, has increasingly played a role in providing for children in need and protecting children from abusive parents. Local authority powers and duties are contained in the Children Act (CA) 1989 which seeks to strike a balance between the rights of parents and giving powers to a local authority to intervene to protect a child.

10.2 Key points

Accommodating children

The student must understand the distinction between the local authority *accommodating* children at the request of their parents (which is a voluntary arrangement) and the local authority taking children into care through *care proceedings* (which allows the local authority to compel the parents to hand over care of the child to the authority).

Every local authority has a general duty to safeguard and promote the welfare of the children in their area who are in need and so far as is consistent with that duty to promote the upbringing of such children by their families: see s17 Children Act 1989.

As required by s20(1) CA 1989, every local authority must provide accommodation for any child in need within their area who appears to them to require accommodation as a result of:

a) there being no person who has parental responsibility for the child;

b) the child being lost or having been abandoned; or

c) the person who has been caring for the child being prevented (whether or not

'ly and for whatever reason) from providing the child with suitable
tion or care.

...nority may not provide such accommodation if any person who has parental
.esponsibility for the child and is willing and able to provide or arrange
accommodation for the child objects: see s20(7) CA 1989. Any person with parental
responsibility for a child may at any time remove the child from such accommodation:
see s20(8) CA 1989. There is no need for written notice or otherwise. If the local
authority wishes to prevent the child's removal it will have to apply for compulsory
powers using the emergency protection order and care proceedings.

Significant harm

Where a child is suffering or is likely to suffer significant harm due to a lack of
reasonable parental care a local authority can take action to compulsorily remove the
child. The key phrase is 'significant harm'. There is no definition of this important
phrase. 'Harm' includes ill-treatment or impairment of health or development. Ill-
treatment includes sexual and emotional abuse. Development includes physical,
intellectual, emotional, social and behavioural development. Health includes physical
or mental health: see s31(9) CA 1989. In deciding whether any harm is 'significant' the
court can compare the child's health and development against what would be
reasonably expected of a similar child: see s31(10) CA 1989. 'Similar' child' means a
child of equivalent intellectual and social development not merely an average child of
that age: see *Re O (A Minor) (Care Proceedings: Education)* [1992] 1 WLR 912.

One definition of 'significant harm' is that it is any harm which the court should take
into account in considering a child's future: see *Humberside County Council v B* [1993] 1
FLR 257.

Emergency protection order, police protection and child assessment orders

If there is an emergency the local authority can apply for an emergency protection
order: see s44 CA 1989. Application would be made to the local family proceedings
court and could be made ex parte with the permission of the justices' clerk. In order to
obtain an emergency protection order the local authority would have to satisfy the
court that there is reasonable cause to believe that the child is likely to suffer significant
harm if he/she is not removed to local authority accommodation or does not remain
where he/she is then being accommodated: see s44(1)(a). There is a second ground,
namely that enquiries made by the local authority are being frustrated by access to the
child being unreasonably refused and the local authority has reasonable cause to
believe that access to the child is required as a matter of urgency: see s44(1)(b).

If the emergency protection order is granted it operates as a direction to produce the
child to the local authority and authorises the child's removal to local authority
accommodation or prevents the child's removal from where he/she is presently
accommodated (eg a hospital). It also gives the local authority parental responsibility
for the child: see s44(4).

An emergency protection order can only last for up to eight days. It can be renewed once for a further seven days: see s45 CA 1989. The local authority must decide within that time whether to apply for a care order. The child's parents can apply to discharge the order 72 hours after it was made: see s45(8) and (9). If the order was made ex parte it must be served on the parents within 48 hours of being made.

An alternative to the emergency protection order is for the police to take the child into police protection. This can be done where a police constable has reasonable cause to believe that the child would be likely to suffer significant harm if he/she did not remove the child to suitable accommodation or prevent the removal of the child from his/her present accommodation. A child may only be kept in police protection for up to 72 hours: see s46 CA 1989.

If the situation is not so serious that it requires an emergency protection order or police protection, the local authority can apply for a child assessment order. It must satisfy the court that it has reasonable cause to suspect that the child is suffering or is likely to suffer significant harm, and an assessment of the child is required to enable the local authority to determine whether or not the child is so suffering or likely to so suffer and it is unlikely that such an assessment will be made (or be satisfactory) without a child assessment order being made: see s43(1) CA 1989. If made the order lasts for seven days and obliges any person named in the order to produce the child for the assessment or otherwise comply with the order. If the court believes the situation to be more serious it can treat the application as one for an emergency protection order.

Applying for a care or supervision order – the threshold criteria

Under s31(2) CA 1989 the local authority can apply for a care or supervision order if it can satisfy the court:

'(a) that the child is suffering significant harm or is likely to suffer, significant harm; and
(b) that harm, or likelihood of harm, is attributable to –
(i) the care given to the child, or likely to be given to him if the order were not made, not being what it would be reasonable to expect a parent to give him; or
(ii) the child's being beyond parental control.'

This single ground is called the *threshold criteria*.

The phrase 'is suffering significant harm' means that where a child has suffered significant harm but arrangements have been made to protect the child (eg via an emergency protection order and interim care orders), and those arrangements have continuously been in place up to the date when the court was deciding whether s31(2) is satisfied, the relevant date is the date when the local authority initiated its child protection procedures. If, after initiating child protection procedures the need for them ended (eg the child was returned to the parents) then the court could not look back to the date when child protection procedures first started but has to be satisfied that the child *is suffering significant harm* on the date it considered whether s31(2) had been satisfied: see *Re M (A Minor) (Care Order: Threshold Conditions)* [1994] 3 WLR 558.

The phrase 'is likely to suffer significant harm' was defined in *Re H and R (Child Sexual Abuse: Standard of Proof)* [1996] 1 FLR 80. The word 'likely' means a real possibility. The standard of proof is on a balance of probabilities. The court has to decide how highly it evaluates the risk of significant harm befalling the child on the basis of facts either admitted or proved on the balance of probabilities. A care order could not be made on the basis of suspicions.

The phrase 'attributable to ... the care given to the child ... not being what it would be reasonable to expect a parent to give to his or her child' was considered in *Lancashire County Council v B* [2000] 1 FLR 583, in which it was not clear who had caused injuries to the child – her mother, her father or the child-minder. The House of Lords held that the phrase 'given to the child' could embrace the care given by any of the carers. The attributable conditions may be satisfied where there was no more than a possibility that the parents were responsible for harming the child. This permitted the court to intervene to protect a child at risk where the individual responsible could not be identified.

Applying for a care or supervision order – the second stage

If the threshold criteria is satisfied the court has to consider the no order principle and the welfare checklist in deciding what order (if any) to make: see s1(3), (4) and (5) CA 1989.

In particular, the court must consider its full range of powers (eg making a residence order instead of a care or supervision order): see s1(3)(g) CA 1989 and *Humberside County Council v B* (above).

In *Re O (Supervision Order)* [2001] 1 FLR 923 it was held that in the context of the Human Rights Act 1998 proportionality was the key. Article 8 of the European Convention on Human Rights obliges a court to ensure that any intervention by the state between parents and children is proportionate to the legitimate aim of protecting family life. A supervision order was the proportionate response in this particular case, as opposed to a care order which would have been a disproportionate response. A similar view was taken in *Re C (Care Order or Supervision Order)* [2001] Fam Law 580 in which the risk to the child from the mother in the future was low and his welfare was safeguarded by the mother having parental responsibility. A supervision order was a proportionate response to the risks presented.

Miscellaneous matters

The court will appoint a children's guardian to investigate the case from the child's point of view: see s41 CA 1989. The guardian will appoint a solicitor to act for the child. The court will also lay down a timetable for hearing the application and will direct that each party serves its evidence in the form of written statements on the court and the other parties. Since it is likely to take some time before the final hearing can be arranged the local authority can ask the court to make an interim care or supervision order during the period of an adjournment. The court can only make an interim care or supervision order if it is satisfied that there are reasonable grounds for believing that the circumstances with the respect to the child satisfy the threshold criteria: see s38 CA 1989.

If a care order is made it gives parental responsibility for the child to the local authority. The parents share parental responsibility with the local authority but the parent's parental responsibility is limited by the care order and may be limited by the local authority: see s33(3) and (4) CA 1989. Before making a care order the court must consider what arrangements will be made to allow contact between the child and his/her parents: see s34(11) Children Act 1989. There is a presumption of reasonable contact between the child and his/her parents unless the court orders otherwise: see s34(1) and (2) CA 1989.

A supervision order gives the local authority the duty to advise, assist and befriend the supervised child: see s35(1) CA 1989. The order can only be made for one year though it can be renewed for up to three years.

Role of unmarried father

An unmarried father has no party status in care proceedings. As a result he may not be able to play any part in those proceedings unless he acquires parental responsibility or is made a party to the proceedings by the court.

The Human Rights Act 1998 and arts 6 and 8 of the European Convention of Human Rights are likely to persuade the courts to involve an unmarried father who has some involvement in the child's life and should be heard in the care proceedings: *Re P (Care Proceedings: Father's Application to be Joined as a Party)* [2001] 2 FCR 279.

Limitations on local authority applying for s8 orders

A local authority cannot apply for a residence order and a court cannot make a residence order in favour of a local authority: see s9(2) CA 1989. A local authority is also prohibited from applying for a contact order: see s9(2) CA 1989. A local authority cannot apply for a prohibited steps or specific issues order with a view to achieving a result which could be achieved by making a residence or contact order: see s9(5) CA 1989 and *Nottinghamshire County Council v P* [1993] 3 All ER 815.

Family Law Act 1996

The Family Law Act 1996 provides a solution to a problem identified in *Nottinghamshire County Council v P (No 2)* [1993] 2 FLR 134, whereby a local authority was prevented from applying for a prohibited steps order to exclude an abuser from the family home. An attempt by a local authority to apply for an ouster order under the inherent jurisdiction of the court failed: see *Re S (Minors) (Inherent Jurisdiction: Ouster)* [1994] 1 FLR 623. The same restriction applies in private law situations: see *Re M (Minors) (Disclosure of Evidence)* [1994] 1 FLR 760. The court may, when making an emergency protection order or interim care order, make an 'exclusion requirement' requiring a named individual to leave the home in which he or she is living with the child or to prevent him or her from entering the home in which the child lives. The court must be satisfied that: (i) there is reasonable cause to believe that if the person is excluded the child would cease to suffer or cease to be likely to suffer significant harm; and (ii) the caring parent remaining in the home can provide reasonable care and consents to the inclusion of the exclusion requirement. The court can attach a power of arrest or accept undertakings in place of the exclusion requirement.

The court may also be able to make a non-molestation order either on application or of its own motion: see s42(2) and (3) FLA 1996.

Wardship

The use of wardship is now more restricted. A local authority cannot use wardship as an alternative to care proceedings: see s100 CA 1989. If a local authority wishes to apply to make a child a ward of court it must obtain leave. Leave may only be granted if the High Court is satisfied that the result which the local authority wishes to achieve could not be achieved in other way open to the local authority, and there is reasonable cause to believe that if the child is not made a ward of court the child is likely to suffer significant harm: see s100(4) and (5) CA 1989.

An example of where leave was granted is *Devon County Council v S* [1995] 1 All ER 243 where children were made wards of court to protect them from a potential abuser, Y, married to the eldest child. Care proceedings were not appropriate because the mother's care of the children was good, though she did not appreciate the risk posed by Y.

A person cannot use wardship to challenge the decisions of a local authority: see *A v Liverpool City Council* [1981] 2 WLR 948.

Otherwise wardship can be used to make important and difficult decisions concerning a child (eg whether or not to provide medical treatment for a profoundly handicapped child as in *Re Baby J* [1990] 3 All ER 930).

Review of care plan by the court

In *Re W and B; Re W (Care Plan)* [2001] Fam Law 581 it was held that there was no fundamental incompatibility between the Children Act 1989 and the European Convention on Human Rights. The courts could construe statutory provisions in a manner compatible with the Convention. In the past the CA 1989 had been construed and applied in a way which exposed it to challenge on human rights' grounds. For example, there might be a failure by a local authority to advance a child's life from its family of birth to an alternative family or a failure to provide a child with access to the courts by depriving the child of representation through the children's guardian. The courts could seek to control how the local authority implemented its care plan.

In *Re S; Re W (Children: Care Plan)* [2002] 1 FLR 815 the House of Lords quashed *Re W and B; Re W (Care Plan)* holding that the courts had no power to interfere with local authorities in the way in which they implemented care orders. Once care orders had been made the local authority had the responsibility for deciding what should happen to the children.

10.3 Key cases and statute

- *Re H and R (Child Sexual Abuse: Standard of Proof)* [1996] 1 FLR 80
  Threshold conditions – likelihood of harm

- *Lancashire County Council v B* [2000] 1 FLR 583
  Threshold conditions – who has caused the harm

- *Re M (A Minor) (Care Order: Threshold Conditions)* [1994] 3 WLR 558
  Threshold conditions – is suffering significant harm

- *Re O (Supervision Order)* [2001] 1 FLR 923
  Care or supervision – proportionality

- *Re P (Care Proceedings: Father's Application to be Joined as a Party)* [2001] 2 FCR 279
  Care proceedings – role of unmarried father

- *Re S; Re W (Children: Care Plan)* [2002] 1 FLR 815
  Review of local authority care plan

- Children Act 1989 – grounds for care proceedings

10.4 Questions and suggested solutions

QUESTION ONE

Sarah, whose husband Tim died in 1990, has two daughters, Ursula and Veronica, who were born in 1982 and 1987 respectively. Sarah's boyfriend, William, who is unemployed, moved in with the family in 1994. Since early 1995, Ursula has been a regular school truant and has been cautioned by the police for shop-lifting on more than one occasion. In September 1995, Veronica complained to her teacher that William had been sexually abusing her. Her teacher alerted Zoe, a social worker at the Grantchester Local Authority, of Veronica's allegation and investigations followed which revealed that William had been convicted ten years previously of a sexual offence involving a young boy. Sarah assured the local authority that William had left the house and that she would not have him back. Criminal charges were brought against him in respect of Veronica, but were later dropped.

Zoe has recently been told that contrary to Sarah's assurances, William regularly visits Sarah and the children and that he and Ursula spend a great deal of time together. Ursula has denied that she is in contact with William, but she has not attended school for the last month and has begun to behave in a disturbed manner. Zoe has recently learned that Sarah is two months pregnant.

Advise Zoe, who is concerned about the welfare of Ursula and Veronica, of the steps she can take to protect them. Are there any steps that she may take to protect Sarah's unborn child?

University of London LLB Examination
(for External Students) Family Law June 1996 Q6

General Comment

The question is timely in light of the recent House of Lords judgment in *Re H and R (Child Sexual Abuse: Standard of Proof)* (1996) which dealt with a not dissimilar situation to the facts in the question. The student is given the opportunity to apply the decision to these facts and explain how a court is likely to approach an unproved complaint of sexual abuse in asking whether the threshold criteria in s31(2) Children Act 1989 is satisfied. The questions also allows an outline of local authority powers to protect children to be given and the various factors a court is likely to consider in determining any applications made to it. Finally, the status of an unborn child must be explained.

Skeleton Solution

Definition of phrase 'significant harm' – application for emergency protection orders (s44 CA 1989) or child assessment orders (s43 CA 1989) to meet the immediate situation – application for care orders: the threshold criteria in s31(2) CA 1989; meaning of 'suffering significant harm'; meaning of 'is likely to suffer significant harm' – no order principle (s1(5) CA 1989) and welfare checklist (s1(3) and (4) CA 1989) – exclusion requirement (ss38A and 44A CA 1989) – alternatives to care proceedings through prohibited steps order or wardship – status of unborn child.

Suggested Solution

Zoe seeks advice on what steps she can take to protect Ursula and Veronica and whether there are any steps she can take to protect Sarah's unborn child. Her concerns in relation to Ursula, who is now aged 14 years, can be summarised as the regular truancy from school since early 1995, her cautions for theft and the fact that she spends a lot time with her mother's boyfriend, William, who has a previous conviction for a sexual offence on a young boy and against whom her sister has made a complaint of sexual abuse. This has led to further truancy and disturbed behaviour. Zoe's concerns about Veronica are centred on Veronica's complaint of sexual abuse by William. It is noted that criminal proceedings in relation to her complaint were dropped but that William continues to spend time with both children. It is also noted that the children's mother, Sarah, does not appear to be co-operating with Zoe and that Zoe may have to resort to statutory intervention to protect the children.

Zoe can be advised in relation to Ursula and Veronica that she could apply to her local magistrates' court for emergency protection orders to authorise the removal of them from the family home to local authority accommodation. She can ask the clerk to the justices at the court for permission to make the application ex parte (ie without informing Sarah). If permission is not given, she must serve application forms on the court and at least one day's notice must be given to Sarah of the applications. At the hearing Zoe would have to satisfy the court that there is reasonable cause to believe that each child is likely to suffer significant harm if each child is not removed to local authority accommodation: see s44(1)(a) Children Act 1989 – hereinafter referred to as CA 1989. Zoe can be advised that 'harm' means ill-treatment or the impairment of health or development and that 'development' means physical, intellectual, emotional, social or behavioural development. 'Health' means physical or mental health and 'ill-treatment' includes sexual abuse and forms of ill-treatment which are not physical. Where the question of whether harm suffered by a child is significant depends on the child's health or development, her health or development shall be compared with that which could reasonably be expected of a similar child: see s31(9) CA 1989. 'A similar child' means a child of equivalent intellectual and social development: see *Re O (A Minor) (Care Proceedings: Education)* [1992] 1 WLR 912. This means that in terms of Ursula's truanting the court may compare her with a girl of equivalent intellectual and development who is attending school as opposed to an average child of her age who may or may not have gone to school. If the court grants the emergency protection orders then they can only last for a maximum of eight days (with an single option to extend them for a further seven days): see s45 CA 1989. On the information given, Zoe appears to have a strong case for the grant of emergency protection orders.

Alternatively, Zoe could apply for child assessment orders with respect to the two girls. Such orders would allow the girls to be assessed (eg to see if they had been sexually abused by William) rather than being removed from the family home. To obtain child assessment orders, Zoe would have to satisfy the court that she had reasonable cause to suspect that each child is suffering or is likely to suffer significant harm, and that an assessment of the state of each child's health or development or the way in which each child is being treated is required to enable Zoe to determine whether or not each child is suffering or is likely to suffer significant harm, and it is unlikely that such an assessment will be made or be satisfactory in the absence of an order: see s43 CA 1989. It is not clear whether Sarah has been asked to co-operate with such an assessment or what her attitude would be if this was suggested. This may have to be explored with her before Zoe could make applications for child assessment orders. The circumstances of the girls suggests that they are in real danger of harm so Zoe may be better advised to apply for emergency protection orders.

The above applications deal with the immediate situation. In the long term Zoe would be advised that she may have to apply to the court for care or supervision orders to be made. Such proceedings would take some time to reach a final hearing so her initial applications would be for interim care or supervision orders. Interim care orders would mean that the local authority maintained parental responsibility for the girls alongside Sarah and maintained control over where the girls lived. Interim supervision orders would only provide for Zoe advising and assisting Sarah and the children. The court could only make such interim orders if it was satisfied that there are reasonable grounds for believing that the circumstances with respect to each child satisfied the 'threshold criteria' in s31(2) CA 1989. The court would be concerned to deal with the applications with the minimum delay since it has to assume that delay in dealing with them is likely to be prejudicial to each child's welfare: see s1(2) CA 1989. It will lay down a timetable for the filing of evidence and for the final hearing which all the parties will be expected to comply with. It will also appoint a guardian ad litem (an independent social worker) to investigate the applications from the children's point of view. The children will also be separately legally represented so that their point of view can be put before the court.

The key to whether care or supervision orders would be made at the final hearing would be whether the threshold criteria in s31(2) CA 1989 were satisfied. The court must be satisfied that each child is suffering or is likely to suffer significant harm and that the harm of likelihood of harm is attributable to a lack of reasonable parental care or each child's being beyond parental control. As to whether the court was satisfied that either child 'is suffering significant harm', if the child concerned had been constantly subject to local authority protective procedures since the start of the applications (eg emergency protection order and interim care orders) then the court would look back at the time when those emergency measures were first applied for. If such protective procedures had not applied for all of the period up to the final hearing (eg the children had remained or been returned home without interim orders being made) the court would look at the situation as it was at the date of the final hearing: see *Re M (A Minor) (Care Order: Threshold Conditions)* [1994] 3 WLR 558. In interpreting the phrase 'is likely to suffer significant harm' the court would have to find that there was a real possibility of the child suffering significant harm based on admitted facts or on facts proved on the balance of probabilities: see *Re H and R (Child Sexual Abuse: Standard of Proof)* [1996] 1 FLR 80. This may pose difficulties for Zoe. She can seek to rely on the fact of William's previous conviction to persuade the court that there is a real possibility that he will harm both girls by sexually abusing them. However, that conviction was ten years ago and involved a young boy. She could seek to rely on Veronica's recent complaint even though criminal charges for that were dropped. If she considers that there is good evidence to substantiate her complaint she may seek to prove sexual abuse on a balance of probabilities (bearing in mind that this is a lower standard than the criminal standard of proof beyond reasonable doubt). However, if she fails to establish the fact of abuse the court may not be able to find a likelihood of harm even though it may be more than a little suspicious of William. Having said that, Ursula's persistent truanting for over a year, her offending and now her disturbed behaviour, coupled with her association with a known sexual offender, amount to a strong case that she is suffering significant harm. Veronica's case may be less strong. However, the proof of the harm which her older sister is suffering may be sufficient to persuade the court that Veronica is likely to suffer significant harm even if it finds it is not satisfied of the truth of her complaint against William in September 1995. If the court makes such findings it is also likely to find that Sarah has not provided reasonable care for her daughters, and in particular has failed to protect them from William despite being warned and despite agreeing with Zoe to do so.

If the court does find that the threshold criteria are satisfied it must consider a number of other matters before deciding whether to make care or supervision orders. It must treat the welfare of each girl as the paramount consideration outweighing all other considerations: see s1(1) CA 1989. It must consider that making any orders would be better than making no orders at all (ie that the orders will improve the girls' lives): see s1(5) CA 1989. Given the girls' circumstances it is likely to assume that orders should be made. It must also consider the welfare checklist: see s1(3) and (4) CA 1989. This includes the ascertainable wishes and feelings of each child considered in the light of her age and understanding: see s1(3)(a). Since Ursula is aged 14 her wishes and feelings are likely to carry weight with the court, though not if it is clear that she does not recognise the harm being done to her. Veronica is nine years old so may not be sufficiently mature for her wishes and feelings to carry great weight with the court. The court must also consider each child's physical, emotional and educational needs and must consider their sex, ages, background and other relevant characteristics: see s1(3)(b) and (d). It must also consider the likely effect on each child of any change in her circumstances: see s1(3)(c). If the children are to be removed from their home, and possibly from their mother, the consequences of this must be considered along with the harm they have suffered or are at risk of suffering: see s1(3)(e). The court must consider Sarah's capabilities as a mother (see s1(3)(f)) and its full range of powers: see s1(3)(g). In considering the orders available to it the court will take into account that only a care order gives the local authority the power to control the children's lives should Sarah choose not to co-operate with or try to deceive Zoe. This may persuade the court that a supervision order or any other orders which do not give the local authority such powers do not meet the needs of the case. In addition, the court must consider the recommendations of the guardian ad litem and the care plan provided by the local authority mapping out the children's future.

Zoe can also be advised that she can ask the court to make an exclusion requirement as part of an emergency protection order or interim care order whereby William is excluded from entering the children's home. Such a requirement can only be made if the court finds that there is cause to believe that if William is excluded either child will cease to be likely to suffer significant harm: see ss38A and 44A CA 1989. However, the court would also have to be satisfied that Sarah is able and willing to give the children reasonable care and agrees to William being excluded. Given Sarah's apparent lack of co-operation and lack of reasonable care for the children, the court may feel unable to make an exclusion requirement.

Zoe should be advised that there is an alternative to taking care proceedings but that this approach has not found favour with the courts, so cannot be recommended. This would involve the local authority not applying for care proceedings but applying for a prohibited steps order (under ss8 and 10 CA 1989), which is an order prohibiting William from having contact with the girls. The courts disapprove of such an application being used instead of care proceedings since it does not give the local authority any powers to deal with the situation and prevents it from having the powers and discretion conferred by a care order: see *Nottinghamshire County Council* v *P* [1993]

3 All ER 815. If Zoe does not want to bring care proceedings because she considers this would do more harm than good there is the possibility of her applying to make the children wards of court. This is only likely if Zoe is satisfied that Sarah's care of the girls is otherwise good and the local authority do not wish to invade her parental responsibility and risk destabilising the children's care. The court would only allow the children to be made wards if it accepted that there were valid reasons why care proceedings were not appropriate and if it was satisfied that was reasonable cause to believe that if the court's powers were not exercised the children would suffer significant harm: see s100 CA 1989 and *Devon County Council v S* [1995] 1 All ER 243. Since Sarah's care of the children does not appear to fall into this category this does not seem to be a likely option.

In relation to Sarah's unborn child Zoe can be advised that no statutory proceedings can be taken to protect the unborn child since he or she is not treated as having a separate existence to Sarah: see *Re F* [1988] 2 All ER 193. Proceedings could be started as soon as the child was born on the basis of likelihood of significant harm if Zoe was able to satisfy the court that the harm caused to the baby's half sisters was sufficient to show that there was a real possibility that the baby would suffer significant harm.

QUESTION TWO

To what extent, in your opinion, has the Children Act 1989 achieved the aim of diminishing the powers of the state while asserting the autonomy of the family? What is the right balance? What part have the courts played in striking the appropriate balance?

University of London LLB Examination
(for External Students) Family Law June 1997 Q7

General Comment

This essay-style question invites a discussion about the 'public law' parts of the Children Act 1989. The Act laid down a code for local authorities to respond to requests for help for parents in difficulties with their children, to deal with the emergency protection of children and the taking of children into the care or their supervision. The Act tried create a balance between family autonomy and the powers of the local authority to protect. Has the Act created the right balance? This requires an outline of the relevant parts of the Act and how the courts have played their role in striking the appropriate balance, particularly *Re H and R (Child Sexual Abuse: Standard of Proof)*.

Skeleton Solution

Part III of the Children Act 1989: provision of accommodation for children with the consent of the children (ss20–22 CA 1989) – Part V CA 1989: protection of children; emergency protection orders (s44); child assessment orders (s43); police protection (s46); ex parte applications – Part IV CA 1989: application for care/supervision orders

make an interim care order (which allows a local authority to remove a child from his/her parents for up to eight weeks on the first order) if it is satisfied that there are reasonable grounds for believing that the circumstances with respect to the child meet the threshold criteria. The court can only make a care order if it is satisfied that that the child is suffering or is likely to suffer significant harm, and that the harm, or likelihood of harm, is attributable to a lack of reasonable parental care or the child being beyond parental control: see s31(2) CA 1989. The key to removing a child from his/her parents is the threshold criteria. This one criteria replaced a series of grounds for the making of care orders under s1(2) CYPA 1969 which were not entirely consistent. For example, the commission of a single criminal offence by a child could lead to a care order being made: see s1(2)(f) CYPA 1969. The threshold criteria was designed to provide a single criterion which would promote a more consistent and fairer approach, particularly from the parents' point of view. It appears that the Children Act 1989 has succeeded to a large extent in this respect. The Act provides a wide definition of harm: see s31(9) CA 1989. The word 'significant' is not defined except to the extent of comparing a child's development with that of a similar child: see s31(10) CA 1989 and *Re O (A Minor) (Care Proceedings: Education)* [1992] 1 WLR 912. The courts have attempted various definitions of varying degrees of usefulness. One attempt was to liken 'significant harm' to an elephant, difficult to describe but one knew it when one saw it! This appears to reflect how courts have applied the phrase. There have been some difficulties in defining the phrase 'is suffering significant harm' until the House of Lords resolved the matter in *Re M (A Minor) (Care Order: Threshold Conditions)* [1994] 3 All ER 298. That decision appears to have resolved that particular difficulty so that both the local authority and parents know how the courts will interpret the phrase. More controversially, the House of Lords has given guidance on the phrase 'is likely to suffer significant harm' in *Re H and R (Child Sexual Abuse: Standard of Proof)* [1996] 2 WLR 8. This phrase involves an assessment of risk. The majority decision was that s31(2) marked the boundary line between the interests of the parents in caring for their own children and the interests of the child, particularly where it was in the child's interests to be cared for by others. The word 'likely' meant a real possibility, namely a possibility which could not be ignored having regard to the nature and gravity of the feared harm in the particular case. A court had to make findings on disputed facts and then evaluate the risks of significant harm befalling the child. It was held that parents were not to be at risk of having their children taken away on the basis only of suspicions. This decision swung a delicate balance in favour of the parents. It may make the threshold criteria more difficult to satisfy in cases of suspected sexual abuse in which suspicions are many but hard proof thin on the ground. Even if the threshold criteria is satisfied the court has a discretion as to which kind of order to make. It must consider the welfare checklist: see s1(3),(4) CA 1989. This includes considering a full range of orders including a supervision order or a residence order: see *Humberside County Council v B* [1993] 1 FLR 257. This contrasts with the previous situation when either a care order could be made or no order at all.

If a care order is made then the local authority shares parental responsibility with the child's parents, though the exercise of the parents' parental responsibility can be limited by the local authority, particularly in terms of with whom the child lives: see s33(3) CA 1989. There is a presumption of reasonable contact in favour of the parents which can only be limited by court order: see s34 CA 1989. The courts have emphasised that any local authority plans which involves limiting or ending parental contact do not bind the court: see *Re B (Minors) (Termination of Contact: Paramount Consideration)* [1993] 3 All ER 525. The court can require the local authority to justify its plans to the extent that they limit or exclude contact between a child and his/her parents. In that particular case a local authority wished to terminate contact between two children in care and their mother. The court refused to allow this since it recognised that the mother's potential to improve and care for her children needed to be investigated. Both the courts and local authorities recognise the importance of a child's parents continuing to play a part in the child's life even after the making of a care order. Their right to withhold consent to an adoption remains as under the pre-existing law.

The Children Act 1989 also restricted the use of wardship, particularly as an alternative to care proceedings: see s100(2) CA 1989. This again reflects the need for consistency in deciding when a child should be removed from parents.

The Children Act 1989 removed a whole series of powers to make care orders in the context of private law applications. These powers were seen to be inconsistent and arbitrary. There is now no power to make a care order as a result of concerns raised during a private law application. The only power is to ask the local authority to investigate the circumstances with a view to deciding whether to bring care proceedings: see s37 CA 1989. This reform of the law has been most welcome since it again promotes consistency and removes powers which could be exercised unfairly and arbitrarily.

In general terms the Children Act 1989 has encouraged local authorities to work with parents rather than against them. This is reflected in the no order principle in s1(2) CA 1989, whereby a court cannot make an order unless it is satisfied that it would provide some positive benefit for the child. Applications for emergency orders or for care orders are seen as something of a last resort, eg when agreement between the parents and the local authority has broken down or where the nature of the harm or risk of harm to the child is too great and immediate to allow the local authority to wait to work with the parents. In conclusion, the Children Act 1989 appears to have achieved a much better balance between the powers of the state and the autonomy of the family. When compared with the law under the Child Care Act 1980 (particularly parental rights resolutions) and the Children and Young Persons Act 1969, the Children Act 1989 provides a much fairer and coherent code for child protection. The courts appear to have recognised the importance of this balance and have laid guidelines to protect parental autonomy (particularly in *Re H and R*).

QUESTION THREE

In your view, does Part IV of the Children Act 1989, as interpreted by the courts, go far enough to protect the integrity of family units against the power of local authorities?

University of London LLB Examination
(for External Students) Family Law June 2000 Q6

General Comment

This essay-style question allowed the student to discuss Part IV of the Children Act 1989 and the checks and balances within it in terms of powers given to local authorities to protect children while respecting the integrity of family units. First, the single ground for the making of a care order required discussion. The 'threshold criteria' has been subject to a good deal of judicial scrutiny, particularly by the House of Lords. The consequences of making a care order or a supervision order also required discussion, as did the provisions dealing with contact with children in care. The safeguards provided by children's guardians should be included. In order to provide an up-to-date suggested solution the impact of the Human Rights Act 1998 and relevant European case law has also been included in the answer.

Skeleton Solution

Reforms brought in by Children Act 1989 – Parts III and Part IV; Part IV of the Children Act 1989: the threshold criteria in s31 CA 1989 – the concept of significant harm – case law on 'is suffering significant harm' and 'is likely to suffer significant harm' – case law on 'attributable to a lack of reasonable parental care'; consequences of: care order – supervision order; contact between children in care and parents; interim orders; discharge of care or supervision orders; the role of the children's guardian; the Human Rights Act 1998 and the impact of art 8 (the right to family life) of the European Convention on Human Rights.

Suggested Solution

The question asks whether Part IV of the Children Act (CA) 1989, as interpreted by the courts, goes far enough to protect the integrity of family units against the power of local authorities. The Children Act 1989 came into force in 1991. Part IV of the 1989 Act introduced a single ground for local authorities (and other authorised persons) for applying for care orders. The Act replaced a number of separate provisions which were inconsistent and wide-ranging and could lead to a child being taken into care without due regard to the integrity of family units. Has the single code provided by Part IV of the 1989 Act gone far enough to protect that integrity against the power of local authorities?

Before discussing Part IV of the 1989 Act mention should be made of Part III of the 1989 Act. Part III imposes a duty on local authorities to safeguard and promote the welfare of children within their area who are in need and, so far as is consistent with te the upbringing of such children by their families: see s17 CA 1989. y has a duty to provide accommodation for any child in need if, for ·son who has been caring for the child is prevented from providing uitable accommodation or care: see s20(1) CA 1989. However, the local not provide such accommodation against the wishes of a parent with onsibility who is able to provide accommodation for the child (see s20(7) CA 1989), a..id a parent with parental responsibility may remove the child voluntarily accommodated with the local authority: see s20(8) CA 1989. The local authority must also consult the parents and give them due consideration in making any decision about the child: see s23 CA 1989. Part III therefore provides the basis for the local authority working with parents and respecting the integrity of family units, in particular the rights of the parents with parental responsibility. It should be noted that unmarried fathers, who do not have parental responsibility, do not have the right to remove children: under s20(7) and (8) CA 1989.

Part IV of the Children Act 1989 deals with the powers of a local authority (or authorised person) to compulsorily take a child into its care against the wishes of the parents. There is a single criteria for the making of a care or supervision order, called the 'threshold criteria', and set out in s31(2) Children Act 1989, namely that the court is satisfied:

1. that the child concerned if suffering or is likely to suffer significant harm; and

2. that the harm or likelihood of harm is attributable to a lack of reasonable parental care or the child being beyond parental control.

'Harm' is defined as ill-treatment or the impairment of health or development. 'Development' means physical, intellectual, emotional, social or behavioural development and 'health' means physical or mental health. 'Ill-treatment' includes sexual abuse and forms of ill-treatment which are not physical: see s31(9) CA 1989. Where the court is asked whether the harm suffered by the child is significant turns on the child's health or development, and his or her health or development must be compared with that which could reasonably expected of a similar child (see s31(10) CA 1989). This means a child of equivalent intellectual and social development to the child in question, as opposed to an average child: see *Re O (A Minor) (Care Proceedings: Education)* [1992] 1 WLR 912. The courts have held that 'significant harm' means any harm which the court should take into account in considering a child's future: see *Humberside County Council v B* [1993] 1 FLR 257.

On a number of occasions the courts have been asked to interpret aspects of the 'threshold' criteria. In *Re M (A Minor) (Care Order: Threshold Conditions)* [1994] 3 WLR 558 the House of Lords considered the phrase 'is suffering significant harm'. The court interpreted the phrase as meaning that where a child has suffered significant harm but arrangements were then made to protect the child (eg via emergency protection orders and interim care orders) and those arrangements had continuously in been in place up to the date of the court hearing then the relevant date is the date when the local authority initiated its protection procedures. If such procedures had either not been used or had not continuously been in place then the court must look back to the situation when the protective arrangements started. This enabled the court to confirm a care order with respect to a child who had seen her father murder her mother but who later had the prospect of being cared for by her aunt. It rejected the argument that, since the father was in prison and the aunt could provide the child with a home, the phrase 'is suffering significant harm' could not apply at the time of the hearing. Protection procedures had continuously been in place and the local authority could use the care order to manage the arrangements for the child living with her aunt.

The House of Lords then had to wrestle with an even more difficult situation in *Re H and R (Child Sexual Abuse: Standard of Proof)* [1996] 2 WLR 8. It was required to consider the phrase 'is likely to suffer significant harm'. The case concerned four daughters, the eldest of whom alleged sexual abuse against her mother's partner. The local authority applied for care orders on the basis of the likelihood of harm to the younger daughters. The partner was acquitted of rape. The court found it could not be sure to the requisite high standard of proof that the eldest daughter's allegations were true and dismissed the applications for care orders. The Court of Appeal and the House of Lords dismissed the appeals. It was held that s31(2) of the 1989 Act marked the boundary line between the interests of the parents in caring for their own children and the interests of the child in terms of protection from harm. 'Likely' meant a 'real possibility', a possibility which could not be ignored having regard to the nature and gravity of the feared harm in the particular case. It did not mean 'more likely than not'. The burden is on the local authority. The standard of proof is on a balance of probabilities. However, the more serious the allegation the less likely it is that the event occurred and the stronger the evidence needed before the allegation can be established. Parents were not to be at risk of having their children taken away on the basis only of suspicions. The House of Lords was protecting the integrity of the family unit against the power of local authorities acting on insufficient proof.

More recently the House of Lords considered s31(2)(b)(i) of the 1989 Act and in particular the word 'attributable' in *Lancashire County Council v B* [2000] 1 FLR 583. The case concerned firstly a child who suffered serious injuries as a result of violent shaking. It was not clear who had harmed the child, the parents or a child minder. Care proceedings were brought in relation to that child and in relation to the child of the childminder. The House of Lords held that s31(2)(b)(i) normally referred to the care given by the parents or other primary carers. Different considerations applied where there was shared caring and the court was unable to identify which carer provided deficient care. The attributable condition could be satisfied where there was no more than a possibility that the parents were responsible for inflicting the injuries. This interpretation was necessary to permit the court to intervene to protect a child at risk where the individual could not be identified. It by no means followed that because the threshold conditions were satisfied that the court could make a care order. The court's discretion would have to take account of the fact that the parents had not been shown to be responsible for the child's injuries. In the particular case a care order was confirmed for the child who had been injured. No care order was made with respect to the childminder's child. The proceedings were based on the likelihood of harm. In the absence of proof of injury to that child, and in the absence of proof to the requisite standard that the childminder had injured the first child, there was not sufficient proof to satisfy the threshold criteria. The House of Lords also considered arguments by the parents pursuant to art 8 (the right to family life) of the European Convention on Human Rights. The House of Lords held that the local authority could interfere with the right to family life, provided the local authority took reasonable steps to pursue the legitimate aim of protecting the child from further injury (applying art 8(2)).

If the threshold criteria is satisfied the court is not obliged to make a care order. It must consider the welfare checklist in s1(3) and (4) of the 1989 Act, including the full range of orders available to it, before determining what order to make. The range of orders include not only a care order but a supervision order or a residence order. A care order gives the local authority parental responsibility for the child which is shared with the parents, but with the local authority determining where the child should live and limiting the extent to which the parent may meet his or her parental responsibility for the child: see s33 CA 1989. A supervision order has far less force and obliges the local authority to advise, assist and befriend the child but does not allow the local authority to control the parents' exercise of parental responsibility: see s35 CA 1989. Following the Human Rights Act 1998 which applied the European Convention on Human Rights to English and Welsh law from October 2000, the courts have been advised to consider the least interventionist response needed to protect the child, namely to make a supervision order where for example the balance between that and a care order was equal: see *Re C and B (Care Order: Future Harm)* [2001] 1 FLR 611.

The other sections in Part IV of the 1989 Act deserve mention. Section 34 deals with contact between children in care and their parents. There is a presumption of reasonable contact whereby a local authority must seek a court order to restrict or prevent contact between the parents and their child: see s34(1) CA 1989. Section 38 deals with interim care and supervision orders and provides that a court cannot make such orders unless satisfied that there are reasonable grounds for believing that the threshold criteria is satisfied: see s38(2) CA 1989. There are also provisions allowing the court to make an exclusion requirement as part of an interim care order in order to exclude, for example, the perpetrator of harm, and allowing the children to remain at home with the 'innocent' parent (provided he or she is able to provide proper care and consents to the perpetrator being excluded): s38A CA 1989. There are also provisions allowing a parent (or the local authority) to apply to discharge or vary a care or supervision order: see s39 CA 1989. There are provisions too requiring the appointment of a children's guardian and legal representative to represent the interests of the child: see s41 CA 1989. This is an important factor in enabling the court to know the child's wishes and feelings and have an independent view on what the best course of action is for the child. The role of the guardian is significant in that the court must give reasons for not following a reasoned recommendation made by a guardian.

Though not strictly relevant the restrictions on local authorities to intervene in family life through wardship should also be highlighted. Section 100(2) of the 1989 Act prevents the local authority from using wardship as an alternative to care proceedings. Indeed, any application for wardship by a local authority requires the leave of the court (see s100(3) CA 1989) and leave will not be granted if the local authority can achieve its aims through the 1989 Act: see s100(4) and (5) CA 1989. Having said that the courts have allowed local authorities to use wardship where the flexibility of wardship would be more appropriate than the blunt instrument of care proceedings: see *Devon County Council* v *S* [1995] 1 All ER 243.

Finally mention must be made of the Human Rights Act 1998 and the impact of art 3 (the duty to protect a person from inhumane and degrading treatment), art 6 (the right to a fair trial) and art 8 (the right to family life) of the European Convention on Human Rights (ECHR). The English and Welsh courts must now apply domestic law in a way which is consistent with the ECHR and decisions of the European Court of Human Rights. This provides a separate check on the power of local authorities in relation to the integrity of family units and, in particular, the right to family life in art 8. There is a duty on local authorities to take care proceedings in order to protect children: see *Z* v *United Kingdom* [2001] 2 FLR 603. This must be balanced against only interfering with family life where it is necessary and proportionate in a democratic society: see art 8(2). The European Court requires a fair balance to be struck between the need to protect children from harm and the interests of a parent in being reunited with his or her child. As under the Children Act 1989, the European Court stresses the importance of maintaining or reuniting the family unless this would clearly harm the child. The courts must ensure that any action of the local authorities balances the interests in a proportionate and reasonable manner: see *K and T* v *Finland* [2000] 2 FLR 79 and *Scott* v *United Kingdom* [2000] 1 FLR 958.

In conclusion, Part IV of the Children Act 1989, as interpreted by the courts, does go far enough to protect the integrity of family units against the power of local authorities. The balancing act within Part IV of the 1989 Act has been scrutinised and approved by the European Court of Human Rights (eg in *Scott* v *United Kingdom*). Second, the House of Lords has shown an awareness of the need to protect the integrity of family units in such decisions as *Re H and R (Child Sexual Abuse: Standard of Proof)* and particularly not to sanction the removal of children without clear proof of harm or the likelihood of harm. If there is any criticism it may be that the courts have gone too far in recognising the rights of parents as against the difficulties for local authorities in adducing the required sufficiency of evidence in difficult cases (eg of sexual abuse) and being unable to protect children because of the absence of clear proof.

QUESTION FOUR

In early 1999, the social services department of Blankshire local authority was informed that two children in their area, Mary and Steven, aged seven and five respectively, were left on their own for long periods of time, sometimes overnight. The local authority was also told that the children appeared dirty, malnourished and uncared for.

In May 1999 a social worker called at the children's home and spoke to their mother, Sally, about the children. Sally said that the children were visiting their grandparents for a few days and would not allow the social worker into the home.

Making enquiries, the social worker discovered that Sally was working as a prostitute in the King's Cross area of London, and that as a child Sally herself had been regarded as being at risk of abuse from her step-father.

Advise Blankshire local authority, and Sally, of their respective rights and duties in relation to the children under the Children Act 1989.

University of London LLB Examination
(for External Students) Family Law June 1999 Q7

General Comment

This is a general question on care proceedings and preliminary steps which could be taken to protect children at risk from harm. It requires discussion of parental responsibility and what that entails. It also requires discussion of emergency protection orders, child assessment orders, interim care orders and care proceedings generally. In order to provide the student with an up-to-date suggested solution reference is made to the impact of the Human Rights Act 1998 and the effect of the European Convention on Human Rights.

Skeleton Solution

Parental responsibility, in particular: the duty to financially maintain the children – the duty to protect the children from harm – the duty to ensure they receive a proper education; working with the local authority by consent; duties of local authority in relation to children in need; emergency protection order application; child assessment order application; interim care orders; threshold criteria for care proceedings and other considerations (eg the welfare checklist); ancillary matters: children's guardian – disclosure of evidence – contact with children in care.

Suggested Solution

The question asks for advice to both Sally and Blankshire local authority on their respective rights and duties to the children under the Children Act 1989.

There is no reference to the father of the children. It is assumed that he or they are unmarried fathers with no parental responsibility for the children. As a result it appears likely that Sally has sole parental responsibility for Mary and Steven: see s2(2)(a) Children Act (CA) 1989. Though parental responsibility has no precise definition it includes the responsibility to financially maintain the children, the responsibility to protect them from physical and emotional harm and the responsibility to see that the children receive education. Breach of the responsibility to protect the children from physical or emotional harm may result in Sally being criminally liable. Sally should be advised that it is a criminal offence for her to neglect, abandon or expose the children in a manner likely to cause them unnecessary suffering or injury: see s1 Children and Young Persons Act 1933. A prosecution must show a deliberate or reckless neglect on Sally's behalf if they wish to successfully prosecute her: see *R v Shepperd* [1981] AC 394. In addition, it is Sally's duty to ensure that Mary and Steven receive suitable education: see s7 Education Act 1996. Both children are of compulsory school age. If Sally is not ensuring that they regularly attend school then she may be guilty of an offence: see s444 Education Act 1996. Repeated non-school attendance can also be grounds for the local authority applying for a care order: see *Re O (A Minor) (Care Proceedings: Education)* [1992] 1 WLR 912. Details of how the local authority might make such an application are given below.

Sally can be advised that Blankshire local authority have no power to act in relation to the children without either her consent or a court order. She would be advised to co-operate with the local authority to avoid any need for the local authority applying for court orders. For example, if she is having problems coping with the children she can agree to them being accommodated by the local authority (eg with foster parents): see s20(1) and (7) CA 1989.

The Blankshire local authority can be advised that it has a duty to safeguard and promote the welfare of any child in need in its area: see s17(1)(a) CA 1989. So far as is consistent with that duty the local authority must promote the upbringing of Mary and Steven by their mother: see s17(1)(b) CA 1989. As a result the local authority should attempt to work with Sally as far as is possible. Blankshire local authority can also be advised that if it considers that it has reasonable cause to suspect that Mary and Steven are suffering, or are likely to suffer, significant harm it must make all necessary enquiries to enable it to decide whether it should take action to safeguard or promote the children's welfare: see s47(1) CA 1989. It is noted that enquiries have already been made and the local authority can be advised as to what steps they can now take.

A key concept is that of 'significant harm'. Harm is given a wide meaning and includes ill-treatment or impairment of health or development. Ill-treatment includes emotional abuse. Development includes physical, intellectual, emotional, social and behavioural development. Health includes physical or mental health: see s31(9) CA 1989. The court can judge a child's health and development against what would be expected of a similar child: see s31(10). 'Significant harm' has been held to mean harm which the court should take into account in determining a child's future: see *Humberside County Council v B* [1993] 1 FLR 257. In this case it appears likely that Mary and Steven are suffering significant harm or are likely to do so. If such young children are being left alone for such long periods of time, including overnight, they are likely to have suffered, or be at considerable risk of, significant harm. Young children of that age need supervision to protect them from physical harm. They also need to be provided with food and drink. They also require emotional care and support. If in addition the children are dirty, malnourished and uncared for is likely to confirm significant harm or the risk of such harm. There also seems some indication that Sally has her own needs because of her own history which may emphasise the risks to the children. If the local authority take the view that they cannot work with Sally because she has unreasonably refused access to the children it can be advised that it can apply to the magistrates' court (through the family proceedings court) for orders allowing the local authority to act to protect the children without the consent or co-operation of Sally.

The local authority do have a duty to act to protect the children. If they fail to act and the children are harmed then the authority could be liable in negligence and under the Human Rights Act 1998: see *Z* v *United Kingdom* [2000] 2 FCR 245. Not to act to protect the children from inhumane and degrading treatment would infringe art 3 of the European Convention on Human Rights (ECHR). If the local authority wish to take emergency action in relation to the children it can be advised that it can apply to the family proceedings court for emergency protection orders: see s44 CA 1989. If granted the orders would require Sally to produce the children to the local authority if so requested and authorises the authority to remove the children to local authority accommodation. The orders would also prevent Sally from removing the children from such accommodation. The orders would also give the authority parental responsibility for the children to the extent of what is reasonably required to safeguard or promote the welfare of the children. The local authority can seek to apply for emergency protection orders ex parte, namely without notifying Sally. It must obtain the leave of the justices' clerk of the magistrates' court to make ex parte applications: see r4 Family Proceedings Courts (Children Act 1989) Rules 1991. The justices' clerk will not grant leave unless the need to protect the children is so important that it overrides the right of the mother to a fair trial. He or she will consider the ECHR which was incorporated into English law by the Human Rights Act 1998 in October 2000. He or she will consider the need to protect the children from degrading or inhuman treatment (see art 3 ECHR) and the right of Sally to a fair hearing (see art 6 ECHR) and the right to a family life with her children: see art 8 ECHR (though this right can be restricted if necessary and proportionate in a democratic society). If leave to make the applications ex parte is refused then at least one day's notice must be given to Sally. The local authority must satisfy the court that there is reasonable cause to believe that the children are likely to suffer significant harm if they are not removed to local authority accommodation: see s44(1)(a) CA 1989. An alternative ground is that enquiries are being made by the local authority under s47 CA 1989 and these enquiries are being frustrated by access to the children being unreasonably refused by Sally, and the local authority has reasonable cause to believe that access to the children is required as a matter of urgency: s44(1)(b) CA 1989. It appears on the facts that either ground could be made out. As already discussed above it appears that there are reasonable grounds for believing that the children are likely to suffer significant harm if not removed to local authority accommodation given the apparent neglect (so that s44(1)(a) could be made out). It may be more advisable for the local authority to apply under this ground as opposed to s44(1)(b) since Sally could argue that she has not unreasonably refused access to the children on the basis of one visit, particularly if the children were indeed visiting their grandparents. The local authority could also apply for child assessment orders with respect to the children as a less drastic form of intervention. The authority would have to satisfy the court that it has reasonable cause to suspect that the children are suffering or are likely to suffer significant harm and an assessment of the state of the children's health or development or the way in which they have been treated is required to enable it to determine whether or not the children are suffering or are likely to suffer significant harm: see s43(1) CA 1989. The order would require Sally to produce the children to the local authority and comply with any directions given by the court. The authority can be advised that applications for child assessment orders are rare. Emergency protection orders provide the authority with much greater powers particularly in relation to an uncooperative parent.

Should emergency protection orders be granted they would be for a maximum period of eight days with the possibility of renewing them for a further seven days: see s45 CA 1989. Sally could apply for the orders to be discharged once 72 hours had elapsed from the making of the first order: s45(9) CA 1989. If the orders were made ex parte they have to be served on Sally within 48 hours so that she is aware of them. During the period of any emergency protection orders the local authority would have to decide whether or not to apply for care orders. If it does so it must give Sally a minimum of three days' notice. It can then apply for interim care orders with respect to the children. The court must be satisfied that there are reasonable grounds for believing that the 'threshold criteria' is made out: see s38(2) CA 1989. The 'threshold criteria' (set out in s31(2) CA 1989) require the court to be satisfied that each of the children is suffering or is likely to suffer significant harm and the harm or likelihood of harm is attributable to a lack of reasonable parental care. The phrase 'is suffering significant harm' either relates to the period when the children are first taken into the care of the local authority (eg through an emergency protection order and then interim care orders), provided interim care orders have continually been in place up to the date of the final hearing, or to the situation as it exists at the final hearing: see *Re M (A Minor) (Care Order: Threshold Conditions)* [1994] 3 WLR 558.

It appears that the grounds for making interim care orders could be made out on the basis of the apparent neglect of the children. More information is required in relation to the extent of the neglect and the effect on the children. If interim care orders are made then the children could be taken into local authority for initially up to eight weeks and then for periods of up to 28 days at a time while preparations are made for the final hearing: see s38(4) CA 1989. The local authority is advised to try to work with Sally. Equally Sally is advised to co-operate with the local authority. If she co-operates then it could apply for interim supervision orders instead and ultimately ask the court to make supervision orders for the children (using the same threshold criteria in s31(2)). A care order gives the local authority parental responsibility for the children (which would be shared with Sally) but the power to determine where the children should live: see s33 CA 1989. A supervision order gives the authority the duty to advise, assist and befriend the children and work with Sally: see s35 CA 1989. With the advent of the

Human Rights Act 1998 and the impact of art 8 ECHR the authority will be expected to adopt the order which least interferes with Sally's and the children's right to family life consistent with protecting the children: see *Re C and B (Care Order: Future Harm)* [2001] 1 FLR 611.

The authority can be advised that the court will lay down a timetable to ensure any care or supervision proceedings are dealt with speedily: see s32 CA 1989. It will assume that any delay in determining the future of the children is likely to cause them harm: see s1(2) CA 1989. It will appoint a children's guardian to investigate the application from the children's point of view: see s41 CA 1989. If satisfied that the threshold criteria are made out it will take into account particular factors in deciding what orders, if any, to make: see s1(3) and (4) CA 1989. It will take into account the wishes and feelings of Mary and Steven in light of their age and understanding: see s1(3)(a). The children's guardian will assist in putting the children's wishes and feelings across, particularly those of Mary given her age. It will consider their emotional, physical and educational needs and their ages, sex and relevant characteristics: see s1(3)(b) and (d). It will also consider the likely effect on any change in their circumstances: see s1(3)(c). This could include the distress caused by being removed from their mother's care. It will consider the harm they have suffered or are risk of suffering (see s1(3)(e)) and how capable Sally is of meeting the children's needs: see s1(3)(f). It will consider the full range of the court's powers: see s1(3)(g). These will include a care order or a supervision order. There is also the possibility of a family assistance order which provides up to six months' assistance to Sally: see s16(3) CA 1989. This order seems unlikely if the problems are more deep rooted and long lasting. The court will also consider the 'no order' principle, namely not making an order unless it will make things better for the children: see s1(5) CA 1989. Given the harm the children are likely to be suffering or at risk of suffering it seems likely that some kind of order will have to be made to protect the children. The welfare of the children will always be the paramount consideration: see s1(1) CA 1989.

Sally will have the right to be fully involved in the court proceedings. She will be entitled to be legally represented. The local authority, Sally and the children's guardian will disclose their evidence to the each other and the court before the hearing so that everyone knows in advance the issues in the case and what arguments are being advanced. If the children are removed from her care she has the right to reasonable contact with them (see s34 CA 1989) subject to any court order to the contrary.

Chapter 11

Property Disputes between Unmarried Couples (or Married Couples Who Are Not Divorcing)

11.1   Introduction

11.2   Key points

11.3   Key cases and statutes

11.4   Questions and suggested solutions

11.1   Introduction

The incidence of cohabitation outside marriage is increasing, as is the number of children born to cohabiting couples. Traditionally the English and Welsh legal system only acknowledged rights as existing within marriage. This has led to problems for unmarried couples. In particular, an unmarried 'wife' may be left in a much worse position on the breakdown of the relationship than would be the case if the parties were married. The classic example of this is *Burns* v *Burns* [1984] Ch 317 in which a woman who had given over 20 years of her life to her partner and the three children of the relationship received nothing on the breakdown of the relationship. Had she been married it is probable that she would have been granted a sufficiently large lump sum to enable her to purchase suitable alternative accommodation for herself. The student must be aware of what remedies are available to an unmarried couple in resolving property disputes.

A spouse may also have a need to resolve property disputes outside the scope of divorce or other statutory provisions. For example, if one spouse is made bankrupt the other spouse may need to establish his/her property rights against the trustee of bankruptcy. Such a spouse may need to use the same remedies as the unmarried partner.

11.2 Key points

Establishing property rights

Courts have a wide discretion to make orders concerning the matrimonial home in divorce proceedings pursuant to the Matrimonial Causes Act (MCA) 1973. The courts can make orders which are just and reasonable in light of the particular considerations in ss25, 25A–25D of the 1973 Act. Where the 1973 Act does not apply (eg where a couple are not married) the main remedy is to ask the courts to declare property rights in accordance with strict property law principles. Where a couple is married but does not wish to make use of the Matrimonial Causes Act 1973 either spouse can apply for an order under s17 Married Women's Property Act (MWPA) 1882, whereupon the court can consider any question as to the title or possession of property and make such order with respect to the property in dispute as it thinks fit.

An application for a declaration or for an order under s17 MWPA 1882 only allows the court to declare what property rights exist under property law – the court is not allowed to give title which does not already exist. It is not allowed to make orders as it considers just and reasonable but must declare property rights as it finds them: see *Pettitt* v *Pettitt* [1969] 2 WLR 966 and *Gissing* v *Gissing* [1970] 3 WLR 255.

The conveyance

All conveyances of land or any interest in land must be by way of deed: see s52 Law of Property Act (LPA) 1925. A declaration in a conveyance as to the beneficial interests of the parties is conclusive evidence of ownership unless the conveyance can be set aside on the grounds of fraud or mistake: see *Goodman* v *Gallant* [1986] 1 All ER 311 and *Turton* v *Turton* [1987] 2 All ER 641.

An unsigned deed or conveyance may be used to decide interests: see *Re Gorman* [1990] 2 FLR 284, but contrast *Huntingford* v *Hobbs* [1993] 1 FLR 736.

By written document

An equitable interest may be evidenced by a document in writing (see s53(1)(b) Law of Property Act 1925). From 27 September 1989 such an interest can only be created by a written contract incorporating all the terms which the parties have expressly agreed to and which must be signed by or on behalf of each party: see ss2(1) and 3 Law of Property (Miscellaneous Provisions) Act (LP(MP)A) 1989.

By resulting, implied or constructive trust

In everyday life spouses or unmarried couples often fail to comply with the strict requirements of s52 LPA 1925 or s53(1)(b) LPA 1925 or ss2(1) and 3 LP(MP)A 1989. As a result s53(2) LPA 1925 and s2(5) LP(MP)A 1989 allow a person who cannot establish his or her interest in the home by the conveyance or by a written and signed contract to nevertheless ask the court to declare his or her interest under a resulting, implied or constructive trust. The court will not therefore allow one party with the legal interest to stand on his or her strict legal rights when it is clear that the other party has a beneficial interest.

A resulting or constructive trusts requires:

a) Clear evidence of a common intention between the parties that at the time of the purchase of the property (or exceptionally some time after the purchase) though one party has the legal title to the property *both* parties clearly intended that the other party has a beneficial interest in the property; and

b) the other party has acted to his or her detriment based on that common intention.

In practice there now appear to be only two ways to satisfy these requirements:

a) the other party making direct financial contributions towards the purchase of the property (where there is an obvious inference that there must have been a common intention between the parties that the contributing party should acquire a beneficial interest) – this gives rise to a presumption of *resulting trust*; or

b) clear evidence of conversations between the parties showing that they formed a common intention that the party without legal title has a beneficial interest and that party acting to his or her detriment based on that common intention – this gives rise to a *constructive trust*.

See *Lloyds Bank* v *Rosset* [1990] 2 WLR 867.

The courts are unlikely to refuse to infer any common intention based on how the parties behaved towards each other if there is no evidence of direct financial contributions or no evidence of direct conversations establishing a common intention. An uncommunicated belief by one party that there is a common intention is insufficient: see *Springette* v *Defoe* [1992] 2 FLR 437.

If a common intention is established by constructive trust the courts appear to give themselves a broad discretion to determine the shares under that trust on the basis of inferences as to the parties' common understanding about the ownership. The court may not limit itself to the direct contributions made: see *Midland Bank* v *Cooke* [1995] 4 All ER 562 and *Drake* v *Whipp* [1996] 1 FLR 826. However, this broad approach to quantifying shares under a resulting or constructive approach may not be in keeping with earlier authorities and with the spirit of *Lloyds Bank* v *Rosset*, so it remains to be seen whether this approach will continue.

Contractual licence

A lesser form of protection of property rights is the contractual licence. Where no resulting or constructive trust exists a partner may have a right of occupation protected by contractual licence, namely a contract giving him or her a licence to remain in occupation which, if breached, gives rise to a claim for damages. In order for a contractual licence to exist there must be an intention to create a legally binding contract and the claimant must show he or she has provided consideration for the contract: see *Tanner* v *Tanner* [1975] 1 WLR 1346 and *Hardwick* v *Johnson* [1978] 1 WLR 683.

Proprietary estoppel

Where one person has acted to his or her detriment in reliance on a belief, which was known of and encouraged by another person, that he or she has or is going to be given a right in or over the other person's property, the other person cannot insist on his or her strict legal rights if to do so would be inconsistent with the person's belief. The other person would be 'estopped' from relying on his or her strict legal rights: see *Re Basham* [1986] 1 WLR 1498.

This is similar to a constructive trust but there is no need to establish a common intention, only that the claimant has been misled in the manner described above. Examples of proprietary estoppel can be found in *Maharaj* v *Chand* [1986] 3 All ER 107, *Matharu* v *Matharu* [1994] 2 FLR 597, *Wayling* v *Jones* [1995] 2 FLR 1030 and *Gillett* v *Holt* [2000] 2 FLR 266.

Equitable accounting

After one party has left the other party may remain in the home. The party in the home may continue to pay the mortgage and make improvements to the property and may ask the court to take these payments into account. The other party may argue that the party in occupation has enjoyed the occupation of the property while he or she has had to find alternative accommodation and that this should be taken into account. The court can adjust the shares of the parties to take these factors into account. This is called *equitable accounting*.

Credit can be given for the capital element of mortgage payments paid by the party in occupation. The court will credit one-half of those repayments to the party in occupation who paid them (see *Cracknell* v *Cracknell* [1971] 3 WLR 490 and *Leake* v *Bruzzi* [1974] 1 WLR 1528). Mortgage payments relating to interest may not be credited, though they can be counted towards occupation rent (see below): see *Suttill* v *Graham* [1977] 1 WLR 819.

If one party leaves voluntarily then the occupying party is not expected to pay occupation rent to the other party to reflect the benefit of occupation. However, if one party is forced to leave then the occupying party can be liable to pay occupation rent to the party who was forced to leave: see *Dennis* v *MacDonald* [1982] 2 WLR 275 and *Re Pavlou (A Bankrupt)* [1993] 3 All ER 955. Interest only mortgage payments can be taken into account in deciding on occupation rent.

Improvements by the occupying party after the other party has left will also be taken into account: see *Re Pavlou* (above).

Improvements to the property

There is a special provision for married people whereby a contribution in money or money's worth by a spouse to the improvement of real or personal property shall, if the contribution is of a substantial nature and subject to any contrary intention, be taken to increase the beneficial interest of that spouse in such amount as agreed between the spouses or, in the absence of such agreement, as may seem just in all the circumstances to the court: see s37 Matrimonial Proceedings and Property Act 1970.

Any improvement must be of a substantial nature: see *Re Nicholson (Deceased)* [1974] 1 WLR 476. Minor improvements of a DIY nature are unlikely to suffice: see *Pettitt* v *Pettitt* (above) and *Gissing* v *Gissing* (above).

Allowances for housekeeping and maintenance

In the absence of any agreement any allowance made by the husband for the expenses of a matrimonial home, or for similar purposes or any property acquired out of such money, shall be treated as belonging to them in equal shares: see s1 Married Women's Property Act 1964.

Bank accounts

Ownership of money in a joint bank account and property bought therewith depends on the intention of the parties and, in particular, where there is an established common purse. If a bank account is regarded as for their joint use then, regardless of who puts money into it, the parties are entitled to it equally and to any investments bought using money from the account equally: see *Jones* v *Maynard* [1951] 1 All ER 802. However, in *Re Bishop (Deceased)* [1965] 2 WLR 188 a contrary view was taken in relation to property bought using money from the joint account. The spouse who bought the chattel or investment in his or her own name owns that chattel or investment.

Engaged couples

Engaged couples may use s17 MWPA 1882 to resolve property disputes: see s1 Law Reform (Miscellaneous Provisions) Act 1970 and *Shaw* v *Fitzgerald* [1992] 1 FLR 357.

Protection of overriding interests against third parties

A person with an overriding interest who is in 'actual occupation' of the property can protect his/her interest against a claim for possession by a third party (eg a bank) because the interest is an overriding interest under s70(1)(g) Land Registration Act 1925: see *William & Glyn's Bank Limited* v *Boland* [1980] 2 All ER 408. This applies to registered land, but the situation appears to be the same for unregistered land: see *Kingsnorth Finance Co Ltd* v *Tizard* [1986] 1 WLR 783.

For there to be an overriding interest the person has to show that he/she has a beneficial interest in the property and that he/she was in actual occupation of the property before the charge to the third party took effect and that he/she was unaware of the charge (eg had been deceived by his/her spouse or partner). If the claimant was aware of the charge before it took effect then it is not an overriding interest: see *Bristol & West Building Society* v *Henning* [1985] 2 All ER 606. It also does not apply if the house has been conveyed into two names and the claimant is a third person. See *City of London*

Building Society v *Flegg* [1987] 3 All ER 435 where the house was in the names of a husband and wife. The wife's parents had a beneficial interest. The spouses mortgaged the house to a bank without the knowledge of the parents. The parents could not claim an overriding interest because there were two trustees, namely the spouses.

In other cases a spouse or partner can have a charge set aside because the document on which it was based was signed by him/her under duress, undue influence or misrepresentation. This is because it is recognised that a spouse or partner is likely to have an emotional involvement with the debtor (normally the husband) which makes her vulnerable. Any lending situation is expected to take reasonable steps to satisfy itself that the spouse/partner entered into the obligation freely and in knowledge of the true facts. The lending institution should warn the spouse/partner in the absence of the principal debtor of the consequences of the liability and advise her to take independent legal advice. If the bank fails to take such steps it will be fixed with constructive notice of the duress, undue influence or misrepresentation: see *Barclays Bank* v *O'Brien* [1993] 3 WLR 786 and *CIBC Mortgages* v *Pitt* [1993] 3 WLR 802.

The House of Lords revisited the law in this area in *Royal Bank of Scotland* v *Etridge (No 2)* [2001] 2 FLR 1364 in which it was held that a bank is put on inquiry when a wife offers to stand surety for her husband's debts. On its face such a transaction is not to the financial advantage of the wife and there is a substantial risk that the husband has acted wrongly, whereby the wife could set aside the transaction. There is no need for the wife to prove financial disadvantage or any wrongdoing by the husband. The wife does not have to show to the bank that she is cohabiting or that she placed implicit trust and confidence in the husband in relation to financial affairs. There is no need for the wife to show 'manifest disadvantage'. This term has caused difficulty and misunderstanding and should be discarded. In future banks should be put on inquiry in every case where the relationship between the surety and the debtor is non-commercial. The types of relationship which give scope for misuse cannot be listed exhaustively. The greater the disadvantage to the vulnerable person, the more cogent the explanation for the transaction must be (applying *Allcard* v *Skinner* (1887) 36 Ch D 145). The court can then infer that, in the absence of a satisfactory explanation, the transaction could only have been procured by undue influence. The House of Lords then outlined the steps a bank should take to ensure that the wife's interests were protected.

11.3 Key cases and statutes

- *Barclays Bank* v *O'Brien* [1993] 3 WLR 786
  Undue influence

- *Gillett* v *Holt* [2000] 2 FLR 266
  Proprietary estoppel

- *Gissing* v *Gissing* [1970] 3 WLR 255
  Property rights by resulting or constructive trust

- *Lloyds Bank* v *Rosset* [1990] 2 WLR 867
  Property rights by resulting or constructive trust

- *Pettitt* v *Pettitt* [1969] 2 WLR 966
  Property rights by resulting or constructive trust

- *Royal Bank of Scotland* v *Etridge (No 2)* [2001] 3 FCR 481
  Constructive nature of undue influence

- *Tanner* v *Tanner* [1975] 1 WLR 1346
  Contractual licence

- *Williams & Glyn's Bank* v *Boland* [1980] 2 All ER 408
  Overriding interest in land

- Land Registration Act 1925 – overriding interests in property

- Law of Property Act 1925 – property rights in land

- Married Women's Property Act 1882 – declaration of property rights

- Matrimonial Proceedings and Property Act 1970 – improvements to property

11.4 Questions and suggested solutions

QUESTION ONE

Imogen and Bruce were married in 1984. They have one child, Deborah, who was born in 1986 and Imogen is expecting a baby in August 1991. The matrimonial home, 'Misrule', which was purchased by Imogen out of funds provided by her parents, is registered in her name alone. Bruce, who is a builder, has been unemployed since December 1987, and since that time he has taken care of Deborah and carried out various improvements to the house which include the installation of central heating and an ornamental gas fire. In return, Imogen, who works as a doctor, has paid him a weekly allowance, some of which he has invested in a deposit account.

Unknown to Bruce, in 1988 Imogen borrowed £25,000 from the bank using the house as security, but she has been unable to keep up the repayments. The bank would like 'Misrule' to be sold so that it can recover the money. Further, Imogen and Bruce have been unhappy since January 1991, often arguing in front of Deborah. Imogen, who is concerned about Deborah and the effect the situation is having on the unborn child, has asked Bruce to leave 'Misrule'.

University of London LLB Examination
(for External Students) Family Law June 1991 Q4

General Comment

Note that the establishment of a beneficial interest in property by cohabitees is similar in principle to a spouse establishing an interest under the Married Women's Property

Act. This question requires a detailed answer on ownership of the matrimonial home, applying the principles under s17 Married Women's Property Act 1882, and on protecting rights of occupation against the bank and the other spouse.

Skeleton Solution

Discuss ownership of the matrimonial home: s17 MWPA 1882 – have direct or indirect contributions towards the acquisition of the property been made? – consider s37 Matrimonial Proceedings and Property Act 1970; discount s1 MWPA 1964 in relation to the deposit account – consider whether Bruce can resist the bank's claim; discuss the effect of the decision in *Williams and Glyn's Bank Ltd* v *Boland*; establish whether the conditions applicable under that case can be made out – in the event Bruce cannot establish an equitable interest, discuss s14 Trusts of Land and Appointment of Trustees Act 1996 application for sale; principles to be applied – consider dispute over occupation with Imogen; s30 Family Law Act 1996; right of occupation; application for occupation order (s33 FLA 1996).

Suggested Solution

Bruce requires advice as to his general position with regard to the property 'Misrule' in respect of ownership and his continued occupation of the same. The ownership of the deposit account must also be considered.

On the assumption that divorce proceedings are not contemplated at this time and therefore that the provisions of the Matrimonial Causes Act 1973 cannot be invoked to settle the dispute over the ownership of the property, the issue could be resolved by reference to s17 Married Women's Property Act 1882 (hereinafter MWPA 1882). Under s17 an application may be made by either a husband or wife to settle any question between them as to the title to or possession of property.

Under s17 MWPA 1882 the matter will be resolved by the application of general principles of property law. The legal estate in 'Misrule' is vested in Imogen's name and therefore, prima facie, the legal title is vested in her absolutely and Bruce has no interest in the property. However, a proprietary interest may exist in equity and the court may look behind the title deeds and may establish the existence of a trust, that is that Imogen holds the property on trust for herself and Bruce. Under s17 the court may not create an interest in the property because it considers it fair to do so; it may declare existing interests only: *Pettitt* v *Pettitt* [1970] AC 777.

The legal estate may be displaced where there is evidence of a contrary intention on the part of the spouses. If there is evidence of a contrary intention at the date of acquisition of the property the court will give effect to it by imposing a trust in the shares agreed upon. The court may draw inferences which a reasonable person would draw from the parties' conduct at the date of acquisition and subsequently and in *Gissing* v *Gissing* [1971] AC 886 it was recognised that the parties may have agreed to hold property jointly without having used express words to communicate that intention to each other.

In this case, 'Misrule' was purchased by Imogen out of funds provided by her parents. It is not clear when the property was purchased, that is, before or after the marriage, or whether the funds provided were a gift from Imogen's parents to her and intended to be used for the purchase of the house. If so the next question must be whether the gift of the money was intended for Imogen alone or for both herself and Bruce. If the funds were provided to Imogen to purchase a home for herself and Bruce then it is likely that Bruce would be deemed to have a joint interest in the property on that basis alone. However if the funds were provided for Imogen alone then Bruce will have to rely on agreements or conduct which took place subsequent to the acquisition of the property to establish the existence of a trust.

It can be inferred that the parties intended both to have an interest in the property conveyed to one of them if both contributed towards the acquisition of the property either directly (through payment of the deposit or mortgage repayments) or possibly indirectly (for example by meeting household expenses which the owner could not otherwise afford to make, although in *Lloyds Bank plc* v *Rosset* [1990] 2 WLR 867 the House of Lords doubted the possibility of establishing a trust by indirect contributions.

There is no evidence of direct or indirect contributions of the nature referred to above having been made by Bruce. However he would acquire an interest in 'Misrule' by virtue of his works of improvement carried out at the property. Section 37 Matrimonial Proceedings and Property Act 1970 (hereinafter MPPA 1970), provides that where a husband or wife contributes in money or money's worth to the improvement of real or personal property in which, or in the proceeds of sale of which, either or both of them has or have a beneficial interest, the husband or wife so contributing shall, if the contribution is of a substantial nature, and subject to any agreement between them to the contrary, be treated as having acquired, by virtue of his or her contribution, a share or an enlarged share in that beneficial interest, of such an extent as may then have been agreed, or in the absence of such agreement, as may, in all the circumstances, seem just.

The contribution must be substantial and in money or money's worth. In this case Bruce carried out the work himself. Certainly the installation of the central heating will be considered a substantial improvement within the terms of s37 (*Re Nicholson* [1974] 1 WLR 476), but the installation of the ornamental gas fire will not be considered substantial enough. It is not clear what other improvements were carried out by Bruce. To come within the terms of s37 the contribution must effect an improvement to the property as distinguished from merely maintaining it (*Pettitt* v *Pettitt*), and so, depending on the nature and extent of those other improvements, Bruce may be deemed to have an interest in 'Misrule' by virtue of them as well as the installation of the central heating.

The next question to consider is whether there was any agreement between Imogen and Bruce as to an interest, if any, he was to have in the property by virtue of these improvements. We are told that 'in return' for the works carried out by Bruce, Imogen paid him a weekly allowance. Such an allowance would not come within the terms of s1 Married Women's Property Act 1964, which, in the absence of contrary agreement, establishes that where a husband pays a housekeeping allowance to a wife, it shall be treated as belonging to them equally. This payment by Imogen to Bruce may not be a housekeeping allowance and in any event the Act only covers payments made by a husband to a wife. Prima facie therefore monies paid by a wife to a husband as an allowance would remain the property of the wife unless a contrary intention could be established and so prima facie the deposit account would belong to Imogen.

If Imogen made the allowance to Bruce in payment for the works carried out at 'Misrule' and the intention was that he was not to take any interest in the property by virtue of these improvements, then the deposit account belongs to Bruce. However if the allowance was not intended for that purpose then Bruce will take an interest in the property but the deposit account is likely to be deemed to belong to Imogen. When deciding the extent of Bruce's interest, if any, in 'Misrule' the court will consider the increase in value attributable to the improvements and calculate Bruce's share accordingly.

The next problem to consider is whether the sale of the property, desired by the bank, can be prevented. It is not clear what Imogen's position with regard to such a sale would be. In the event of a dispute between Bruce and the bank as to whether the sale should take place, Bruce may be able to protect his occupation of 'Misrule' on the strength of his beneficial interest, if he has one.

Since Bruce is married he has a right of occupation by virtue of s30 Family Law Act 1996. This is a right not to be evicted if in occupation and if not in occupation a right to enter and occupy the dwelling-house by court order. This is a personal right which can be registered and if registered the right binds all subsequent purchasers. It is unlikely that Bruce has registered his right of occupation. However, even if this is the case there is the possibility that Bruce could resist the bank's claim in any event. It is clear that in 1988, when the mortgage came into effect, Bruce was in occupation so is likely to have an overriding interest under s70(1)(g) Land Registration Act 1925: see *Lloyds Bank v Rosset*. This will depend on the matters referred to previously, such as the intention of Imogen's parents when they supplied the funds to purchase the home and whether Bruce's works of improvement give rise to an interest. If he can establish an equitable interest then, following *William and Glyn's Bank v Boland* [1981] AC 487, it will mean that he can resist the bank's claim for possession. If he has no equitable interest he would be unable to resist the bank's claim: *Midland Bank v Dobson* [1986] 1 FLR 171. In this context the bank could obtain judgment against Imogen and then obtain a charging order on her interest in the property and apply for the house to be sold under the Trusts of Land and Appointment of Trustees Act 1996. Generally the bank's claim is likely to prevail, although in exceptional circumstances the court may delay sale to prevent hardship to the family.

If Imogen asks that he leave 'Misrule' because of their matrimonial difficulties and he refuses she can apply for an occupation order under s33 FLA 1996 requiring him to leave.

In deciding whether to make such an order the court would have regard to all the circumstances including particular matters: see s33(6) FLA 1996. The court would consider the housing needs and housing resources of each of the parties and Deborah as well as the financial resources of the parties. The financial position of the parties is not clear. Imogen and Deborah are likely to have greater housing needs than Bruce. The court will also consider the likely effect of an order on Bruce's health, safety or well-being and the likely effect of a refusal to make an order on the health, safety or well-being of Imogen and Deborah. The court will also consider the conduct of Bruce and Imogen in relation to each other and otherwise. If it appears to the court that Imogen and Deborah are likely to suffer significant harm attributable to Bruce's conduct if an exclusion order is not made the court must make the order, unless it appears to the court that Bruce is likely to suffer significant harm if the order is made and the harm he is likely to suffer is as great as or greater than the harm which Imogen and Deborah are likely to suffer if the order is not made: see s33(7) FLA 1996. It is noted that there are arguments which appear to be verbal rather than violent. It is not clear what effect the arguments have had on Deborah. As a result it is not clear whether the balance of harm test favours Imogen. In the absence of further evidence it seems doubtful that an occupation order would be made in Imogen's favour.

QUESTION TWO

In January 1990, on Francesca's 30th birthday, Francesca and Graham announced their engagement. Graham gave Francesca an emerald and diamond ring, now valued at £20,000, and a matching bracelet, valued at £10,000. They moved into a flat which was a birthday present from Francesca's grandmother. The flat, which was registered in Francesca's name alone, was dilapidated and required structural improvements and decoration.

Although Graham is a tax consultant, he is a competent builder and he devoted each weekend of 1990 to improving the flat. He installed central heating, rewired the flat and decorated it and in 1991 he completely replaced the bathroom with units that he and Francesca bought together out of a joint bank account. According to Francesca's brother, a property surveyor, the improvements effected by Graham doubled the value of the flat.

Francesca has now decided that she no longer wishes to marry Graham and has asked him to leave the flat.

Advise Graham who is curious to know if he has any interest in the flat and who would like the jewellery he gave to Francesca returned to him together with his share of the bank account.

University of London LLB Examination
(for External Students) Family Law June 1993 Q4

General Comment

This is a straightforward question about property disputes between an engaged couple. The provisions of the Law Reform (Miscellaneous Provisions) Act 1970 have to be discussed in relation to the engagement ring, the bracelet and the bank account. The property dispute requires discussion of s37 Matrimonial Proceedings and Property Act 1970 (which appears to provide the most direct answer to the consequences of the work Graham has done on the flat). Given s37 of the 1970 Act there appears to be no need to explore the uncertain world of resulting and constructive trusts.

Skeleton Solution

Engagement ring is presumed to be an absolute gift (s3(2) LR(MP)A 1970) – bracelet may be an absolute gift or conditional on getting married – what was the intention of the parties in relation to the money in the joint bank account? – bank account may be held in equal shares but property bought with money from account may belong to individual – application of s37 Matrimonial Proceedings and Property Act 1970 in terms of substantial improvements made to the flat – application for declaration under s17 Married Women's Property Act 1882.

Suggested Solution

Graham asks for advice as to whether he has any interest in the flat. He also asks whether he is entitled to have the engagement ring and bracelet returned to him. He also wants the return of his share of the bank account.

In relation to the emerald and diamond ring it is assumed that this was an engagement ring. The engagement ring is presumed to be an absolute gift by Graham to Francesca: see s3(2) Law Reform (Miscellaneous Provisions) Act (LR(MP)A) 1970. Graham could seek to rebut that presumption by proof that the ring was given with a condition that it be returned should the engagement be broken off. For example if the ring was a family heirloom Graham might persuade a court that the ring was meant to be kept in his family and that on the breaking of the engagement it should be returned. There is no evidence suggesting that this is the case. In the absence of such evidence it would appear that Francesca is entitled to keep the ring.

Whether Francesca can keep the bracelet will depend on the circumstances of Graham giving it to her. If he intended it as an absolute gift Francesca may keep it. If he intended it as a gift conditional on the parties marrying then it should be returned to him. Since the bracelet matches the ring the fate of the ring is likely to determine that of the bracelet. Therefore it appears that Francesca is entitled to keep the bracelet.

Ownership of the money in the joint bank account will depend on the intention of Graham and Francesca. If the bank account was intended to be held equally and used as a common purse (as opposed to being held in the shares each contributed to it) then a court is likely to order that Francesca and Graham receive the money in the bank account in equal shares (even if Graham put in more money than Francesca or vice versa): see *Jones* v *Maynard* [1951] 1 All ER 802. However, property bought by one party for his or her own benefit using money from the joint account may be held to belong to that party since a joint bank account not only allows one party to spend money for the mutual benefit of both parties, but also to spend money for the sole benefit of one party: see *Re Bishop* [1965] 2 WLR 188.

Graham can be advised that the work he has done in the flat is likely to have given him an interest in it. He has contributed in money and money's worth to the improvement of the flat by the work he has done for many weekends over 1990 to improve the flat. His contribution appears to be substantial. The installation of central heating has been held to be a substantial contribution in this context: see *Re Nicholson* [1974] 1 WLR 476. Rewiring the flat is also likely to have been a substantial contribution as was the replacement of the bathroom. The redecorating in itself may not amount to a substantial contribution since that may be likened to normal DIY work (see *Button* v *Button* [1968] 1 WLR 457) but taken in the context of the other work may become 'substantial'. The substantial nature of the work is underlined by the effect that the work has had on the value of the flat Unless there was an express or implied agreement between Graham and Francesca otherwise, Graham will be treated as having acquired a share in the beneficial interest of such an extent as seems just in all the circumstances (in default of any agreement between the parties as to the quantification of shares): see s37 Matrimonial Proceedings and Property Act 1970. Since Graham's contribution appears to have doubled the value of the flat he is likely to be entitled to a one half beneficial interest in it. Graham can be advised that the work he has done to the flat may give rise to an interest under a resulting or constructive trust. However the law covering resulting or constructive trusts is not easy to apply and is not always clear. Unless there is clear evidence of a common intention between Francesca and Graham that Graham have a beneficial interest in the flat and that Graham acted to his detriment based on that common intention it is likely to be difficult for Graham to establish a beneficial interest in the property: see *Lloyds Bank* v *Rosset* [1990] 2 WLR 867. He has not made any financial contribution to its purchase which might give rise to a resulting trust. In a case concerning an unmarried couple one party did substantial work to improve a house. It was held that he had no beneficial interest in the property in the absence of an express agreement or common intention. Since the man did the work without a clear understanding as to the financial basis on which the work was done he did so at his own risk: see *Thomas* v *Fuller-Brown* [1988] 1 FLR 237. As Graham's position by virtue of the engagement appears to be covered by clear statutory provision there appears to be no need to advise him further with respect to this difficult area of trust law.

Graham can be advised that he may apply to the court under s17 Married Women's Property Act 1882 for a declaration as to his interests in the jewellery, the bank account and the flat, provided that he makes the application within three years of the termination of the engagement: see s2(2) LR(MP)A 1970.

QUESTION THREE

It is said that legal developments in relation to cohabitation are examples of interference with family autonomy. Those who exercise their right not to marry should not have the consequences of matrimony thrust upon them.

What do you understand this to mean? Do you agree with the statement? Consider it with particular reference to financial provision and property entitlements and the status of children.

University of London LLB Examination
(for External Students) Family Law June 1997 Q1

General Comment

The question invites a comparison between the legal position of married and unmarried couples in relation to financial provision and property and in relation to the status of children. It also invites a discussion on how the law has developed in these areas and whether it can be said that such developments amount to interference with family autonomy.

Skeleton Solution

Law relating to the financial provision between cohabitants – financial provision of a child of an unmarried relationship: s15 and Sch 1 Children Act 1989; Child Support Act 1991; Social Security and Administration Act 1992 – law relating to property entitlements between unmarried couples – occupation of the family home by unmarried couple: Part IV Family Law Act 1996 – status of child of unmarried parents and status of unmarried father: Children Act 1989.

Suggested Solution

To answer the issues posed by this question one first has to identify what developments in the law in relation to cohabitation there have been with particular reference to financial provision and property entitlements and the status of children.

The law has not developed a great deal in relation to the financial provision between cohabitants. There still remains no statutory right for one cohabitant to apply for financial provision from another. This contrasts with the statutory framework dealing with the financial provision between married couples who divorce: see ss21–26 Matrimonial Causes Act (MCA) 1973. There are also provisions to allow for financial provision between married couples who separate: see s27 MCA 1973 and ss2, 6 or 7 Domestic Proceedings and Magistrates' Courts Act 1978. To this extent the consequences of matrimony have not been thrust on cohabiting couples.

The situation is different if there is a child of the unmarried couple. The cohabitant with whom the child is living can apply for financial provision from the other cohabitant for the child: see s15 and Sch 1 Children Act (CA) 1989. Such an application can be for maintenance or lump sum orders to the child, or to the applicant for the benefit of the child, or the transfer of property to the child, or to the applicant for the child's benefit. In deciding whether to make an order the court has to have regard to all the circumstances and to matters such as the income and outgoings of the parties, the financial needs and responsibilities of the parties and the child and certain other matters: see para 4(1), Sch 1 CA 1989. Of even greater importance is the Child Support Act (CSA) 1991, which now largely deals with the financial support of children when parents separate. Under the Act both married and unmarried parents are equally liable to be assessed for child support. The CSA 1991 emerged from a perceived failure of the courts to use their various powers to order reasonable financial provision for children – as a result the burden of financially supporting children fell largely to the state through benefits being paid to lone parents. The application of the CSA 1991 means that parents who choose not to marry cannot avoid the financial consequences of parenthood traditionally associated with the responsibilities of married parents. This development has long been part of the law. The Affiliation Proceedings Act 1957 and the Guardianship of Minors Act 1971 (both predecessors to the CA 1989 and then the CSA 1991) placed an obligation on the unmarried father to provide for a child of his unmarried relationship. This development has been partly 'child centred' (so that children are not brought up without the financial support of an absent parent) and partly 'state based' (trying to reduce the burden on the state of supporting children after parents have separated). Similar rules have applied in relation to social security legislation (see s26 Social Security Act 1986 and now s78(6) Social Security Administration Act 1992). This aspect of the law contradicts the assertion that those who exercise their right not to marry should not have the consequences of matrimony thrust upon them. There is a political imperative (to reduce the financial burden on the state) and a moral imperative (that unmarried parents should have the responsibility of financially supporting their children) which means that it is difficult to agree with the statement in the question.

The law relating to the property entitlements between cohabitants has not developed a great deal since the landmark decisions of *Pettitt* v *Pettitt* [1969] 2 WLR 966 and *Gissing* v *Gissing* [1970] 3 WLR 255. The courts still apply strict rules of property law when dealing with property disputes between unmarried cohabitants. There was a period when the courts appeared to adopt a more flexible approach to dealing with such property disputes, but the more strict approach was confirmed in *Lloyds Bank* v *Rosset* [1990] 2 WLR 867. As a result unmarried couples must regulate their property interests either through the conveyance or by resulting, implied or constructive trust. Establishing an interest under a resulting, implied or constructive trust has proved difficult. In *Hammond* v *Mitchell* [1991] 1 WLR 1127 the difficulties were described as 'the judicial quest for the fugitive or phantom common intention' or as a 'detailed, time consuming and laborious' process. In *Midland Bank* v *Cooke* [1995] 4 All ER 562 the difficulties in establishing property entitlements were such that the court called for law reform (as recommended by the Law Commission) to save a lot of human heartache and public expense. This situation sharply contrasts with married couples who can ask a divorce court to exercise a wide and generous discretion in allocating property as is fair and just following the marriage breakdown. To this extent the consequences of matrimony have not been thrust upon those who choose not to marry.

The law in relation to financial provision on death has developed in relation to unmarried couples. Under the rules of intestacy an unmarried partner is not entitled to any part of the estate of his/her partner if no valid will has been made. The law has developed to the extent of allowing an unmarried partner who immediately before the death of the deceased was wholly maintained, either wholly or in part by the deceased: see s1(1)(e) Inheritance (Provision for Family and Dependants (I(PFD)A) Act 1975. More recently, the law has been changed where the deceased died on or after 1 January 1996. If during the whole of the period of two years before the deceased died the claimant lived with the deceased as his/her husband or wife then a claim can be made from the deceased's estate: see ss1(1)(ba) and (1A) I(PFD)A 1975. This has partly thrust the consequences of matrimony on a person in an unmarried relationship who dies either intestate or makes no provision for the partner in his/her will.

Changes in taxation have tended to reduce the difference in the tax treatment of married and unmarried couples. However, such legal developments have largely affected the taxation of married couples rather than changing the taxation of an unmarried partner. It has been confirmed that an unmarried relationship cannot attract the married person's allowance: see *Rignell* v *Andrews* [1991] Fam Law 217.

Rights of occupation between unmarried couples have been codified in Part IV of the Family Law Act (FLA) 1996. The law in relation to unmarried couples has developed from the Domestic Violence and Matrimonial Proceedings Act 1976. This allowed an unmarried partner to apply to exclude his/her violent partner and apply for an order prohibiting further harassment. Section 33 FLA 1996 allows an unmarried partner who is entitled to occupy the home to apply for a occupation order to exclude the other partner. Section 36 FLA 1996 allows an unmarried partner with no right to occupy the home to apply for an occupation order against the partner who has a right to occupy, while s38 FLA 1996 allows an unmarried partner with no right to occupy for an occupation order against his/her partner also with no right to occupy. The considerations which apply differ according to the kind of application. In particular, a balance of harm test applies to a s33 occupation order whereby if it appears to the court that the applicant or any relevant child is likely to suffer greater significant harm (attributable to the respondent's conduct) if an occupation order is not made than any significant harm the respondent or any relevant child would suffer if an order was made, then the court must make an occupation order. This balance of harm test does not apply to s36 or s38 occupation orders. Also in considering the nature of an unmarried relationship the court must have regard to the fact that they have not given each other the commitment involved in marriage: s41 FLA 1996. A married partner is normally allowed to make a s33 application because s/he either is entitled to occupy or is given 'matrimonial home rights': see 30 FLA 1996. Therefore a married partner has greater scope for obtaining an occupation order than an unmarried partner. Despite this it could be said that some of the consequences of matrimony have been thrust upon unmarried couples in terms of regulating occupation of the home. Married couples and unmarried couples have the same right to apply to the courts for non-molestation orders: see s42 FLA 1996. This development in the law has been designed to protect the victims of domestic violence or other forms of unacceptable behaviour. As a result it is perceived as an acceptable development as opposed to an imposition of the consequences of matrimony on cohabitees.

The law has developed in relation to the status of children of unmarried parents. The main theme of these developments has been to reduce the legal consequences of the child being of unmarried parents when compared to the legal status of a child of married parents. Put in another way, the law has sought to reduce the consequences of birth outside marriage, particularly in the context of the growing number of children born to unmarried parents. Examples of such developments include s1 Family Law Reform Act 1987, whereby references to any relationship between two persons must be construed without regard to whether or not the father or mother of either or them, or the father and mother of any person through whom the relationship is deduced, have or have not been married. Rights of children under intestate succession have also been improved: see s18 FLRA 1987. The position of the unmarried father in relation to his child has improved. Before the Children Act 1989 the law left the unmarried father with a confused and unsatisfactory legal status – he was described by one commentator as a 'beached whale'. His position is now much clearer as a result of the Children Act 1989. He starts with no rights in relation to his child (ie he has no automatic parental responsibility, this vests exclusively in the mother: s2(2)(a) CA 1989). The father must acquire parental responsibility either by agreement with the mother or by a parental responsibility order or by obtaining a residence order. This legal position clearly distinguishes between a married father who automatically shares parental responsibility with his wife. The unmarried father must earn parental responsibility, eg by establishing a relationship with, and showing commitment to, his child: see *Re P (A Minor) (Parental Responsibility Order)* [1994] 1 FLR 578.

In conclusion, it is difficult to agree with the statement posed by the question. The consequences of matrimony have been thrust on those who choose not to marry to a limited extent but only where there has been a clear moral or political imperative for this to be done. The financial obligations of supporting the children of an unmarried relationship are justified in terms of the moral judgment that parents, whether married or unmarried, should be responsible for the financial support of their children. There is also the political imperative that the state does not wish to bear a financial burden which parents should bear. Rights to regulate occupation have been extended to unmarried couples but this is so an unmarried partner can protect herself from violence. In other respects, such as the right to financial support from an unmarried partner and property entitlements on the breakdown of an unmarried relationship, the law has not developed and the consequences of matrimony have not been thrust upon cohabitees. This has left some unmarried partners in a weak and disadvantaged position compared to those who choose to get married. The position of the unmarried father remains a relatively disadvantaged one when compared to a married father.

The unmarried father has to take steps to gain the status of a married father. Where the law has developed it is difficult to say this amounts to interference with family autonomy. The law has moved to provide protection and rights where a clear need has been identified (eg the need to protect the victims of domestic violence). Indeed the present law could well be criticised for not developing more to provide greater protection for unmarried partners, particularly in resolving property and maintenance matters following the breakdown of a relationship.

QUESTION FOUR

Is it possible to develop, legislatively and judicially, a coherent approach to cohabitants' rights and duties and at the same time treat cohabitants (heterosexual and homosexual) differently from spouses? Should there be such differentiation?

University of London LLB Examination
(for External Students) Family Law June 1999 Q8

General Comment

This is a general question inviting the student to describe the legal status, rights, duties and remedies of cohabitants compared to married spouses. The student needs to look at rights and duties concerning children, financial support (including pension rights), property, provision after death and occupation of the family home. The student then needs to discuss whether the present state of the law can be developed coherently and whether differences in rights and duties can be justified. In order to provide an up-to-date solution the effect of the European Convention on Human Rights is included in the suggested solution, particularly in relation to arts 8 and 14. This provides a wider European perspective on English and Welsh law which assists in answering the question.

Skeleton Solution

Rights and duties of spouses and cohabitants and how they have developed legislatively and judicially: concerning children (in particular parental responsibility – rights in relation to care proceedings – rights in relation to adoption proceedings) – concerning financial support and property rights (financial support for spouses or cohabitants (including pension rights) – property rights for spouses or cohabitant – occupation orders for spouses or cohabitants – provision on death for spouses or cohabitants) – the impact of the ECHR and arts 8 and 14 – the right to family life and marriage; do the above provide a coherent approach?; can any differentiation be justified?

Suggested Solution

The question asks whether it is possible to develop through statute and case law a coherent approach to the rights and duties of cohabitants and at the same time treat cohabitants (heterosexual and homosexual) differently from spouses? It is necessary to describe the approach to the rights and duties of cohabitants compared to spouses in terms of different areas of the law.

With regard to the rights and duties concerning children, the Children Act (CA) 1989 gives the married parents of their child automatic parental responsibility: see s2(1) CA 1989. Parental responsibility means all the rights, duties, powers, responsibilities and authority which a law a parent has in relation to his/her child or property: see s3(1) CA 1989. In practical terms this means the status to determine important aspects of the child's life, such as where he or she lives, his or education and important aspects of his/her health. In the case of unmarried parents parental responsibility vests solely in the mother: see s2(2)(a) CA 1989. The unmarried father has no legal status in relation to his/her child unless he acquires it by agreement with the mother or by court order: see s4(1) CA 1989. An unmarried father has no status in adoption proceedings because he is not treated as a parent. His consent is not required to the adoption of his child: see s72(1) Adoption Act 1976. An unmarried father has no automatic party status in care proceedings in which a local authority may seek to remove a child from his care. This distinction in status between married fathers and unmarried fathers may seem hard to justify as more and more children are born to couples who choose not to get married.

However, case law has much improved the status of the unmarried father to the extent that where he has played an important role in his child's life he is usually accorded an equivalent status of a married father. Gaining the status of parental responsibility via a parental responsibility order requires an unmarried father to demonstrate commitment to his child, a positive relationship with his child and the right motivation to be involved in his child's life: see *Re C (Minors)* [1992] 2 All ER 86. In relation to adoption proceedings the courts have held that any father who has played an important role in his child's life must be notified of the adoption proceedings and be given the opportunity to be heard: see *Re H; Re G (Adoption: Consultation of Unmarried Fathers)* [2001] 1 FLR 646. In relation to care proceedings the courts will readily grant an unmarried father who has been involved in his child's life party status: see *Re B (Care Proceedings: Notification of Father without Parental Responsibility)* [1999] 2 FLR 408. The distinction between married and unmarried fathers under English and Welsh law was considered by the European Court in *B v United Kingdom* [2000] 1 FLR 1. It was held that the distinction was not discriminatory and did not contravene art 14 European Convention on Human Rights (ECHR). The relationship between unmarried fathers varied from ignorance and indifference to a close stable relationship indistinguishable from the conventional family unit. There was an objective and reasonable justification for the difference in treatment between married and unmarried fathers in relation to the automatic acquisition of parental rights. In this respect the courts do appear to have developed a reasonably coherent approach to the rights and duties of unmarried parents, giving them equivalent rights to married parents where a family life has been established. In relation to same sex couples the courts will recognise that where a child benefits from the parenting of homosexual parents then parental responsibility can be vested via the making of a residence order: see *B* v *B* *(Minors)* *(Custody: Care and Control)* [1991] 1 FLR 402. Though a homosexual couple cannot apply for adoption an adoption order can be made in favour of one parent and a residence order in favour of the other where this is in the interests of the child: eg *Re W (A Minor) (Adoption: Homosexual Adopter)* [1997] 2 FLR 406.

Where there is a more fundamental difference between married and unmarried couples is in the area of financial and property rights. In relation to financial support when married couples separate there are a number of legislative provisions allowing the courts to order appropriate financial support from one spouse to another: eg the Matrimonial Causes Act 1973, the Domestic Proceedings and Magistrates' Courts Act 1978. There is no similar provision when unmarried couples separate. There are no statutory provisions allowing an unmarried partner to claim maintenance from the other unmarried partner. There is little difference in terms of children. Most claims for child maintenance are now dealt with by the Child Support Agency through the Child Support Act 1991. Child support makes no distinction between married or unmarried parents of children. Both are equally liable to be assessed for child support. Similarly, married or unmarried parents can apply to the courts for lump sum payments and/or property orders (and maintenance orders if the CSA does not have jurisdiction) for the children under Schedule 1 of the Children Act 1989.

In relation to property rights the distinction is more stark. When a married couple separates and divorces either spouse can apply for lump sum and/or property orders and/or pension orders under the Matrimonial Causes Act 1973. The court can make such orders as it considers fair in all the circumstances and taking into account particular considerations: see ss25(1), (2) and 25A MCA 1973. The House of Lords in *White* v *White* [2000] 2 FLR 981 encouraged the courts to apply a yardstick of equality in looking at matrimonial assets, strengthening the position of a non-working and financially vulnerable spouse. As a result a non-earning spouse in a long marriage who has brought up the children and looked after the household can receive a substantial contribution via lump sum orders, property orders and pension orders for his/her future maintenance. The clean break provisions discourage spouse maintenance orders but the courts have applied the clean break cautiously in terms of spouses in a weak financial position. However, when unmarried couples separate there is no such generous scope for making fair provision. The court applies strict property law principles based on who owns property according to the conveyance and the law on resulting, implied and constructive trusts: see *Gissing* v *Gissing* [1970] 3 WLR 255. An unmarried partner can find it extremely difficult to establish property rights unless he/she has made direct financial contributions to the purchase of the home or there is a specific agreement that he/she has a share of the property: see *Lloyds Bank* v *Rosset* [1990] 2 WLR 867. The mere fact of a long standing relationship does not in itself give rise to property rights. This was graphically illustrated in the case of *Burns* v *Burns* [1984] 2 WLR 582 where an unmarried partner of 19 years was left with no rights in the home when the relationship ended. The courts have consistently declined to give unmarried couples greater property rights and have left it to Parliament to act.

In terms of financial provision on death there is a distinction in relation to intestacy whereby a spouse takes most property on death under intestacy whereas an unmarried partner would not: see Administration of Estates Act 1925. A wife or husband of the deceased can apply for provision from the spouse's estate: see s1(1)(a) Inheritance (Provision for Family and Dependants) Act (I(PFD)A) 1975. However, so can an unmarried partner subject to him/her living with the deceased as 'husband and wife' for at least two years: see s1(1)(ba) I(PFD)A 1975. This would not apply to a same sex couple. However, any person being maintained wholly or partly by the deceased may be able to make a claim: see s1(1)(e) I(PFD)A 1975.

In relation to occupation of the matrimonial home the distinction between married and unmarried couples is less stark. A married spouse with no right to occupy the matrimonial home is able to claim 'matrimonial home rights' under s30 Family Law Act (FLA) 1996 which can provide that spouse with protection of the right of occupation of the home against the other spouse or a third party. This is not available to an unmarried partner. However, there is less of a distinction in terms of applying to the court for occupation orders (namely orders regulating who should occupy and who should be excluded from the matrimonial home). An unmarried partner with the right to occupy the home can apply for an occupation order in the same way as a married partner with the right to occupy the home: see s33 FLA 1996. A married couple with matrimonial home rights could make the same application. An unmarried cohabitant with no right to occupy can also apply for an occupation order: see s36 FLA 1996. The considerations for a s33 order and a s36 order are similar. The distinctions include the balance of harm test in s33(7) being binding on the court, whereas under s36(7) it is not. They also include the court being obliged to look at the quality of the unmarried relationship (see s36(6)) and the court being obliged to have regard to the fact that unmarried partners have not given each other the same commitment as marriage: s41 FLA 1996. The period of a s33 order can be unlimited whereas a s36 order can only be for up to six months (with one extension for up to six months). These distinctions are unlikely to prevent a court from acting to protect an unmarried partner who is the victim of domestic violence in the same way as it protects a married partner in a similar situation. There is no distinction in protecting married or unmarried partners from molestation through non-molestation orders: see s42 FLA 1996.

From 2 October 2000 the Human Rights Act 1998 made the European Convention on Human Rights (ECHR) binding in terms of interpreting English and Welsh law. It is possible for the higher courts to declare a statute incompatible with the Convention and thereby inviting Parliament to amend the statute. Article 8 ECHR guarantees the right to family life subject to any restrictions which are necessary and proportionate in a democratic society. Article 14 prohibits any discrimination in applying Convention rights. Unmarried couples are able to challenge UK law which infringes any Convention right. This is already obliging courts to recognise the rights of the unmarried father though not to the extent of the law on parental responsibility being declared to be in contravention of the Convention. However, the ECHR does give the courts the opportunity to judicially provide a coherent approach to cohabitant's rights and duties subject to reasonable and proportionate distinctions with married spouses. The right to marry under art 12 has been the subject of much litigation by transsexuals wishing to marry. The European Court has repeatedly upheld the British authorities' refusal to recognise a transsexual's right to marry: see *Sheffield and Horsham v United Kingdom* [1998] 2 FLR 928. However, the Court has required the UK authorities to keep the position under review as it increasingly recognises the rights of transsexuals.

In conclusion there is an increasingly coherent approach to the rights and duties of cohabitants which reflects their rights to a family life and not to be treated substantially differently from married couples. Both the courts and statute have lessened the distinction between them particularly in light of the Human Rights Act 1998. There are still greater distinctions in terms of homosexual couples. The most glaring distinction between married and unmarried couples concerns property rights. This is the one area in which is it increasingly difficult to justify the stark differentiation. However, the courts have felt unable to act and have left it to Parliament. Despite repeated requests for reform Parliament has yet to act.

Law Update 2003 edition – due March 2003

An annual review of the most recent developments in specific legal subject areas, useful for law students at degree and professional levels, others with law elements in their courses and also practitioners seeking a quick update.

Published around March every year, the Law Update summarises the major legal developments during the course of the previous year. In conjunction with Old Bailey Press textbooks it gives the student a significant advantage when revising for examinations.

Contents

Administrative Law • Civil and Criminal Procedure • Commercial Law • Company Law • Conflict of Laws • Constitutional Law • Contract Law • Conveyancing • Criminal Law • Criminology • English and European Legal Systems • Equity and Trusts • European Union Law • Evidence • Family Law • Jurisprudence • Land Law • Law of International Trade • Public International Law • Revenue Law • Succession • Tort

For further information on contents or to place an order, please contact:

Mail Order
Old Bailey Press
at Holborn College
Woolwich Road
Charlton
London
SE7 8LN

Telephone No: 020 7381 7407
Fax No: 020 7386 0952
Website: www.oldbaileypress.co.uk

ISBN 1 85836 477 9
Soft cover 246 x 175 mm
450 pages approx
£10.95
Due March 2003

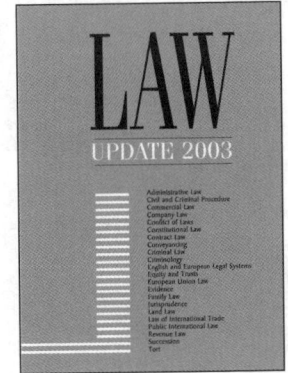

Unannotated Cracknell's Statutes for use in Examinations

New Editions of Cracknell's Statutes

£11.95 due 2002

Cracknell's Statutes provide a comprehensive series of essential statutory provisions for each subject. Amendments are consolidated, avoiding the need to cross-refer to amending legislation. Unannotated, they are suitable for use in examinations, and provide the precise wording of vital Acts of Parliament for the diligent student.

Commercial Law
ISBN: 1 85836 472 8

European Community Legislation
ISBN: 1 85836 470 1

Conflict of Laws
ISBN: 1 85836 473 6

Family Law
ISBN: 1 85836 471 X

Criminal Law
ISBN: 1 85836 474 4

Public International Law
ISBN: 1 85836 476 0

Employment Law
ISBN: 1 85836 475 2

For further information on contents or to place an order, please contact:

Mail Order
Old Bailey Press
at Holborn College
Woolwich Road
Charlton
London
SE7 8LN

Telephone No: 020 7381 7407
Fax No: 020 7386 0952
Website: www.oldbaileypress.co.uk

Suggested Solutions to Past Examination Questions 2000–2001

The Suggested Solutions series provides examples of full answers to the questions regularly set by examiners. Each suggested solution has been broken down into three stages: general comment, skeleton solution and suggested solution. The examination questions included within the text are taken from past examination papers set by the London University. The full opinion answers will undoubtedly assist you with your research and further your understanding and appreciation of the subject in question.

Only £6.95 Due December 2002

Constitutional Law
ISBN: 1 85836 478 7

Jurisprudence and Legal Theory
ISBN: 1 85836 484 1

Criminal Law
ISBN: 1 85836 479 5

Land Law
ISBN: 1 85836 481 7

English Legal System
ISBN: 1 85836 482 5

Law of Tort
ISBN: 1 85836 483 3

Elements of the Law of Contract
ISBN: 1 85836 480 9

For further information on contents or to place an order, please contact:

Mail Order
Old Bailey Press
at Holborn College
Woolwich Road
Charlton
London
SE7 8LN

Telephone No: 020 7381 7407
Fax No: 020 7386 0952
Website: www.oldbaileypress.co.uk

Land Law

2000–2001 LLB Examination Questions and Suggested Solutions

University of London External Examinations

Solutions by Allan Coverley

Old Bailey Press

The Old Bailey Press integrated student law library is tailor-made to help you at every stage of your studies from the preliminaries of each subject through to the final examination. The series of Textbooks, Revision WorkBooks, 150 Leading Cases and Cracknell's Statutes are interrelated to provide you with a comprehensive set of study materials.

You can buy Old Bailey Press books from your University Bookshop, your local Bookshop, direct using this form, or you can order a free catalogue of our titles from the address shown overleaf.

The following subjects each have a Textbook, 150 Leading Cases/Casebook, Revision WorkBook and Cracknell's Statutes unless otherwise stated.

Administrative Law
Commercial Law
Company Law
Conflict of Laws
Constitutional Law
Conveyancing (Textbook and 150 Leading Cases)
Criminal Law
Criminology (Textbook and Sourcebook)
Employment Law (Textbook and Cracknell's Statutes)
English and European Legal Systems
Equity and Trusts
Evidence
Family Law
Jurisprudence: The Philosophy of Law (Textbook, Sourcebook and
    Revision WorkBook)
Land: The Law of Real Property
Law of International Trade
Law of the European Union
Legal Skills and System
    (Textbook)
Obligations: Contract Law
Obligations: The Law of Tort
Public International Law
Revenue Law (Textbook,
    Revision WorkBook and
    Cracknell's Statutes)
Succession

Mail order prices:	
Textbook	£14.95
150 Leading Cases	£11.95
Revision WorkBook	£9.95
Cracknell's Statutes	£11.95
Suggested Solutions 1998–1999	£6.95
Suggested Solutions 1999–2000	£6.95
Suggested Solutions 2000–2001	£6.95
Law Update 2002	£9.95
Law Update 2003	£10.95

Please note details and prices are subject to alteration.

To complete your order, please fill in the form below:

Module	Books required	Quantity	Price	Cost
		Postage		
		TOTAL		

For Europe, add 15% postage and packing (£20 maximum).
For the rest of the world, add 40% for airmail.

ORDERING

By telephone to Mail Order at 020 7381 7407, with your credit card to hand.

By fax to 020 7386 0952 (giving your credit card details).

Website: www.oldbaileypress.co.uk

By post to: Mail Order, Old Bailey Press at Holborn College, Woolwich Road, Charlton, London, SE7 8LN.

When ordering by post, please enclose full payment by cheque or banker's draft, or complete the credit card details below. You may also order a free catalogue of our complete range of titles from this address.

We aim to despatch your books within 3 working days of receiving your order.

Name

Address

Postcode   Telephone

Total value of order, including postage: £

I enclose a cheque/banker's draft for the above sum, or

charge my   ☐ Access/Mastercard   ☐ Visa   ☐ American Express
Card number

☐☐☐☐ ☐☐☐☐ ☐☐☐☐ ☐☐☐☐

Expiry date   ☐☐☐☐

Signature: ....Date: ....